Population and Community in Rural America

POPULATION AND COMMUNITY IN RURAL AMERICA

LORRAINE GARKOVICH

PRAEGER

Westport, Connecticut
London

The Library of Congress has cataloged the hardcover edition as follows:

Garkovich, Lorraine.
    Population and community in rural America.
    (Contributions in sociology, ISSN 0034–9278 ; no. 84)
    Bibliography: p.
    Includes index.
    1. United States—Population, Rural—History.
  2. Rural-urban migration—United States—History.
  3. United States—Rural conditions.   I. Rural Sociological Society. II. Title. III. Series.
    HB2835.G37   1989b   307.2′4′0973   89–11802
    ISBN 0–313–26620–4 (lib. bdg. : alk. paper)

British Library Cataloguing in Publication Data is available.

A hardcover edition of *Population and Community in Rural America* is
available from Greenwood Press, an imprint of Greenwood Publishing
Group, Inc. (Contributions in Sociology, Number 84; ISBN 0–313–26620–4).

Library of Congress Catalog Card Number: 89–11802
ISBN: 0–275–93350–4

First published in 1989

Praeger Publishers, 88 Post Road West, Westport, CT 06881
An imprint of Greenwood Publishing Group
www.praeger.com

Printed in the United States of America

∞™

The paper used in this book complies with the
Permanent Paper Standard issued by the National
Information Standards Organization (Z39.48–1984).

10 9 8 7 6 5 4 3 2

This book is dedicated to my parents, a first generation son of immigrant parents and an immigrant herself. Their lives exemplify the dreams and hopes that have brought millions to our shores in search of a better life for their children. Thank you for encouraging me to dream.

And to Rex Campbell, my faculty advisor in graduate school, my mentor, and my friend. For many years Rex has encouraged me and given me the confidence to reach for my dreams. Thank you for keeping the dream alive.

Contents

Figures and Tables   ix

Preface   xiii

1. Why Do People Move?   1

2. The Socioeconomic and Political Context of
    Rural Population Change   25

3. Migration and Population Change During the
    Era of Rural Dominance (1650–1880)   49

4. Migration Streams in the Urban Era (1880–
    1970)   83

5. Consequences of Migration During the Urban
    Era   111

6. The Era of Residential Diversity (1960–?)   129

7. Institutional and Scientific Forces Influencing
    Rural Population Studies   163

8. Research Challenges for the Future   177

Appendix   185

Bibliography   199

Name Index   219

Subject Index   225

Figures and Tables

FIGURES

1. Change in the Rural Population in the
   United States, 1790–1880   50
2. Geographic Location of the U.S. Center of
   Population, 1790–1980   55
3. Census Geographic Divisions   62
4. Rural-Urban Distribution of U.S. Population,
   1790–1880   63
5. Proportion of U.S. Population Living in
   Places of 10,000 + and 50,000 +, 1790–1880   65
6. Rural-Urban Distribution of U.S. Population,
   1890–1980   85
7. Net Immigration as a Proportion of Total
   Population Growth, 1900–1985   88
8. Foreign-Born as a Proportion of Total U.S.
   Population, 1850–1980   90
9. Urban and Rural Distribution of Black and
   White Population, 1890–1980   96
10. Farm Population as a Proportion of Total
    U.S. Population, 1880–1980   98

11. Proportion of U.S. Population in Places of
    50,000+ and 1 Million+, 1890–1980   135

12. Change in Rural Population in the United
    States, 1890–1980   138

13. Farm Population as a Proportion of the Rural
    Population, 1880–1980   142

TABLES

1. Theoretical Approaches to the Study of
   Migration   3

2. Increases in Labor Productivity and Out-
   migration of the Farm Population   103

APPENDIX TABLES

A–1 Definitions of Rural and Urban in
     Successive U.S. Censuses   186

A–2 Geographic Expansion of U.S. Land Area   188

A–3 Rural and Urban Population and Intercensal
     Change, 1790–1980   189

A–4 Regional Population Growth and
     Distribution, 1790–1880   190

A–5 Fertility Ratios by Residence and Region,
     1800–1880   191

A–6 Net Migration of Blacks by Region, 1910–
     1980   192

A–7 Regional Population Growth and
     Distribution, 1890–1980   192

A–8 Fertility Ratios by Residence and Region,
     1890–1970   193

A–9 Urban Population Change by Size of Urban
     Place, 1880–1980   194

A–10 Regional Migration Interchanges, 1955–
1980   195

A–11 Population in Urban and Rural Territory by
Metropolitan and Nonmetropolitan Status,
1950–1980   196

A–12 Percent Change in Metropolitan and
Nonmetropolitan Population,1950–1980   197

Preface

Change is the hallmark of the American experience, and perhaps the most significant change has been the shift from a predominantly rural society to one where three-quarters of our people reside in urban areas. Migration from rural communities to urban areas has accounted for a substantial proportion of this population shift. The streams of migration from rural to urban areas have shaped the social and economic development of both the rural communities of origin and the urban destinations. Despite the slight turnaround in rural-to-urban migration in the 1970s, the dominant pattern of population movement throughout American history has been toward our cities. Thus, within the U.S. and rural communities, migration has been and remains the most important demographic process in determining population change.

Migration as the primary force for population change in rural America is the focus of this book. Population change is of vital interest for many reasons to all those concerned about rural America, but perhaps the most fundamental reason is that rural areas, by definition, have smaller, more dispersed populations. Any changes in the number of births or deaths, or the movement of people into and out of rural areas produce immediate and visible effects on community and family structure.

Migration studies have been the single largest area of rural population research over the last half century for several reasons. First, changes in migration are usually more rapid and visible within a rural community than changes in birth and death rates. Vacant houses and farmsteads with "for sale" signs, or new houses and apartments appearing on yesterday's farmland are daily reminders of population losses or gains due to in- or out-migration. Moreover, because migration generally involves the loss or arrival of entire family units, the consequences of migration for a community's population size and socioeconomic structure are often much greater than for shifts in mortality and fertility.

Perhaps the most important reason for the abiding interest in migration is that migration streams bind the nation's communities together. When rural migrants move to cities, they bring with them a subcultural heritage both similar and different to that of their new urban neighbors. The interchange of population through migration intermingles urban and rural perspectives, contributing to the development of a national character. Furthermore, rural and urban areas depend on each other for human resources. The arrival of rural migrants represents an important infusion of workers for urban industries, while urban migrants to rural areas bring occupational and educational skills often absent in these places. Finally, migration streams are an important factor in the gradual convergence of rural and urban vital rates, reducing the demographic extremes that once distinguished rural and urban areas.

Migration has been and will continue to be the key population process in rural America. The relationship between migration and the other components of population change, and their joint effects on the population structure of rural America are the overarching themes of this monograph. Two questions guide this discussion: What do we know about migration and its effects on other population processes and characteristics? Why have particular patterns of migration and population change occurred at certain points in the historical development of rural America?

Migration and the other population processes—fertility and mortality—are influenced by demographic composition; social and economic conditions; cultural values and expectations; racial, ethnic, religious, and socioeconomic characteristics of the population; and the interactive effects of migration, fertility, and mortality on each other. Population change is rooted in the sociocultural dynamics of a particular historical epoch, as well as in the pressure for change built into a population by prior levels of migration, fertility, and mortality. In other words, the population structure of a society is both a consequence of prior population dynamics and a cause of future population changes. Moreover, the social and economic environment; technological innovation; political agendas, policies, and programs; and dominant values and beliefs all modify the expression of these population processes and are influenced by them. Thus, the particular configuration of vital rates—levels of fertility, mortality, and migration—and the age, sex, racial, ethnic, and socioeconomic composition of a nation's population at a particular moment in time represent the confluence of prior population and historical dynamics, as well as current conditions.

The organization of this monograph is as follows: Chapter one describes various theoretical and methodological issues in the study of migration. The purpose of this account is not to provide a comprehensive overview of migration theory, but rather to identify factors conceptually associated with rates and patterns of migration, and to highlight some methodological constraints on migration research. Chapter two presents a brief description of the major social, economic, and political events of the three historical eras of rural population change—the era of rural dominance (1650–1880), the urban era (1880–1970), and the era of residential diversity (1960–?)—establishing the social environment within which the population restructuring of rural America has occurred.

Chapters three through six describe in greater detail rural population changes throughout American history. Included in these chapters are major migration streams, factors associated with these population movements, and their consequences for the population structure and community life in rural America. Chapter seven focuses on some institutional forces that have shaped the study and interpretation of rural population change, suggesting that what we know about rural population change is often a function of who asks the questions and the purpose of the research. The final chapter summarizes the major changes in rural America and the role of migration in shaping the rural population of today. It also identifies critical issues that must guide migration research in the future if we are to understand the process of rural population change.

While one author is credited for this book, no work is done in isolation. My deepest appreciation is expressed to Rex R. Campbell, who, with good humor and a most discerning mind, reviewed several versions of this book. John Wardwell carefully reviewed the manuscript and offered many helpful comments, as did J. Allan Beegle and Thomas W. Ilvento. Nancy Strang labored many weeks as technical editor to ensure that the ideas are expressed appropriately, Aneen Boyd carefully typed the manuscript and tables, and Bruce Gage prepared the figures. James Zuiches spent many hours helping me organize my ideas and nursing this and the other books in the series through publication. Finally, my colleagues at the University of Kentucky provided the professional critiques and personal encouragement that help one stick to a task as large as this.

Population and Community in Rural America

1

Why Do People Move?

INTRODUCTION

From the beginning, mobility has been the hallmark of America. We are a nation on the move, a people restlessly searching for more opportunities, a more amenable place to live, or any number of other hoped-for dreams. The nation has been populated by successive waves of immigrants, the territorial expansion of the nation fueled by the westward movement of settlers, and regional growth and decline a function of internal mobility. Migration has been and will continue to be the key component of community population change in rural areas, and for this reason the study of migration has been the pre-eminent focus of rural population studies.

This chapter briefly reviews the various ways in which social scientists have studied and explained migration. The purpose of this presentation is to highlight the factors social scientists have linked to

1. the decision to move,
2. the selection of a destination,
3. the actual process of migration, and
4. the adjustment to the consequences of this mobility by the migrants, the communities they left, and the communities receiving them.

These theoretical explanations provide the "lenses" through which migration has been perceived and interpreted (Kuhn, 1970). Thus, they have shaped our understanding of migration as a process of population and social change.

For decades, the nearly exclusive focus of migration research has been the stream of persons leaving rural places for urban or metropolitan areas. The reasons for the out-migration, the characteristics of the migrants, and their adjustment to urban life and social structure have been the main topics of interest. This orientation tends to focus on differences between rural and urban places and the characteristics of persons attracted to urban places as opposed to those who have chosen to remain in rural or to seek other rural destinations.

From this research, two general approaches to the theoretical understanding of migration have been developed. In the macro approach, migration is viewed as a function of aggregate or area attributes, that is, it focuses on the characteristics of places that prompt differential flows of migration. In the micro approach, migration is viewed as a function of individual attributes, that is, individuals' positions in a social structure, or their social psychological attitudes affecting their propensity to move or not move. This perspective includes a focus on the subjective process of decision making based on individual choices, preferences, and motivations.

While we can theoretically distinguish between these perspectives, and while much research tends to focus on one to the exclusion of the other, in reality both of these explanations contribute to the understanding of migration. Table 1 illustrates how the various theories used to study migration fit within these two perspectives. A brief review of these theoretical perspectives illustrates their points of convergence and divergence.

AREA OR MACRO APPROACHES

A macro approach to migration considers migration a function of aggregate or area attributes. Migration is viewed, from this perspective, as a population process linking two different areas through the influences of both labor market and nonla-

Table 1
Theoretical Approaches to the Study of Migration

I. Area or Macro Approaches	II. Individual or Micro Approaches
A. Economic Models	A. Economic Models
1. Labor mobility	1. Human capital maximization
2. Labor market differentials (wage levels, unemployment, composition or structure of the labor market area)	2. Household maximization
3. Welfare programs and levels	3. Social mobility or social Status attainment
B. Noneconomic Models	B. Noneconomic Models
1. Amenities (climate, recreational resources)	1. Life cycle stage
2. Population structure and dynamics (ethnic/racial composition, marriage market differentials, rates of growth)	2. Affinity models (community or (kinship ties)
3. Ecological models (population, organization, environment, technology)	3. Value-based models (life style preferences, risk-uncertainty, residential satisfaction, decision-making styles)
C. Methodological Approaches	C. Methodological Approaches
1. Unit of analysis: Places or areas	1. Unit of analysis: Individuals, families or households
2. Common measures:	2. Common measures:
a. Gross interchanges	a. Residential histories
b. Net migration rates	b. Event history analysis
c. Migration systems or streams	c. Reasons for moving

bor market conditions (Ritchey, 1976). The economic factors influencing migration in this approach are variations in the opportunities among areas as measured by earnings, unemployment levels, or job availability. Nonlabor market factors include such things as the presence of relatives and friends, amenities and services, public assistance, or racial inequality (Ritchey, 1976: 375).

Studies using economic models examine labor mobility, labor market differentials, or variations in welfare programs and levels of public assistance to explain migration interchanges among areas. Labor mobility studies view migration as a mechanism for the effective allocation of labor in response to market needs. "Theoretically, the potential migrant will select the locality in which the real value of the expected net benefit from migration is greatest. A full test of the model involves an explicit comparison of area of origin and area(s) of destination on the discounted value of expected future net returns" (De Jong and Fawcett, 1981: 23). The bulk of these studies use area or aggregate data to specify the factors in this model.

Studies of labor market differentials compare wage levels, unemployment rates, or the composition or structure of labor market areas to explain variations in migration among areas. Clearly, these factors would also enter an analysis of labor mobility, since they will affect the net benefits expected from migration to one destination as opposed to another.

In the 1960s, as state-sponsored programs of public assistance expanded, the effects of area differentials in levels of assistance on patterns of migration became a research focus. Theoretically, it can be argued that migration will be toward areas of easier eligibility requirements or higher levels of assistance, and away from areas with more rigid eligibility requirements or lower levels of assistance. From a macro perspective, these differences will affect the value of expected benefits associated with migration, such that the costs of remaining in areas of low levels of assistance exceed the costs of migration to areas with better levels of assistance. However, most of the research examining this factor has found that area differences in welfare programs account for an insignificant amount of the variation in migration direction or volume.

Geographic areas also vary in their natural amenities, population structures, and in other ways. Noneconomic models explore how variations in these factors are related to migration differentials. During the 1970s, the differences in amenities among areas frequently appeared in analyses of rural-urban migration trends. For example, differences in mean annual temperatures or the availability of recreational resources were used to explain the flow of migrants to the Sunbelt and to more remote recreational communities in the Ozarks or Michigan's upper peninsula.

Differences in the population structures of areas have also been used to account for migration patterns. Concentrations of particular ethnic or racial groups in some metropolitan areas have been associated with in-migrations of similar persons. The out-migration of young women from areas with small pools of eligible mates, or the in-migration of single adults to areas with large pools of single adults represent the effects of marriage market differentials on migration. It has also been demonstrated that the rate and direction of population change in an area is associated with patterns of migration. For example, areas experiencing population growth attract migrants, while those experiencing population decline have net migration losses. While this may appear to be a circular argument, it in fact reflects the assumption of an aggregation effect.

Another macro approach employs an ecological framework. Ecological models consider migration to be a mechanism of population adjustment to life chances (Hawley, 1968: 331). The ecological approach uses indicators of level and change in technology, environment, social organization, and population to explain migration patterns (Frisbie and Poston, 1978; Poston and Coleman, 1983). Ecological models do not consider individual motives, rather, changes in the organizational or technological base of areas are viewed as conditions requiring population adjustments. For example, a national study by Frisbie and Poston (1976) found that counties experiencing population growth through migration have more distinct sustenance functions and greater organizational complexity than counties losing population.

INDIVIDUAL OR MICRO APPROACHES

To consider migration as a function of individual attributes is to assess the influence of an individual's position in a social structure and/or his or her social psychological characteristics.

As with area or macro approaches, studies using this perspective examine the influences of both economic and noneconomic factors on migration patterns.

The individual level correlates to area economic models focus on human capital maximization, household maximization, or social mobility. Human capital maximization models assume that migration is based on an individual's analysis of the costs of moving or not moving, as opposed to the benefits of either decision. "Migration becomes a personal investment that will be made only if returns for this behavior are justified" (De Jong and Fawcett, 1981: 24). In other words, migration occurs when individuals believe they can maximize their returns on personal investments in educational and occupational skills elsewhere. Household maximization applies a similar analysis of migration costs and benefits to the household's net gains or losses as opposed to the individual's net gains or losses.

Social mobility or social status attainment models view migration as a mechanism by which individuals or households improve their position in the status hierarchy. Here, individuals with high aspirations with regard to education, occupation, or life style move to places with opportunities for advancement. Geographic mobility as a means to social mobility, especially for persons in upper socioeconomic status occupations, has been well documented (Blau and Duncan, 1967). "To the extent that the motivation for social mobility is enhanced or thwarted by the educational and occupational organization as well as by environment constraints of an area, the social mobility hypothesis may be an individual-level analog to the 'ecological perspective' of migration" (De Jong and Fawcett, 1981: 26).

Noneconomic models focus on the influence of stages in the life-cycle, community or kinship ties, or values and preferences in migration patterns. The key difference between this and macro approaches is that migration is sparked by the life-cycle stage or family composition of the household. A life-cycle approach assumes that individuals and families go through a series of changes in the composition of their family or household, and that these changes may lead to migration. In this approach, migration is defined as a mechanism for adjusting

housing or neighborhood to these changes in family or household composition. In some cases, it may be that life-cycle change
generates dissatisfaction with current residence or neighborhood and leads to migration. In other cases, an individual or
family may simply compare the relative advantages of different
places in the context of their life-cycle stage, moving to the
place with the greatest comparative advantage.

Affinity models argue that community and kinship ties or
minority group status can be conceptualized as "location-
specific capital" or the "generic term denoting any or all of the
factors that 'tie' a person to a particular place" (DaVanzo and
Morrison, 1981: 87). Location-specific capital expands the human capital approach by noting that "two destinations with
equivalent wage levels will not necessarily be equally attractive because of the various other economic and noneconomic
considerations important to migrants" (Williams, 1981: 186).
Location-specific capital can both tie and attract individuals to
various places (Williams and McMillen, 1983), and can explain
why individuals and families are attracted to or remain in
places with limited economic opportunities or many other negative characteristics.

Most micro approaches to the study of migration involve a
consideration, either implicitly or explicitly, of the decision-
making process that produces migration and/or a destination
selection. The decision-making process occurs in a series of
sequential stages. First, individuals must decide whether to
stay or leave, and this decision reflects stress or dissatisfaction
with the current place of residence (Speare, 1974) due to limited
opportunities for advancement (the social mobility or human
capital models) or changing environmental conditions (e.g.,
crowding, pollution, neighborhood composition). If the decision
is to move, individuals then weigh the actual or expected economic and noneconomic costs and returns of migration to alternative destinations (DaVanzo, 1976). Beshers (1967) and
others (De Jong and Fawcett, 1981) suggest that two individuals, confronting the same set of conditions and options, could
arrive at different migration decisions. Individuals vary in
their willingness to take risks, their opportunities or abilities
to obtain and evaluate information, and their "mode of orien-

tation" to decision-making (e.g., short- vs. long-term goal orientation); therefore, each individual evaluates his or her migration options differently. At the individual level of study, migration is implicitly a function of choice or preference as expressed in a rational decision-making process.

A COMPARISON OF MACRO AND MICRO APPROACHES

There are many similarities in the conceptualization and operationalization of these two theoretical approaches, even though these are often implicit rather than clearly articulated. First, the role of individual volition in the decision to move or not to move and in the selection of a destination is a thread running through each of these perspectives. Macro approaches imply that migrants are attracted by positive economic differences, while micro approaches imply migrants are attracted by greater opportunities to achieve desired ends. In either case, migration is quintessentially an act of individuals. As such, any analysis of migration must take into account individual motives and choices.

Second, migration occurs between areas with differing objective socioeconomic conditions. While macro approaches treat these differences as the primary explanatory factor in their models, micro approaches focus on how individuals perceive or encounter these differences. Hence, it must be acknowledged that social and economic structures and other external factors influence the decision to move or not to move. As De Jong and Fawcett (1981: 17) note: "Migration differentials for areas point to potentially important contextual-locational effects that must be considered in testing alternative hypotheses of migration decision making."

Third, migration occurs within a social system, even though micro approaches emphasize the individual as the primary actor in migration, and macro approaches focus on aggregates. For example, the most common unit of migration is the family. Mangalam (1968) argues that migration is a process wherein a social system (the family) relocates from one social system (the community of origin) to another (the community of destination).

Finally, migration as a process of individual geographic mobility contributes to changes in the composition and functioning of areas; it is a key factor in changing the labor force structure, or the racial and ethnic composition of communities of origin and destination. This is not to discount the influence of fertility and mortality, or the effects of such socioeconomic factors as business cycles or investments in the educational system. Yet, migration has a more immediate and potentially long-term effect on areas. In this sense, the very attributes of areas that are the focus of macro analyses are often the consequence of prior migration of individuals with particular status characteristics.

A SYNTHESIS OF MACRO AND MICRO APPROACHES

While there are many similarities among these different theoretical approaches, usually only one is chosen as the primary explanatory framework for research, often with disregard of complementary perspectives. To some degree this is surprising, since most of the factors identified as individual motivations have counterparts in the social structure related to migration as an aggregate or area process. After a review of several approaches to the study of motivation in migration, De Jong and Fawcett (1981: 38) note: "1. Some motivations have counterparts in environmental and structural factors that help explain aggregate mobility patterns; and 2. the key to an integration is the identification of linkage processes through which macro stimuli are translated into relevant considerations for individual decision making." Yet, the most dominant explanatory framework has been economic, emphasizing the importance of macro level economic conditions and, occasionally, micro level economic motivations in the migration process. In other words, the tendency has been to assume that people move toward economic opportunity or away from economic deprivation in search of a better living standard as defined by personally based economic criteria.

In his review of explanations of migration, Ritchey (1976) notes the emergence of a more integrative theoretical approach to migration research, the cognitive-behavioral model. Ritchey (1976: 397) states: "Basic to this approach is the idea that spatial preferences are subjective evaluations, and the perceived attractiveness or perception of residential desirability of alternative locations is a critical element in the decision-making process of migration and a critical determinant of migration and its direction." This approach, Zuiches (1981) suggests, unites both individual and aggregate perspectives by emphasizing the influence of subjective evaluations of alternative places, as well as the objective locational and geographic conditions affecting these perceptions in the decision-making process. Zuiches (1981) goes on to suggest that this approach provides a framework for integrating the growing literature on residential preferences and migration used to interpret the residential turnaround of the 1970s.

The cognitive-behavioral model provides a parsimonious approach for interpreting migration. It acknowledges the importance of both individual and social structural factors in the migration process while being sympathetic to the traditional models of migration. For example, Lee's (1966) elaboration of Ravenstein's (1885; 1889) "laws of migration" indicates that four factors influence both the decision to migrate and the migration process itself: characteristics of the place of origin, the place of destination, and the potential migrants, and intervening obstacles. Lee (1966) emphasizes that while it may be possible to empirically quantify these factors (e.g., rates of unemployment, wage differentials, or distance), what actually influences the migration process is the individual's perceptions of these factors.

The "push-pull" model of Bogue (1969) and others (Peterson, 1975) suggests that people are "pushed" from a place of origin by a set of conditions perceived to be intolerable, and "pulled" to a destination that offsets these intolerable conditions without introducing any equally negative ones. The cognitive-behavioral model, while acknowledging the significance of objective differences between locations, highlights the importance of individual perceptions of these locational values.

Sell and De Jong (1978) offer a motivational theory of migration decision making incorporating many of the same components as the cognitive-behavioral model. Their approach identifies four components or stages that move an individual through the decision process. The first is the possibility of moving. This entails both the physical possibility of migration as a behavioral alternative (e.g., few if any restrictions on leaving or entering places and the types and extent of intervening obstacles), as well as the cognitive or perceptual possibility of migration (e.g., information about alternative designations and level of attachment to place of origin). If migration is both a physical and cognitive possibility, the next factor is the motivation to move. This entails the relative importance people attach to particular values (e.g., economic success, maintaining family ties, freedom of religious expression, recreational opportunities) and serves as the springboard for the third factor or stage—expectancy.

Expectancy involves evaluating the probability of achieving highly desired goals by staying or moving. Expectancy entails people's perceptions of conditions at the place of origin and at the different potential destinations. Regardless of whether these perceptions reflect objective conditions in various places, they strongly affect the decision to move or not to move. The fourth component of the model is incentive—the specific attributes of origin and alternative destinations enabling people to actualize their goals. These incentives are positive (e.g., low unemployment, pleasant climate, presence of family) or negative (high unemployment or crime rates, absence of family) characteristics of places that serve to attract or repel potential migrants.

In this model, each stage or component must be present if a decision to move occurs. In other words, people move when they have the ability to leave (physical possibility); perceive that a destination is available (cognitive possibility); believe or know conditions elsewhere are more likely to enable them to reach a desired goal (motive) than is likely in their current place (incentive); and believe that they can take advantage of these opportunities elsewhere (expectancy). As with the cognitive-behavioral model, Sell and De Jong propose a theoretical explanation of migration accounting for why some people in particular situations move and others do not; why some destinations attract migrants and others do not; and why some origins lose their residents and others retain them.

This brief review of various approaches to the study of migration highlights some common threads in their explanations of why migration occurs, including

1. objective differences among places in economic opportunities or conditions, and/or environmental or social (presence of family or friends) differences;

2. disparities in peoples' knowledge and/or subjective evaluations of these objective conditions;

3. variations in individuals' perceptions of opportunities and obstacles to moving; and finally,

4. differences in individual decision-making strategies.

A final set of factors influencing what we know about migration involve how migration is studied. These methodological issues highlight some of the difficulties in the study of this complex population process.

METHODOLOGICAL ISSUES IN THE STUDY OF MIGRATION

There are probably as many approaches to operationalizing migration and defining the units of analysis as there are population researchers. The great diversity of approaches has both contributed to the extensive base of substantive knowledge on migration and made difficult the synthesis of the empirical findings. To a certain extent, the diversity of methodologies reflects the diversity of theoretical frameworks. However, the types of data that have been employed in migration research have also influenced methodological approaches.

Defining Migration

Unlike international migration, in which a national boundary is crossed, internal migration is not so easily measured or operationalized. In the United States we use, as a matter of convention and convenience, moves across county lines as an indicator and measure of migration, while intracounty movements are defined as "residential mobility." Essentially, this division reflects the influence of a major source of data on migration, the U.S. Census, which defines migration as a move across a county line.

The theoretical assumption underlying this definition is that a move across a political-administrative boundary involves greater change in social attachments and activities than a move not crossing such boundaries. Implicitly, we attribute sociological significance to political-administrative boundaries in conceptualizing them as the indicators of distance, the economic and social obstacles, and the degree of heterogeneity between origin and destination (Goldscheider, 1971). Using the county boundary as a delineation between migration and residential mobility may have some merit so long as we remember that intracounty moves may involve as significant a disruption and reorganization of activities and relationships as cross-county moves, for example, a move from an inner city neighborhood to a suburban residential neighborhood.

There also has been considerable research suggesting that some rural migrants to urban areas re-establish their old social attachments in enclaves filled with friends and kin from their community of origin (Schwarzweller, Brown, and Mangalam, 1971). In these cases, rural-to-urban migrants can reduce or even eliminate the need to adopt urban lifestyles and mores. Finally, the importance of political-administrative boundaries may be diminishing as transportation and communication innovations transform the sociocultural meaning of geographic space. These comments are not meant to imply that the traditional definition of migration is no longer applicable, but rather to suggest that precisely what constitutes migration remains an empirical question.

Types of Migration

A second definitional issue involves differentiating among types of migration, and assessing whether these differences have implications for understanding why migration occurs and its consequences for migrants and communities. The three types of migration most typically identified are

1. primary migration, or a first time geographic movement;
2. repeat migration, or a series of movements within a short period of time; and
3. return migration, or a movement back to an area in which one has previously resided.

By and large, most research on migration treats a move as a unique event in the life history of an individual or family, that is, a primary or first time move (DaVanzo, 1981). If prior moves are taken into account, they are treated as a composite variable that increases or decreases a person's "propensity to move." Yet, several researchers (Goldstein, 1954; Morrison, 1971) have demonstrated that a substantial proportion of all migrants have moved more than once (repeat migrants), and others note that a portion of these persons return to a prior place of residence (DaVanzo and Morrison, 1981).

Intuitively, it would seem that the motives underlying a first time move differ from those producing a series of moves, or those leading a person to move back to a place he or she once left. Yet, these differences in motives have rarely been addressed (DaVanzo, 1981). Indeed, the task is made difficult by data collection methods that produce information only on one move, or only measure the net movement between places.

Furthermore, the conceptual meaning of these different types of migration is unclear. For example, is a person who has moved two times in ten years similar in motivations and personal characteristics to someone who has moved five times in ten years? Is a first time move the same as a fifth move? Does the movement back to a place of origin have the same sociological meaning as a movement to a new place? Is a move to one's state of birth, which one may have left as a child, inspired by the same motives underlying a return to a place left only three years earlier? The tendency to deal conceptually and empirically with migration as a discrete event disengaged from prior residential moves, as well as the inconsistency in the empirical treatment of repeat and return migration reflects both short-comings in the dominant theoretical models and limitations of the major sources of data.

Not only do we often fail to take into account the possible influence of prior migration behavior, we also often discount the influence of significant life events. While research on residential mobility (intracounty moves) has clearly established the relationship between life-cycle changes (marriage, divorce, employment, unemployment, occupational mobility, etc.) and residential moves, the possibility that migration is a result of such events is rarely taken into account in migration studies. These life-cycle events are infrequently included in the dominant theoretical perspectives, and our methods often yield little or no information on them.

Unit of Analysis

A third issue is the unit of analysis. Again, due to the nature of migration data generated by the decennial census, as well as problems of measurement and analysis, most migration research has focused on the individual as the unit of study. Frequently, this individual, the head of the household, is presumed to represent the family unit (spouse and dependents), and both the socioeconomic characteristics of the head of the household and his or her motives for migration are presumed to represent those of all family members.

While this approach "fits" the type of data as well as the statistical methods generally available, it overlooks the reality that a substantial proportion of all migration occurs in a group context—the family—and that the dynamics of the migration process may differ with each family member. It is possible that all members of a family or household may not share the same desire to move or the same preference for the destination; indeed, it is possible that some members are "dragged along" in the migration process. A narrow focus on the individual precludes a consideration of migration as an interactive decision-making process engaged in by all members of a family social system, and so may distort our understanding of the migration process.

Additionally, if we presume that the motives of the head of a family—the individual typically interviewed in migration research—may not reflect those of other members, questions arise as to the consequences of migration for the individual members. Individual approaches to migration suggest that motives influence subsequent adjustment. If true, the fact that family members have different, and possibly incompatible, motives for migration means that addressing this topic based on the responses of one member may mask real differences in the processes of adjustment of all members (Beshers, 1967).

Considering migration as a group process does not necessarily demand new theoretical conceptualizations; rather, it implies a need for new methodological approaches. While family sociologists have developed methods for studying family dynamics, those engaged in rural population studies have not often used these research strategies in the study of migration. This illustrates a needed area of development in rural population studies, possibly involving collaborative research.

Sources of Data

A fourth methodological issue concerns the use and availability of data for different measures of migration. The most typical measure of migration as an aggregate or macro level process is net migration, which represents the net movement of persons into and out of a particular area over a given period (one, five, or ten years). This measure focuses on a given area, then aggregates its in- and out-migration of persons. Since it typically compares persons' residences at one point in time versus another, this approach overlooks multiple moves during the time interval, as well as those who left and returned to their place of origin during the time interval. This approach, with a five-year time interval, is the one employed by the decennial census, the most frequently used source of migration data.

As a measure of migration, net migration is often calculated as a residual in the population equation. That is, net migration is the number of persons remaining after subtracting natural increase or decrease from the total population change in an area over a given period of time. This approach may undercount the actual level of movement into and out of a community because it reports only the difference at the end of the period (DaVanzo and Morrison, 1981). For example, in the beginning of a time period large numbers of persons moved into a coal mining area experiencing a boom, while at the end of the time period, as the coal boom collapsed, a great number of persons moved out. The residual method of calculating net migration would indicate a small net gain or loss for the area, when actually great numbers of persons moved into and out of the area over the time period.

Another measure of migration as an aggregate phenomenon is migration streams—flows of persons between particular places of origin and particular destinations. First developed by Ravenstein (1888) to describe the heavy flow of population moving between rural areas and towns in the nineteenth century, this has been a common approach to measuring migration between rural and urban areas and between states in the United States. Two types of measures of migration streams have been employed: The net interchange is the difference in the number of persons moving from place A to place B (the stream) and those moving from place B to place A (the counterstream). The gross interchange is the sum total of all persons moving between these places. Migration streams provide specific information on how many persons have been attracted to a particular place (e.g., Cincinnati) or area (e.g., nonmetropolitan counties) in a given period of time. In this way, migration streams permit an evaluation of the relative attraction of particular places vis-á-vis others. When migration streams or gross migration interchanges are linked to the economic and noneconomic characteristics of places, this is the most appropriate measure of area or macro models of migration.

However, the analysis of migration streams becomes unwieldy as the analysis moves from general types of places (e.g., metropolitan vs. nonmetropolitan, or the South vs. the Northeast) to specific types of places (e.g., Oklahoma vs. California, or Chicago vs. St. Louis). As a result, migration stream analysis has typically been used to assess the interchange between general types of places. Furthermore, data on migration streams, while implying the relative attraction of one type of area over another, provides no information as to the specific character- istics of an area that make it more or less attractive to mi- grants. Hence, migration stream analysis as a method of testing area or aggregate explanations of migration is usually linked to other data on the socioeconomic characteristics of places, and the factors associated with the attraction of mi- grants imputed.

Residential histories represent a micro approach to the meas- urement of migration, since they present the details of the geographic mobility of particular persons and identify origins and destinations, reasons for moving, and other relevant in- formation for each move. Residential histories most appropri- ately assess both individual or micro approaches to migration and the cognitive-behavioral model, since such histories pro- vide detailed information on the decision-making process lead- ing to choices among destinations. However, residential histories require more extensive interviews with individuals and pose special analytic problems. Hence, even when residen- tial histories are available, the tendency is to aggregate infor- mation about geographic mobility cross-sectionally rather than longitudinally. Hence, the most common measures of migration reflect the conceptual tendency to view migration as an aggre- gate or area phenomenon rather than an individual process.

Operationalizing Migration Concepts

A fifth methodological issue is how we operationalize the concepts underlying the dominant theoretical approaches to migration. Given the primacy of economic models of migration and the accompanying focus on the movement of the working- age population, considerable effort has been devoted to oper- ationalizing economic indicators, especially employment- related indicators, of area differences. A common way to op- erationalize economic models grew out of the availability of decennial census data on migration and the socioeconomic characteristics of places. That is, if people move for employment reasons, "then at the ecological level we may perceive the re- sults of these decisions through observed covariations in patterns of population redistribution and jobs-related indicators" (Williams, 1981: 184). Following this logic, area differences in aggregate wage levels (or an appropriate surrogate, such as income) should be in favor of the place attracting migrants (Tarver and Gurley, 1965; Cebula and Vedder, 1973). De Jong and Fawcett (1981: 23) note: "In general, the results of research from the economic framework support the significance of economic and labor force predictors of net and gross migration flows between areas." However, this approach imputes an economic motivation to migration based, not on the statements of migrants, but on economic differences between areas. There is no attempt to determine if the migrants were aware of these differences, or, if aware, whether the differences actually entered into their decision making.

Therefore, the availability of aggregate level data has made aggregate analyses the most common approach to the study of migration. However, many studies do use individual level data, usually derived from primary data collection efforts. These studies typically focus on reasons for moving, determining individual motivation by asking the question: Why did you move? This approach requires migrants to reflect on their prior behavior, and generally forces them to identify the single most important reason for moving. This is a problem for two reasons. First, this approach focuses on the responses of a single representative of the household. As noted earlier, this precludes the possibility that other household or family members have different reasons for moving. Second, few people make such a significant decision based on a single motive.

In response to this likelihood, Tilly and Brown (1967) introduced the concept of "auspices of migration" to represent the cluster of reasons for migration. While an individual may say that he or she moved for a job, his or her knowledge of an employment opportunity may have come from family members in the destination community, who also offer the migrant a place to live upon arrival and support in his or her adjustment to the new place. In this situation, Tilly and Brown (1967) argue, the main reason for moving may be employment, but the auspice of migration is the family that provides the support for the migration. Few studies address the reasons for moving in sufficient depth to determine underlying motives. Indeed, the census, a primary data source for migration research, does not address the issue of motive at all.

Finally, the pre-eminent explanation for migration, using the individual as the unit of analysis, is economic, especially for long distance moves (U.S. Bureau of the Census, 1966). Whether implicitly or explicitly, the findings from studies of individual migrants typically are translated into presumed differences in economic opportunities among places, reinforcing the dominance of the area or aggregate approach to migration.

Operationalizing Rural and Urban

A final methodological issue concerns how we operationalize the concepts rural and urban. Rural and urban have had different meanings at various times in the history of American population studies (*see* appendix table A–1). To a certain extent, the wide divergence in the criteria used to differentiate rural and urban areas simply reflects our failure to develop a theoretical understanding of the meaning of rural. On a more practical level, the various methods of operationalizing rural and urban produce confusion as to the nature of the unit of analysis in migration studies. This situation has been complicated by the emergence of the Standard Metropolitan Area (SMA) as a unit of analysis.

In 1950, the U.S. Bureau of the Budget introduced the SMA to "define standard areas, by the uniform application of a set of criteria, that would be used by the Federal statistical agencies" (Shryock, Siegel and Associates, 1973: 129). In the 1950 census, these statistically defined, county-based entities became the primary geographic units for data collection and dissemination. Those counties not included in the metropolitan designation became nonmetropolitan areas, and the word "metro" and "nonmetro" have now subsumed "urban" and "rural" in the demographic lexicon. These statistical constructs have, over time, assumed a sociopolitical reality of their own.

The standard metropolitan area is identified based on three criteria: population, metropolitan character, and integration. The population criterion emphasizes a minimum population size of 50,000. ("Sister" cities whose combined population meet the minimum are included.) The metropolitan criteria focus on the attributes of the county as the place of residence and work. In the past, at least 75 percent of the labor force had to be engaged in nonagricultural pursuits, and the county had to have a minimum density of 150 persons per square mile. Because of the declining number of Americans engaged in agriculture, the former criterion has recently been dropped. The integration criterion focuses on the relationship between the county with the central city of more than 50,000 residents and contiguous counties, to determine whether the contiguous counties will be classified as part of the metropolitan area. It is operationalized by the amount of commuting for employment between the adjacent counties and the central city county. The commuting criterion emphasizes the "metropolitan area as an integrated socioeconomic community whose outer boundary would include the residences of nearly all its workers as well as the workplaces of nearly all its residents" (Federal Committee on Standard Metropolitan Statistical Areas, 1980: 339). As a result, the Metropolitan Statistical Area (as it is now called) represents both the built-up, densely settled areas but also the surrounding population in the open countryside of those counties linked through commuting for work or residence.

The introduction of the SMA led to other refinements in how we measure the urban area and, by extension, rural areas. The urbanized area represents the incorporated central city (or cities) and the surrounding closely settled areas, whether incorporated or unincorporated, that total 50,000 or more persons. It is the physical city, the built-up area that would be identified from an aerial view. The urban fringe, on the other hand, is the densely settled residential belt outside the incorporated city limits, and includes those persons who live in incorporated and unincorporated places, as well as those who live in the open countryside.

In 1950, when SMAs were first defined, about 6 percent of the nation's total land area and 56 percent of the nation's population fell within metropolitan boundaries. In 1980, 16 percent of the nation's land area and 75 percent of our population fell within metropolitan boundaries. Expansion of the land area encompassed by metropolitan areas, or lost to nonmetropolitan areas, reflect statistical redefinitions of counties' statuses following each census.

Whether intended or not, introduction of the SMA and its alternate, the nonmetropolitan area, altered our understanding of what is rural as well as the ways in which we study rural life. Essentially, these concepts link the study of the social demography of rural areas to political boundaries—county lines—resulting in a blurred distinction between rural and urban demographic processes. Because these statistical constructs encompass both rural and urban populations and lifestyles, our ability to identify and define the underlying demographic and social processes that differentiate *rural* and *urban* has been, it could be argued, diminished.

Following the introduction of these concepts, rural population studies have tended to use metropolitan and nonmetropolitan county level data to explain rural population dynamics (Humphrey and Sell, 1975; Humphrey, et al., 1977; Kirschenbaum, 1971; Zuiches, 1970). Such an approach is a problem both statistically and conceptually. A significant portion of the rural population lives in metropolitan areas, and, alternatively, a significant portion of the urban population lives in nonmetropolitan areas. Robinson (1965) explored this overlap using the 1960 metropolitan definition and the pre–1950 urban definition. He found that about one-third of the total rural population resided in metropolitan areas representing just over one in every five metropolitan residents. On the other hand, more than one out of three nonmetropolitan persons actually resided in urban places. In 1980, nearly one of every five persons residing on a farm were found in metropolitan areas. These comments illustrate one reason why it is a problem to use *metropolitan* and *nonmetropolitan* as interchangeable concepts with *urban* and *rural*.

The use of *metropolitan* and *nonmetropolitan* as synonymous with *urban* and *rural* is a conceptual problem. Sorokin and Zimmerman (1929) suggest and Smith (1953) reaffirms that the delineation of *rural* and *urban* must, at a minimum, encompass size, density, occupational differences, environment, and social heterogeneity as a set of "mutually dependent and functionally related characteristics." Although some of these characteristics are part of the metropolitan criteria, all are not. On the other hand, Namboodiri (1966) argues, while population size is an important factor affecting a person's life, its use as a variable for operationalizing *rural* and *urban* is a function of the amount of correspondence between places classified by size, and their roles as collective, interdependent communities. To a certain extent, this is what the definition of *metropolitan* seeks to accomplish—to assess the interdependence among areas. Yet, *nonmetropolitan* remains a residual, meaning there is no effort to determine the functional characteristics of non-metropolitan areas.

By adopting the census's statistical delineation of *metropolitan* and *nonmetropolitan* as surrogates for *rural* and *urban*, the analysis of how demographic processes differentiate rural and urban places has become one of gaining an understanding of metropolitan and nonmetropolitan demographic processes. There is a long tradition of developing theoretical sociological definitions of *rural* (Willits and Bealer, 1963 and 1967; Falk, 1978; Redfield, 1943) and *urban*. But, while there is a history of theoretical rigor underlying the delineation of *metropolitan*, the delineation of *nonmetropolitan*, although statistically meaningful, has no such history of theoretical rigor. Our understanding, then, of nonmetropolitan lifestyles or demographic processes has no comparable foundation in sociological theory to that of *rural* and *urban*.

Hence, area and population data from the decennial census on metropolitan and nonmetropolitan areas continue to attract our empirical attention and influence how we study rural population processes. Introducing the statistical concepts, *metropolitan* and *nonmetropolitan*, as the basis for gathering and disseminating census and other data has altered our concept of rural and urban areas. Instead of viewing rural and urban population dynamics as functions of social processes rooted in the structural and cultural characteristics of place, we have moved to a view of population dynamics as definers of place.

SUMMARY

The theoretical underpinnings of rural population studies on migration have attempted to explain the causes and consequences of migration within either a micro (individual) or a macro (aggregate) context. These approaches are not mutually exclusive. The cognitive-behavioral model has the potential to integrate these perspectives, enhancing our ability to understand the dynamics of migration. The next chapter describes significant changes associated with three major stages in the history of rural America, and is based on the factors or conditions that these theoretical models have identified as associated with migration.

2

The Socioeconomic and Political Context of Rural Population Change

INTRODUCTION

The theoretical frameworks that guide research on migration identify social, economic, and political conditions influencing both the decision to move and the choice of a destination. This chapter identifies some of the significant social, economic, and political events during the three eras of rural history (chapters three through seven will examine them in terms of major population changes), setting the stage within which the population changes take place. The three eras to be discussed, as adapted from Johnson and Beegle (1982), are

1. the rural dominance stage (1650–1880),
2. the era of urban growth (1880–1970), and
3. the era of residential diversity (1960–?).

The last two eras overlap because the socioeconomic and demographic events characterizing the era of residential diversity have their roots in earlier times, while many of the significant trends of the era of urban growth have persisted into the post-industrial era.

THE RURAL DOMINANCE STAGE (1650–1880)

The rural dominance stage is characterized by five major events:

1. the expansion of the nation's geographic territory,
2. land-use policies,
3. settlement patterns,
4. technological innovations, and
5. economic developments.

Each of these influence the physical distribution of population, people's daily work and life styles, and, indirectly, cultural values related to family formation and size.

Expansion of Geographic Territory

In less than a century, the geographic territory encompassed by the United States increased threefold, from less than one million square miles in 1790 to over three million square miles in 1867 (*see* appendix table A–2). The expansion occurred through simple occupation of territory or outright purchases from European colonial powers. During this period of expansion, the young nation extended its land ownership across the vast, vacant (at least of European settlers), and abundant continent.

Unlike the Old World nations that had too many people and not enough land, America had a surfeit of land and national resources to be exploited. As Potter (1954) notes, the challenge was to transform physical abundance or natural wealth into social wealth by establishing a national system of production and distribution. The physical availability of land and raw materials, Potter and others (Merk, 1963; Smith, 1970) argue, was the basis for a belief in a "continental" or "manifest" destiny, encouraging European expansion westward to the Pacific. Promoting the exploitation of this boundless land and its natural wealth influenced national policies on land dispersal and use.

But the continent was not empty. Over six hundred independent nations containing around one million American Indians populated the land. Initial relations wavered between peaceful coexistence and outright warfare, depending on the extent of the white settlers' intrusion into tribal hunting lands and the economic potential of tribal lands. The Dutch established the precedent of buying tribal lands from the Indians, while the British crown in 1754 guaranteed the inalienable right of the Indian nations to their lands and enforced this policy against the intrusion of colonial settlers. The American government periodically engaged in warfare with various Indian nations, especially when they allied with the British or the French to stop the territorial expansion of the new nation. In 1828, Andrew Jackson secured passage of the Indian Removal Act, empowering the president to remove all Indian tribes to some place west of the Mississippi River. In 1838, 14,000 Cherokees were herded onto the "trail of tears," which took them from their tribal homelands in the southeast, earlier secured by treaty, to a reservation in the Oklahoma territory, where they joined the rest of the Five Civilized Tribes who had also been removed from eastern lands. Over the next few decades, the Indian territories expanded and then shrank as these lands absorbed into the area available for settlement.

During the Civil War, members of the Five Civilized Tribes fought with the Confederacy. At war's end, Congress abrogated all existing treaties, and the new treaties forced these tribes to cede all their lands in the western Indian territory. Eventually, nearly two dozen other Indian tribes were settled on these lands (Collier, 1947). By the 1880s, federal policy toward Indian tribes focused on breaking down tribal or communal ownership of land in favor of individual ownership. All former tribal lands remaining after this land allotment program were removed from tribal ownership and sold to white settlers. Thus, the Indian nations lost 90 million acres to white settlers between 1887 and 1933 through the "direct and indirect workings of land allotment" (Collier, 1947: 134).

The native Indian tribes gave temporary but costly ($20 million fighting the Seminoles in Florida, $100 million fighting the Cheyenne and Navajo) resistance to the extension of federal control over the continent. In episodes too numerous to count, the American government guaranteed tribal lands and then broke these treaties when gold was discovered (e.g., Georgia in 1828) or when land-hungry settlers trespassed on native lands, forcing hostile confrontation. The forced breakup of com-

munally held land through the policy of "individualization" of
ownership reflected the dominant land-use policy applied to all
federally owned lands.

Land-Use Policies

Perhaps the most significant decision of this era was the one
to dispose of national lands rather than retain them in public
ownership. This decision reflected two assumptions: first, that
land was best developed through private ownership rather than
public control, and, second, that land value could only be measured by its development and use. The government's role in
this dispersal was to define the land in place by actual surveys,
and to dispose of the land in a manner that would protect
against uncontrolled land speculation. To satisfy the first purpose, Congress adopted the rectangular survey in 1785. The
provisions of this act called for the division of land into town-
ships composed of thirty-six sections of one square mile each,
with each section divided into quarter sections of 160 acres.
This approach provided a relatively inexpensive, quick, and
nearly infallible method of defining land in place, and reduced
the likelihood of boundary disputes and title litigation (Nelson,
1965). This approach shaped the physical appearance of farmsteads, counties, and many cities and states as can be seen by
any map of U.S. counties.

To satisfy the second purpose, the federal government sold
nearly 30 percent of all federally owned lands directly to private
individuals. During the 1800s, the minimum price was $2 an
acre on units of 320 acres, with a required down payment of
25 percent of the purchase price and four years to pay off the
remainder. Little land was actually sold, however, as most
individuals did not have access to this much cash, and political
tensions made precarious settlement west of the Alleghenies.
The War of 1812 ended the bottleneck of westward expansion
created by Tecumseh's efforts to unite the various Indian tribes
from the Great Lakes to the Gulf against the settlement efforts
of whites. Land speculation by companies and wealthy entre-
preneurs drove up the price of land, and the furious land market
created temporary shortages of surveyed land. As a result, a

considerable amount of unauthorized settlement occurred; individuals and families cleared land and began farmsteads on unsurveyed land in anticipation of purchasing when it eventually came on the market.

The Pre-emption Act of 1841 tacitly acknowledged the federal government's lack of effective control over lands in the public domain. The act declared that settlers had to establish a residence on public lands released into the private market in order to secure title to it. Moreover, if squatters could prove "asserted occupancy and improvement," they then had the prior right to purchase up to 160 acres at market prices.

In addition to the sale of public land, the federal government also donated large amounts of land, nearly 40 percent of all federally owned lands, to a wide variety of interests, such as transportation companies, state governments, war veterans, and timber and mineral companies. The most memorable of the federal land disposal programs, the Homestead Act of 1862, offered a quarter section (160 acres) of land free to citizens or intended citizens who settled and developed the land. While the Homestead Act symbolized the national commitment to agrarian democracy (Smith, 1970), between 1862 and 1891 more public land was in fact sold to private individuals than dispersed under the act.

The importance of the availability of a vast expanse of land in the nation's early development cannot be overestimated. The national government used land as a form of capital, "spending" land to encourage the development of a basic infrastructure. For example, through the nineteenth century, over 100 million acres were dispersed to state governments and private enterprises to encourage the development and expansion of educational facilities. In 1862, the Morrill Act granted 30,000 acres of public lands to each member of Congress, as an endowment for agricultural and mechanical colleges. If no federal or public lands were available within a state, the acres granted would be located elsewhere, and each state could then sell this land to generate the monies to endow such colleges. The Morrill Act called for colleges that would teach "agriculture and the mechanic arts," as well as other "scientific and classical studies, in order to promote the liberal and practical education of the industrial classes in the several pursuits and professions of life." Furthermore, experimental or "model" farms and mechanical shops would be established in conjunction with these colleges to provide students with practical experience.

Railroad companies received over 128 million acres, one-sixth of all public lands, to encourage the extension of rail lines across the continent. Timber and mining companies received federal lands to encourage the development of these resources in the interest of economic growth. Hence, instead of selling these land resources to generate capital necessary to build an infrastructure, the national government "spent" land to encourage private interests or state governments in this task. Finally, the federal government, following the Revolutionary War, the War of 1812, and the Civil War, settled war veteran claims with public lands, further encouraging the settlement of the continent.

Social historians cite this abundance and accessibility of physical resources to all citizens as a key factor in the shaping of the American character and institutions. Smith (1970: 3) states: "One of the most persistent generalizations concerning American life and character is the notion that our society has been shaped by the pull of a vacant continent drawing population westward." Potter (1954: 165), analyzing Turner's frontier thesis, argues that the physical abundance, when transformed by social and cultural processes into "new industrial potentialities ... perpetuated and reinforced the habits of fluidity, of mobility, of change, of the expectation of progress, which have been regarded as distinctive frontier traits."

Settlement Patterns

The continental expansion and land-use policies devised to facilitate development of land resources profoundly influenced settlement patterns. In the precolonial era, the Crown granted a significant proportion of land in New England to trading companies. The tendency of these companies to make grants to groups of settlers rather than individuals, in conjunction with geographic features (narrow valleys), a preference for town residence, and a well-founded fear of hostile actions by

native tribes produced a pattern of village settlement surrounded by small farmsteads.

In the southern colonies, the Crown granted lands directly
to individuals, and the physical features were conducive to
plantations. Smaller farmsteads could be found on the more
marginal agricultural lands. The plantations specialized in
crop production, initially tobacco, and later cotton, while independent freeholders engaged in diversified crop and animal
production. The middle colonies (New York, New Jersey, Pennsylvania) contained a mix of these two types of settlement.

As settlement moved west of the Alleghenies, the traditional
village surrounded by small farmsteads was often not transplanted successfully. The rectangular survey method encouraged scattered isolated farmsteads, a process facilitated by the
Pre-emption Act of 1841, which required landowners to reside
on their property. A final characteristic of settlement patterns
influenced by land availability and federal policies was the
abandonment of the European tradition of subdividing family
land among heirs; instead, young adults moved westward and
acquired their own property. As Billington (1966: 190) notes,
the young men comprising the bulk of westward migration
sought opportunities for a "better farm, more wealth, and a
higher status in life."

This is not to claim that, during the era of rural dominance,
urban areas languished while the rural population flourished.
While the bulk of the population resided in rural areas during
this time, it was also a time of unprecedented city building.
The growth and geographic dispersion of cities reflected technological advances, economic opportunities, and a spirit of op-
timistic boosterism. From the early 1600s, five small villages
(New York, Boston, Philadelphia, Newport, Charleston) grew
into five towns and then into five cities, providing a template
for urban growth in later centuries. Although these five cities
contained only a fraction of the nation's population, by the late
eighteenth century "each had grown economically mature as
distributing, producing, marketing centers that helped pierce
the back country with a transportation system that forged new
towns and cities, each acted as a magnet luring the native
farmer and the foreign immigrant alike by its opportunities

and amenities" (Callow, 1973: 53). Indeed, from 1820 to 1860, while the total population of the nation increased 226 percent, the urban population exploded by 800 percent!

City building during the era of rural dominance was not just a phenomenon of the coastal areas. In the trans-Mississippi West, enthusiastic town builders worked to bring civilization to the wilderness and to exploit the economic potential inherent in the expanding agrarian frontier. Some cities, such as Denver, San Francisco, and Houston, sprang up before the farmer's arrival in order to provide a focus for further development. Other cities, such as Lawrence, Kansas, emerged to service the needs of farmers; some, such as Salt Lake City, to serve the needs of travelers; and some, such as Portland, Oregon, were the final destinations of westward migrants. In 1865, as Harriet Williams wrote in her diary, one thousand people arrived in Portland, Oregon, one Saturday (Jeffrey, 1979).

Technological Innovations and Economic Developments

The power of cities rested, in great part, on the pace of technological innovation undergirding their economic expansion. Technological innovations during the first half of the nineteenth century were oriented toward basic needs—food, clothing, housing, and agricultural tools—plows, scythes, threshers, reapers, and hay rakes—increasing the productivity of farm workers. Food processing innovations—flour mills, assembly line meat processing plants, ice boxes, free-standing stoves, and improved methods for canning meats, fruits, and vegetables—broadened the range of food products available to all persons in any location, in any season (Brady, 1964). By the Civil War, the textile industry produced the bulk of cloth and clothing in the United States. By midcentury, U.S. rifle manufacturers developed the "American system" of interchangeable parts, which later enabled machine shops to build the milling machines and metal working tools that would be the basis of fully mechanized factories in the next fifty years (Pursell, 1967). Finally, innovations in the construction industry—uniformly sized lumber, windows, doors, stairs, and flooring—reduced building costs. The cities provided the capital, land, workers, and transportation routes, enabling these emergent industries to thrive.

Chicago typifies the results of the convergence of technological innovations, access to transportation routes and urban population growth. In 1830, Chicago, a tiny village of fifty persons, had a vision of a great urban hub linked by water (the Great Lakes) and railroads to both the agricultural products of the interior and the markets of the eastern seaboard and Europe. By 1853, Chicago was a city of 60,000 people, translating the continent's physical abundance into the social resources for continued economic growth.

Transportation innovations, such as the steamboat and steam engine railroads, bridged the physical distance isolating the nation's natural resources from the organizational and creative forces that would transform them. From 1865 to 1873 railroad mileage more than doubled to 75,000 miles. Industrial innovations drew workers to the cities, stimulated the influx of new capital, and spurred the investment in the canals, turnpikes, and railroads that extended the urban influence into the hinterlands. Urban growth, then, was as much a part of the era of rural dominance as the expansion of the agrarian frontier. Indeed, it can be argued that the extension of the agrarian frontier depended on access to urban markets that provided both an outlet for products and a source of capital.

The concept of "manifest destiny" justified not only the geographic extension of the nation's boundaries but also the spread of cities across the landscape and the economic exploitation of the continent's resources. In his second inaugural address in 1830, Andrew Jackson asked: "What good man would prefer a country covered with forests and ranged by a few thousand savages to our extensive Republic, studded with cities, towns, and prosperous farms, embellished with all the improvements which art can devise or industry execute" (as cited in Nash, 1967: 41). In this context, the struggle to establish civilization entailed not only "taming" the wilderness by establishing productive farms, but also building cities "from the bosom of the wilderness" (Nash, 1967: 40–41).

In summary, key historical events during the era of rural

dominance (1650–1880) influenced patterns of migration and population change in rural America. First, the nation extended and consolidated control over the continent's physical resources. By the end of this era, the nation's physical boundaries (except Hawaii, acquired in 1898) were established. Second, access to much more physical territory was assured through extending railroads, improving water transportation, and eliminating the threat by native Americans, who were forcibly removed to defined reservations. Third, the nation's physical resources provided, through economic development and growth, for social wealth, a transformation process technologies such as the steam engine (1769), telegraph (1861), telephone (1876), and particular agricultural (mechanical reaper, steel plow, thresher) and industrial (spinning machines, stamping machines, steel production) innovations facilitated.

Fourth, the expanded national and international markets stimulated the demand for both natural resources and manufactured products, fueling the engines of economic growth. In this context, it is important to remember that U.S. farmers, from the earliest days of settlement, produced goods for commercial markets. Sometimes their agricultural products were simply bartered for desired goods, but, in most cases, farmers participated in a cash economy. Finally, the pace of urban and economic growth, territorial expansion, and resource use overwhelmed the social control mechanisms of federal government. Periodic economic crises, emerging monopolistic markets (railroads, grain elevators), the fluctuating value and specie base of the national currency, high protective tariffs, high taxes on farmland, and high-cost credit produced substantial social and income inequalities. Increasingly, opportunities for social mobility flourished in rapidly developing urban areas, not the agrarian heartland.

THE ERA OF URBAN GROWTH (1880–1970)

Changes in the scale of social and economic life and associated economies of scale (agglomeration efficiencies) characterize these decades. Four major trends contributed to these changes: the population concentrated in urban centers, the economy industrialized, the government increased influence over national affairs, and the nation prospered. Each of these influenced the pattern of rural population change and quality of rural life vis-à-vis urban lifestyles. Callow (1973: 155) illustrates the interaction among these trends: "If railroads, heavy industries and technological inventions helped build cities, urbanization in turn helped accelerate the hallmarks of industrialization; mass production, mass consumption, mass distribution of goods and services. If industrialization produced a more coordinated network of economic development, the network of cities became the muscles and sinews of that development—producing, selling, financing, and providing it with a market and a labor force."

Growth of Urban Centers

The 1920 census indicates that over one-half of all Americans resided in urban areas, statistically marking the end of an agrarian America. The increasing concentration of population in urban areas reflected two processes: migration to the cities, and expansion of the cities' physical boundaries. During this stage, cities served as "urban frontiers," offering the opportunities for social mobility once found on the agrarian frontier, and therefore attracting a substantial number of migrants to them. The growth of urban centers demonstrated an agglomeration effect; that is, during this era size was associated with rates of growth. Large urban areas grow more rapidly than smaller urban areas, and incorporated places outside urban centers grow more rapidly than unincorporated places. Overall, the number of places in the smaller population size categories declined during this era, while the number of places in the larger population size categories increased.

The geographic expansion of cities occurred through annexation—the political incorporation of surrounding areas into the jurisdictional control of the city, and the residential-economic integration of the hinterland into the influence of the city. Emerging suburbs typify this latter process, and demonstrate the synergistic effects of transportation innovations, industrialization, and cultural values formulated during the era of rural dominance. The earliest suburbs (pre–1850) were small, semirural communities adjacent to larger places populated by exploiters of business and land opportunities on the urban fringe (Binford, 1985). These early suburbs prospered by developing and then controlling access routes between the hinterland and the city (toll roads, bridges, canals); by assembling, storing, processing, and then transshipping goods in both directions; and by providing ample land for ancillary services, such as craft-based industries or intensive specialized horticultural enterprises producing for city consumption.

While early suburbs thrived because of the difficulty of transportation, later suburbs thrived because of transportation innovations—commuter railroads, fixed-line streetcars, and, ultimately, the automobile. These innovations permitted long-distance commuting for employment and residence, hastening cities' geographic expansion into the countryside. Residential suburbs many miles from urban centers proliferated, especially following World War II, spurred by federal investments in suburban housing through Veteran's Administration loans and Federal Housing Administration (FHA) programs. More critically for rural communities, these innovations enabled urban areas to extend their commercial and industrial influences far beyond their geographic boundaries. When linked with other innovations, such as Rural Free Delivery (the basis for the rise of the great Chicago mail-order houses—Sears, Roebuck and Montgomery Ward), transportation and communication innovations ensured the urban-based mass distribution of goods and services, which is the basis of the urban mass society. By the mid-twentieth century, few rural Americans' lives were untouched by urban-based employment, goods, services, arts, and entertainment.

Industrialization of the Economy

The industrialization of the economy facilitated this urbanization process. Fully mechanized factories, increasingly mechanized agriculture, electricity, and new alloys signalled "a giant leap forward in power, speed, energy, and adaptability. The complex machine ceased to be an innovation and became ubiquitous" (Warner, 1972: 85–86). The industrial transformation of the economy, however, also involved developing a new organization of labor. Warner (1972: 73) states: "Inventions were important . . . but since early machinery served at most as a substitute for a few hand tasks, the principal gains in production accrued to bosses who could organize their shopworkers for a steady production of uniform output." Organizing assembly lines of unskilled workers supervised by craftsmen, contracting work at several different sites, emphasizing product uniformity over artisan quality control, and increasing the sales of manufactured products and producing for mass markets began the "long process of division into two classes within the urban labor force, a social division between hard workers and pen wielders, operatives and clerks, the blue collar and the white" (Warner, 1972: 77).

Expansion of the rail system enabled urban areas to specialize in particular kinds of manufacturing and processing activities (Richmond, Va., cigarettes; Sacramento, Calif., canned fruits and vegetables; Erie, Pa., foundries), and to provide diverse financial and commercial services. In 1916, railroads carried 77 percent of intercity tonnage and 98 percent of the intercity passengers on 254,000 miles of track (Warner, 1972: 89). Ironically, this was also the first year of federal investment in the national highway system. The growing dominance of the automobile for personal transportation and the truck for intercity freight called for rapid expansion of the federal interstate highway system. Further, the development of intrastate road systems gradually eliminated the need to restrict residence and work places to particular areas accessible by rail.

By the 1960s, some manufacturing firms, especially those in highly competitive markets with narrow profit margins, began to leave the cities. They were pushed from the cities by rising employment costs and increased competition for land, but were free from restricted access of fixed transportation routes that had narrowed locational options in the early twentieth century. Firms were attracted to smaller towns and cities by low land values, a low-cost but skilled labor force, and financial incentives. Some rural areas began to capture a greater share of new manufacturing jobs, yet the higher paying, unionized jobs in the durable goods-producing firms (e.g., steel, automobiles) still concentrated in the cities. Furthermore, despite increased manufacturing employment in rural areas, this growth was mostly limited to certain areas (e.g., textile manufacturing in the rural South). As a result, most rural communities continued to depend on a single industrial sector, a situation that would limit their ability to attract new firms and generate new economic growth.

The industrialization of agriculture during this stage involved several significant changes. Tractors were introduced in 1903; by 1920, when the Census of Agriculture first counted them, 246,000 tractors were on U.S. farms, and over 4 million by 1950. Mechanization of agricultural production involved not only the replacement of horses by tractors, but also the acquisition of all the power-driven tools that enabled farmers to maximize their tractors' potential productivity. Mechanization occurred more rapidly and systematically outside the South until the early 1940s, when, within a ten-year period, nearly all cotton production processes were mechanized, displacing thousands of black tenant farmers. To differing degrees, the displacement of farm laborers followed in lock-step with the increased applications of mechanical power to agricultural production.

As in urban-based economic enterprises, the industrialization of agriculture also entailed transforming production's organizational structure. The new technologies (machinery, fertilizers, herbicides, genetically improved seeds or livestock) often necessitated larger production units to fully capture their economic benefits. Hence, larger farms often mechanized first, and were able to capture the larger share of economic benefits of early adoption (Cochrane, 1979). The imperative of economies of scale stimulated the industrialization of agriculture. Farmers could work more land with machinery than with horses, and the tractor expanded agricultural production onto more, often marginal, lands. Moreover, periodic economic crises in the agricultural sector forced many producers out of farming, concentrating production into fewer but larger units—a process echoed in other industrial sectors. Finally, the amount of capital investment required to begin a new farm and to maintain modernization of existing enterprises steadily rose during this era, altering agriculture's opportunity structure.

Federal Influence in National Affairs

The processes of urbanization and industrialization during this era reflected growing governmental influence over national affairs. The Interstate Commerce Commission (1887), Sherman Anti-Trust Act (1890), Meat Inspection Act and Pure Food and Drug Act (1906), Federal Reserve Act (1913), Federal Trade Commission (1914), Agricultural Adjustment Act (1933), Tennessee Valley Authority (1933), Rural Electrification Administration (1935), FHA (1934), Federal Deposit Insurance Corporation (1933), and Securities and Exchange Commission (1934) are only a few examples of the many aspects of economic and domestic life increasingly affected by the national government. The significance of federal involvement lies in its effects on the pace, nature, and distribution of society's economic growth. The following example illustrates this point.

The FHA, a national mortgage insurance program, financed about "one-fifth of all the privately owned nonfarm housing units" (Warner, 1972: 232) built between 1933 and 1970. FHA enabled millions of lower middle-class and upper working-class families to attain private home ownership. FHA also encouraged the construction of residential suburbs away from the inner cities, a locational decision facilitated by the concomitant federal investment in community infrastructure, including a national network of two-lane, all-weather intercity roads.

The program requirements for participation in the FHA loan system further concentrated financial resources in urban areas. In order to participate, banks had to process large quantities of paperwork, maintain detailed records, and encumber a portion of their capital at interest rates often below market levels. As a result, the distribution of FHA loans has been favored by large, urban-based financial institutions with the necessary technical and monetary resources. Similarly, home buyers in rural areas face a smaller pool of mortgage credit, higher required down payments, shorter-term loans, higher interest rates, and/or more restricted credit requirements (Thompson and Mikesell, 1981). The program requirements and operational policies of FHA have unintentionally focused more financial resources for home construction and purchases in suburban and urban areas. As a result, people and the housing industry in urban areas have had greater access to resources facilitating growth and development.

As the federal government assumed a more important role in the nation's economic life, most programs directed funds towards urban centers; the needs of rural communities received scant attention. Federal programs for rural communities focused on developing the rural infrastructure, such as roads, access to electricity and telephones, and, later, water and sewage systems, in order to integrate rural areas into the national economic system. It must be acknowledged that the cost of developing this rural infrastructure outweighed any immediate economic returns: economies of scale produced exceptionally high costs for delivery of such services to a dispersed population. As a result, some of the most remote rural areas still did not have these services by the end of this era. Yet, the commitment to a national strategy of economic development begun over a century earlier justified these costs by their potential long-term economic benefits for the nation as a whole.

National Prosperity

Each of these factors contributed both to the rising national prosperity and the growing income gap between rural and urban areas. Urbanization, industrialization, and federal investments in economic and social developments stimulated unprecedented expansion in national and personal wealth. The growth in national wealth is exemplified by the per capita Gross National Product, which nearly doubled between 1915 ($4,660) and 1950 ($8,855) (real constant dollars). The doubling of worker productivity during the first half of this century was a critical factor in this national prosperity. Moreover, the average worker in 1950 earned more than three times per hour (in real dollars) what the worker in 1915 did, and, finally, the number of persons in the labor force increased faster than the rate of population growth (Linden, 1987).

The national economy's expansion was not without setbacks. A seemingly endless series of economic crises, culminating in the Great Depression of the 1930s, produced numerous economic troughs, and impoverished large numbers of farm and working-class families. The Great Depression is notable not only for its depth and duration, but also for the wide variety of federal programs initiated to stabilize the economy, guarantee a minimum standard of services for most Americans, and stimulate economic recovery. While the complete recovery of the economy depended on the war mobilization, the rapid economic growth following the Great Depression implied to many national boosters that the American engine of prosperity was unstoppable.

This national prosperity steadily improved the standard of living. During this era, the quantity, quality, and range of consumer goods increased dramatically. Technological innovations improved the working conditions of millions, while federal oversight guaranteed the quality and safety of consumer products. Federal, state, and municipal investments in public water systems, health care, and fire protection improved everyone's access to a healthier and safer environment. The Rural Electrification Act (1934) provided access to cheap electricity and to all consumer goods and mass media dependent on electricity, in even the most remote areas. However, these public investments in infrastructure development came earlier to and were greater in urban areas, creating a quality of life gap between urban and rural areas.

Rural areas and rural people, then, did not equally share in the nation's prosperity and growth. Businesses interested in access to workers, supplies, and markets invested in urban economic development. Governments invested in urban areas because a substantial proportion of voters resided there, a result, in great part, of the steady stream of migration from rural to urban areas. The traditional rural economic enterprises— agriculture, mining, and forestry—did not experience sustained expansion as did other economic sectors, and, as already noted, technological advances and structural reorganization reduced the size of the labor force and the number of employing firms in these industries. The limited share of national and personal wealth in rural areas translated into a lower standard of living. Rural areas had a disproportionate share of substandard housing, limited access to health care and public water systems, and more chronic unemployment.

Thus, by the end of this era (1970), urban areas had extended their economic influence over an everwidening geographic area. Mass media, mass-produced consumer goods, and paved interarea roads extended the cities' influence over an ever expanding urban hinterland. The unparalleled pace of technological and scientific innovation generated a continuous flow of goods designed to ease the harshness and difficulty of work, increase productivity, expand the food supply, and improve the standard of living. The federal government redefined the state's role in economic and social life by investing in the national transportation and public services infrastructure, directing economic growth through research and development and various incentives, and establishing subsidy programs that guaranteed most Americans a share in at least some of the national prosperity. National opinion polls during the mid-twentieth century indicated great optimism as to continued economic growth; belief in the continued improvement in the standard of living, both nationally and personally, and interest in the material comforts of the "good life." The changes wrought in the social and economic fabric of national life during this era serve as the foundation for the third stage of national history.

THE ERA OF RESIDENTIAL DIVERSITY (1960–?)

The second half of the twentieth century is marked by both intensifying and discontinuing major socioeconomic trends of earlier eras. The phrase "era of residential diversity" refers to the growing variation of residential choices, resulting in diminished differentials in rural-urban social and economic structures. Four trends or situations are of particular relevance to the restructured population of rural America: continued diffusion of urban influences into rural areas, change in attitude toward urban living, continued structural transformations of the economy, and an emerging reassessment of the federal government's appropriate role.

Diffusion of Urban Influences

During the second half of this century, the influence of urban values, attitudes, and lifestyles continue to diffuse to even the most remote areas. Rural residents have access to the same standardized consumer goods and services as urban residents. Locality-based retailers and financial institutions are increasingly either subsidiaries of state, national, or multinational corporations, or simply bypassed in favor of regional service centers (e.g., shopping malls). Few persons are more than a half-hour drive from major fast food franchises, rural people have access to national distributors through the "800" toll-free mail-order numbers or the booming mail-order catalogue industry, and farm supply cooperatives offer uniform products distributed under the regional cooperative's label. Regional editions of the *Wall Street Journal* and *USA Today* are delivered in rural areas on the day of publication; "VisiCal" and other computer programs are as integral a feature of many farms as discs and plows; and cable systems and satellite dishes link millions of households with over one hundred channels for entertainment, twenty-four hour news and weather reports, and direct marketing (Dillman, 1983).

The federal investments in the national infrastructure, the growing influence of the mass media, and the growing availability of consumer goods and the disposable income to acquire these goods all contribute to the diffusion of urban influences. However, this is not to suggest that rural communities and rural people have become indistinguishable from urban areas and residents. National polls and surveys do indicate measurable differences by place of residence on a host of attitudinal and value measures. Rural peoples remain more conservative in their political views, more traditional in their views on social relations, and more strict in their religious practices and beliefs.

Attitudes toward Urban Areas

As the urban-based mass society extended its influence, providing access to consumer, public service, and entertainment amenities once confined to urban areas, public attitudes towards urban living shifted. The sixties ushered in the "long hot summers," episodes of racial unrest in most major urban areas, along with rising crime rates, pollution, high taxes, illegal drugs, traffic congestion, impersonality, changing moral standards, and overcrowding—all of which converged to make urban life appear more dangerous and stressful, and less desirable than previously (Campbell and Garkovich, 1984). Latent antiurban sentiments re-emerged (White and White, 1962), confirming why urban living represents both the best and the worst of modern life, and suggesting that urban areas have become ungovernable megalopolises. Simultaneously, dormant prorural sentiments have been activated by the increased opportunity to share in desirable aspects of urban life (employment opportunities, higher wages, quality schools, consumer and entertainment opportunities) without the costs or dangers of urban living.

Yet, prourban attitudes remain strong. "Urban gentrification," the renovation of historic areas in urban centers, illustrates the durability of prourban attitudes. In effect, during this era, our historic love-hate relationship with urban life finds new forms of expression and new bases for both our attraction to and our dislike of urban life.

Structural Transformations

Continued structural transformations in the economy further diminish differentials in economic opportunities between rural and urban areas. Agriculture's reorganization, including "a reduction in the number of farms, an increasing capitalization of farms, a shift from family-owned and operated farms to corporate-owned and managerially operated farms, and an absorption of many farm activities by industrial concerns ... has imposed an organizational structure upon a larger segment of agriculture not unlike that which prevails in the metro sector of the economy" (Hawley and Mazie, 1981: 10).

During the 1970s, manufacturing employment grew at a substantially higher rate in rural areas, due primarily to plant expansions and the emergence of new firms, rather than the relocation of existing firms from urban areas. Nondurable goods manufacturing accelerated in rural areas. But of greater consequence has been the rapid expansion of the service industries. Menchick (1981) notes that during the 1970s, the growth of service industries accounted for 74 percent of the new jobs in rural areas. There are many advantages to the growth of the service sector. Service industries are labor-intensive and rarely increase the burden on local public utilities. Fuchs (1968) also suggests that service jobs are relatively resistant to recessions, providing a cushioned income in areas relying on more susceptible specialized industries. Hence, while urban areas continued to offer a significantly larger number of employment opportunities, rural areas captured a significantly larger share of new jobs generated during this era.

As a result of the strength in rural employment growth, the economic differentials once separating rural and urban areas narrowed. Hawley and Mazie (1981: 13) note that the "proportion of workers engaged in professional, clerical, crafts machine tending and transport occupations" became more similar, as did median family incomes. While unemployment and underemployment in rural areas continued to be higher than in urban areas, the standard of living between these places slowly began to converge. Rapidly expanding rural employment opportunities, federal investments in infrastructure development (road construction, public water systems, subsidized health care, etc.), and federal transfer payments (Social Security pensions, disability programs, food and other welfare programs) all contributed in varying degrees to the rising rural standard of living.

The steady march of national prosperity faltered in the late 1970s and early 1980s. Inflationary pressures and declines in worker productivity reduced the competitiveness of American products on the international market, forcing the restructuring and retrenchment of many major industries such as automobiles, steel, textiles, shoes, lumber, and wood products, to name only a few. The American balance of payments burden increased dramatically, so that by the mid–1980s American had become the world's largest debtor nation. The federal deficit exceeded 1 trillion dollars, and a national unemployment rate of 6 percent now appeared to be the new level of "full employment." The economic optimism that carried America through the Great Depression and endless recessions dissipated. National opinion polls revealed that a substantial number of Americans felt their current economic condition was worse than it was five years earlier, and better than it would be in five years.

Changing Role of Federal Government

Finally, public support for an activist federal government softened under inflationary and deficit pressures. Federal infrastructure investments faced cutbacks, as did social support programs, and many programs were transferred to state or local management. The earlier commitment to an active federal government aggressively managing economic development and assisting peoples' access to minimum services seemed to diminish. The consequences of this changing federal role for the pace and nature of economic growth and individuals' opportunities to share in the nation's wealth remain uncertain. Whether this change is temporary or the beginning of a permanent redefinition of federal involvement in economic development is also uncertain.

The era of residential diversity is marked by significant reductions in the differential access to economic opportunities for rural and urban residents that had characterized earlier times. Many accoutrements of a modern, urban, consumptive society have become available directly or through mail order to residents of any size community. Telecommunications innovations have made possible video conferences among persons thousands of miles apart. They have severed the geographic impediment between place of work and place of residence for some industries and occupations, and have enabled people to bypass local service deliverers, such as banks, in favor of regional or national firms, such as money markets. The barrier that place of residence once posed to social mobility or even material comfort has diminished. Rural people have access to a standard of living their ancestors could not have imagined. Although the land frontier of the earlier centuries has disappeared, the frontier of science and entrepreneurship has replaced the opportunities and challenges it once offered.

However, not everyone has shared equally in the technologies that reduced the barriers of distance. Rural people, industries, and businesses have not always been able to take advantage of the opportunities new technologies offer. Limited capital and small populations have prevented some rural communities and people from "linking into" many telecommunications innovations. For example, although nearly half of all American households now have cable television, it is essentially an urban service because of the high per capita costs of laying the cable to individual households. Modems, which link personal computers with central mainframes, require single party telephone service, unavailable in many rural areas. Furthermore, redefining the federal government's role in conjunction with the recession of the 1980s has reduced federal investments in infrastructure development and maintenance. Without these federal monies, many rural communities cannot deal with their deteriorating or inadequate water and sewage systems, roads, bridges, and human services. Finally, the industrial growth in rural communities that had marked the 1970s diminished or simply disappeared in the 1980s as federal monies declined and many manufacturing firms moved overseas. Thus, the era of residential diversity, which began with the promise of population and economic revitalization for rural communities, has become a promise postponed for the 1980s.

SUMMARY

This brief examination of social, economic, and political transformations in American life identifies some of the major factors influencing population changes in rural communities.

1. Sustained economic growth, often marred by temporary recessions, fueled by abundant natural resources and technological innovations that transformed these resources into social wealth.

2. The concentration of employment growth and industrial development in urban centers, so that, increasingly, social wealth and economic power were urban-based phenomena.

3. The expansion of geographic territory encompassed within urban territories.

4. A shift to larger, more capital-intensive, rather than labor-intensive, agriculture, with a corresponding decline in the number of farm enterprises and hired farm laborers.

5. The development of a mass consumer society marked by an ever-expanding range of consumer products and an homogenized American culture. Associated with this trend is the diminished gap between rural and urban standards of living.

6. The emergence of more complex and diverse rural social and economic structures. From primarily agriculturally dependent communities, rural towns and villages have broadened their economic bases and, as a result, diversified their social structures.

As we shall see in the next chapters, these social, economic, and political transformations directed migration away from rural areas and, accordingly, altered the rate and composition of rural population change.

Migration and Population Change During the Era of Rural Dominance (1650–1880)

INTRODUCTION

The desire of European settlers and their descendants to extend political control over a continent and to transform its physical abundance into national wealth shaped the nature and pace of population change during this era. Open door immigration and land dispersal policies exemplify the positive side of the efforts encouraging the population growth necessary to fulfill the nation's "manifest destiny," while the treatment of native Americans represents its darker side. The various migration streams that developed profoundly influenced the distribution and growth of the rural population.

Rural areas during this era had a steadily increasing net gain of population that peaked in the 1870s, when rural areas had a net increase of nearly 7.4 million persons (figure 1; appendix table A–3). This astonishing rate of growth was due to natural increase (the excess of births over deaths), immigration, and migration. However, urban growth was proportionately greater, because the urban population was small. As a result, a small numerical gain in the urban population produced a large percentage gain. For example, between 1790 and 1800 the rural population gained over 1.2 million persons for a 34 percent increase. On the other hand, the urban population increased by 120,000 persons for a 59 percent increase. The

Figure 1
Change in the Rural Population in the United States, 1790–1880

Percent Change

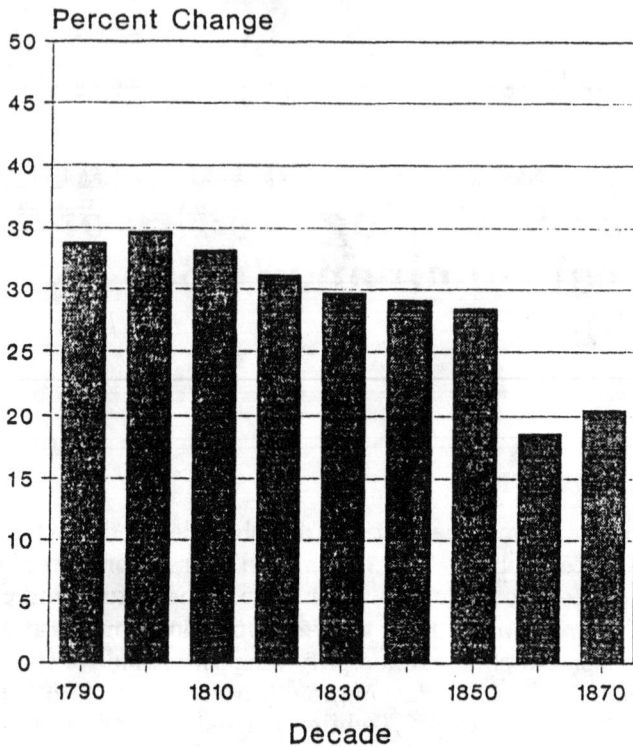

Decade	Population Change (millions)	% Change
1790 to 1800	1.3	33.8
1800 to 1810	1.7	34.7
1810 to 1820	2.2	33.2
1820 to 1830	2.8	31.2
1830 to 1840	3.5	29.7
1840 to 1850	4.4	29.1
1850 to 1860	5.6	28.4
1860 to 1870	4.7	18.6
1870 to 1880	6.1	20.5

Source: Adapted from U.S. Bureau of the Census, Current Population Reports Series p-20 No. 374. Population Profile of the United States: 1981. Washington D.C., Government Printing Office, 1982.

flood of immigrants to our shores and the various streams of migration were critical to the growth and redistribution of the rural population.

The major migration streams of the era of rural dominance were

1. streams of immigrants,

2. westward migration,

3. farm-to-farm migration,

4. rural-to-urban migration, and

5. urban-to-rural migration.

Particular streams were often related, as when immigration was the first stage in westward migration, or when farm-to-farm migration entailed movement to the western frontier. Yet, each was also significant in its own way.

IMMIGRANT STREAMS

To say that America is a nation of immigrants is to mask the great diversity in the composition of and reasons underlying the streams of immigration during the era of rural dominance. Peterson's (1975) general typology provides a useful device for differentiating among several types of this era's immigration streams. Of particular interest here are forced, impelled, free, and mass migrations. Forced migrations are caused by the state or some social institution, and are designed to get rid of some category of persons (native Americans) or to obtain labor (slaves). In either case, those forced to move have no choice in whether to leave or stay. Impelled migrations are also motivated by some external agency for the same reasons as forced migration, but people retain some choice in whether to leave or not (indentured servants). Free migration is the result of an individual's or group's independent decision, but can lead to mass migration if the movement takes on social momentum, for example, the California Gold Rush in the 1840s.

From the earliest settlements to 1808, when the British abolished the Atlantic slave trade, these four types of migration were present. Along with the early individual Spanish, Dutch, German, and English settlers came their white indentured servants and their black slaves. In the northern colonies, almost half of the early white immigrants were indentured servants, but by the early 1700s the rate of black population growth exceeded that of whites, leveling off only at the end of the century (Johnson and Campbell, 1981). For a variety of reasons, including a preference for white workers in skilled trades and a fear of slave uprisings, the northern colonies were primarily settled by "free" immigrants. For example, prior to the Revolutionary War thousands of Scots, Irish, English, and Germans migrated to the colonies, with Philadelphia their port of entry. These immigrants, some arriving as individuals or families, others as members of religious groups, then moved into the western frontiers along the Appalachian valleys (Commons, 1907).

Northern settlers included individuals and their families (free migration), members of religious groups such as the Puritans of New England or the Quakers of Pennsylvania (mass migration), white indentured servants (impelled migration), and black slaves (forced migration). The extent of immigration to the colonies is remarkable given the difficulties of the passage and the uncertainties upon arrival. Smith (1953: 57) estimates that 20,000 Irishmen arrived in the colonies between 1700 and 1730, and 6,000 entered the port of Philadelphia in 1729 alone. In the southern colonies, imported black slaves were a significant component of population growth. For example, between 1714 and 1754 the number of slaves in the colonies increased fivefold—from 59,000 to 298,000—with the vast majority residing in the rural South. The first federal census in 1790 recorded 757,000 blacks in the United States, or 19 percent of the national population; 700,000 of the blacks were slaves, and nine out of ten black slaves lived in the South. (Johnson and Campbell, 1981).

To a certain extent, immigration to America had the characteristics of a mass migration. Handlin (1959: 24) presents a British newspaper account of the German countryside during this period: "In Bavaria especially, whole village communities sell their property for whatever they can get, and set out, with their clergyman at their head. . . . From 1832 to 1835 inclusive, 9,000 embarked every year from Bremen (Germany); from 1839 to 1842, the average number was 13,000; which increased to 19,000 in the year 1844." This is not an unusual tally for one port of debarkation. The New York State Commissioner of Emigration reported that one ship, the Leibnitz, carried about 700 passengers to Quebec in 1866, and 547 passengers to America the following year: this was during a time when hundreds of ships crossed the Atlantic ferrying immigrants to America. However, the hazards of the passage were also noted in this report. Of the 547 passengers embarking on the Leibnitz, only 436 survived.

Peterson's (1975) commentary on Swedish immigrants to America illustrates another mechanism by which many immigrants came to America. In the 1840s, the early Swedish immigrants, about 1,000 a year, were young educated men, primarily from two university towns, Uppsala and Lund. They wrote letters home, and the stories of their experiences appeared in their hometown newspapers; they also provided financial assistance to those who wanted to follow. By the 1860s, nearly 9,000 Swedes were immigrating to America each year. Steamships reduced the length and difficulty of passage, while railroads carried the immigrants to settled family members in Minnesota. As Petersen (1975: 325) notes: "In some districts [in Sweden] there was not a farm without relatives in America, and from many all the young people had gone overseas." This process reflects the transformation of "free" migration by individuals into "mass" migration, wherein migration becomes an institutionalized pattern of behavior. At the individual or family level, this story of Swedish immigration represents "chain" migration, wherein one member of a kinship group moves to an area, and others follow once residence is established and work is found.

With two major exceptions—black slaves in the South in the first century and a half of this era, and Chinese on the West Coast at the end of this era—most immigrants came from northern Europe, especially the British Isles, France, Germany, and Scandinavia. Hansen (1940) identifies this as the "Celtic" period, which reached its crest from 1847 to 1854. Hansen argues

that the Germans, Belgians, Dutch, and Norwegians emigrat-
ing to America during these decades were descendants of Celtic
tribesmen who had settled in the Upper Rhine Valley or along
the coastal districts of Norway and had established agricultural
communities and cultural enclaves. The second great wave of
immigration, from 1860 to 1890, was composed of English,
Scandinavians, Prussian and Saxon Germans, and Austrians.
Again, Hansen (1940: 9) argues that these migrants originated
in regions sharing a common Teutonic heritage, "forming the
most homogenous of all the migrations to America."

The importance of immigration in national population
growth cannot be overestimated. In 1810, 4 percent of the average annual national population growth was attributable to
immigration, rising to 28 percent in 1850 and leveling off at
around 25 percent during the remaining rural dominance
stage. By 1880, fully 15 percent of the American population
was foreign-born, and an additional 19 percent were children
of foreign-born parents. Some areas of the nation had even
greater proportions of foreign-born residents, for example, in
North Dakota nearly 45 percent of the population was foreign-
born; in Minnesota, 35 percent; in South Dakota, 30 percent;
and in Iowa and Nebraska, nearly 20 percent.

This discussion should not obscure the small but measurable
emigration from America to Europe and other destinations.
Some returned to families, while others left in search of opportunities in the Old World. Still others left for religious reasons, as did some Mormons who moved to new settlements in
Mexico, and others left because of political persecution, as did
the British loyalists following the Revolutionary War. Yet, the
movement of persons out of America never rivaled the flow of
immigrants into the nation.

WESTWARD MIGRATION

From the arrival of the first European settlers, people's imag-
inations turned to the frontier. However, the frontier con-
stantly crept westward, as pioneers pushed their settlements
into new lands—first over the Alleghenies, then toward the
Mississippi, and then finally to the Pacific. This is illustrated

Figure 2
Geographic Location of the U.S. Center of Population,
1790–1980

Source: U.S. Bureau of the Census. 1984 Statistical Abstract of the United States. 104th edition. Washington D.C., Government Printing Office.

in figure 2, which shows the westward movement of the U.S. population's geographic center. By the end of the era of rural dominance, the geographic center was just a few miles west of Cincinnati.

By the mid–1840s, settlers had pushed the frontier across the Mississippi. By 1880, the tide of westward movement had swept to the Pacific coast and back again, filling in the "Great American Desert," as the Great Plains were once known. As a result, that half of the continent west of the Mississippi, which, in 1840, was home to less than 1 percent of the nation's population, in 1880 was home to one in five Americans (Jeffrey, 1979). It is estimated that, between 1841 and 1867, over 350,000 persons traveled the overland trails to California and Oregon (Mattes, 1969).

Native Movements Westward

One source for the westward movement was native-born persons. Jeffrey (1979: 28) states that most persons on the overland trails came from "rural and small-town backgrounds in the Midwest and upper South," with a smattering of persons from Midwestern and Eastern cities. A significant proportion of these native-born emigrants to the West were farmers or adult children of farm families searching for new land to cultivate. This migration of the native-born to the western frontier was stimulated in several ways. Schlissel (1982) notes that many associations were formed to encourage westward migration. For example, in 1839 there were ten "Oregon Societies" in communities along the Mississippi; their members pledged to move together to the new frontier. Numerous guidebooks, such as Overton Johnson and William H. Winter's *Route across the Rocky Mountains, with a Description of Oregon and California* (1846), dispensed practical information for the trek westward and sung the praises of the opportunities awaiting newcomers. Magazines of the time, such as *Godey's Lady's Book* or *Western Literary Journal and Monthly Review*, popularized the frontier's adventures and opportunities, and railroad companies aggressively advertised prime agricultural land for sale.

Immigrant Movements Westward

The movement westward was also fueled by the continuing arrival and dispersion of immigrants. During this era, a substantial portion of new arrivals, after pausing for a period of time at their ports of entry, moved to the interior. In the eighteenth century, Charleston served both slaves and white settlers as a major port of entry to the southern colonies. From Charleston and the Virginias, immigrants moved through the Yudkin Valley of the Carolinas, where they then joined the flow of settlers moving westward from the northern colonies. Immigrants from Philadelphia flowed into the Shenandoah Valley during the 1730s, the plateaus of the Carolinas in the 1740s and 1750s, and then southwestward to eastern Georgia, where they were temporarily checked by the Cherokees.

For many, the attraction of America and the American frontier was the vast territory permitting ethnic or religious groups to transplant Old World settlements intact. For example, in 1872 a leader of the Russian Mennonite community came to America, where he met an agent of the Atchinson, Topeka, and Santa Fe railroad. The railroad had three million acres of Kansas land available for settlement, and the two made a satisfactory deal. "The first arrival of Mennonites in Kansas... consisted of 400 families, 1900 people, who brought with them two and a quarter million dollars in gold, and purchased 60,000 acres in the counties of Marion, McPherson, Harvey and Reno" (as cited in McNall and McNall, 1983: 17). Throughout this era, it was not uncommon to enter frontier communities on the plains of Illinois, Kansas, or Nebraska where English was not the spoken language, and where the European countryside had been replicated.

The timing and ethnic composition of the immigrant streams influenced the patterns of settlement in the westward movement and explain the emergence of both rural ethnic communities and urban ethnic enclaves. Of the thirty-eight settlements established in Henry County, Illinois, between 1828 and 1846, nine were established by European immigrants (Hine, 1980). Foreign-born Scandinavian and German residents most frequently settled in homogeneous rural agricultural communities, communities that retain their ethnic identity today. Examples include Lindsborg, Kansas, originally settled in 1869 by thirty-five Swedish families under the leadership of Olaf Olson, a minister of the established Swedish church, and Danneborg, Nebraska, settled in 1871 by Danish immigrants (Hine, 1980).

Hence, nearly one-third of the foreign-born were urban residents, the remainder were distributed throughout the nation's various rural areas. For example, in 1850 nearly three-quarters of the German immigrants resided in the rural areas of the North Central states (Ohio, Illinois, Missouri, Wisconsin, and Indiana) and Pennsylvania, while the second largest foreign-born group in rural America, the Scandinavians, settled in North Dakota, Minnesota, Nebraska, Wisconsin, and Illinois. On the other hand, De Bow (1854) notes that in 1850 over one-third of the foreign-born Irish resided in what he calls the twenty-nine "leading" cities, while only a quarter or less of the foreign-born Germans, English, and Welsh were urban residents.

Not all the immigrants who settled the West came from Europe. On the West Coast, Chinese immigrants comprised a major stream of immigrant settlers. De Bow (1854) estimates that nearly 17,000 Chinese came to America between 1811 and 1855. The rate of immigration then increased dramatically due to the recruitment efforts of, first, the mining companies and, later, the railroads. Chinese immigrants, valued for their industriousness and willingness to work in teams, provided the "coolie labor" that built much of the western infrastructure. At one time, Hill (1973) notes, the Central Pacific railroad employed 10,000 Chinese laborers in the construction of the transcontinental railroad. Chinese immigrants resided almost exclusively on the West Coast. In 1879, only 368 Chinese lived outside the West.

Although only about 100,000 Chinese had entered the United States by 1880, anti-Oriental agitation was common and peaked with the Exclusion Act of 1882, which barred any further immigration of Chinese and denied citizenship to those already here. The characteristics of Chinese workers so attractive to industrial firms—their willingness to work long hours under any conditions and their thriftiness—also appeared as a "threat" to the economic interests of other workers. As a result, popular opinion held that "this cheap coolie labor was largely responsible for the depressed conditions of the American economy after 1873" (Hill, 1973: 45). While the Exclusion Act effectively ended Chinese immigration until the early 1920s, the Chinese were an important component of economic development of the far western frontier. The solicitation of Chinese immigrants reflects the national pattern of economic development during this era: invest human labor, not scarce capital, in transforming physical resources into national wealth.

Another major ethnic group immigrated to the West—people from Spanish-controlled Mexico. Indeed, the first Europeans in many areas (California, Texas, New Mexico, Arizona, Nevada) were first- or second-generation Spaniards settling on land grants from the Crown. As early as the 1690s, Spain extended its influence into Texas by establishing a series of missions with "ranching as the primary economic base" (Rocha, 1985: 3). By 1750, a group of 2,515 settlers and 755 soldiers had traveled from Mexico to north of the Rio Grande to establish twenty-four ranchos. The rate of immigrant settlement of this area is illustrated by one rancho on the north bank of the Rio Grande, the Villa de Dolores, which in 1750 had three families, and by 1753 had 123 people pasturing 5,000 horses and 3,000 cattle (Rocha, 1985: 4). By the mid–1800s, the rancho form of settlement extended from Alta, California, to the Gulf of Mexico (Hine, 1980).

Black Movements Westward

The other westward ethnic stream of consequence during the era of rural dominance was that of the blacks. The domestic slave trade forced the migration of thousands of blacks westward to provide labor for the newly opened agricultural regions of the Southwest (Arkansas, Louisiana, Mississippi, and Texas), and this domestic forced migration flourished after the Atlantic slave trade ended. Johnson and Campbell (1981: 25) estimate that "three-quarters of a million slaves were removed from the old slave states of Delaware, Maryland, Virginia, North Carolina and the District of Columbia to states in the Deep South and the Southwest.... During the 1830s, nearly a quarter of a million slaves were transported over state lines ... for domestic slave trading, 1859–1860, migration accelerated, with 193,000 slaves transported over state lines." The economic expansion of many southern cities benefited from this trade. For example, Johnson and Campbell (1981) note the importance of slave trade for Memphis, favorably situated on the Mississippi River between the slave-exporting states of the Southeast and the agriculturally developing states of the Southwest. The slave trade was a key factor in "the agricultural and economic development" of the East South Central and Southwest states, for it assured a source of cheap labor for the

Southern frontier's economic transformation (Johnson and Campbell, 1981: 31).

The Kansas Exodus of 1879 was the "first planned movement involving a substantial number of blacks relocating to a common distant destination under the leadership of a small group of people" (Johnson and Campbell, 1981: 51). An estimated 10,000 blacks moved to Kansas in search of political and economic independence, but the Kansas migration, while noteworthy, was only a small part of the post-Civil War migration of blacks. A substantial stream of freed blacks from South Carolina, Georgia, Alabama, and Mississippi followed the earlier forced migratory stream to Arkansas, Louisiana, and Texas. Another stream moved from Texas, Louisiana, and Mississippi to Oklahoma, Kansas, and Nebraska. Limited economic opportunities in the war-torn, overcrowded, and impoverished Deep South, combined with increased violence against freed blacks, pushed many from the region. But, the destination for many black migrants was often shaped by the active recruitment of land and railroad agents.

In some cases, these migrants settled on farms or in existing communities, but in many other cases they established their own settlements. Nicodemus, Kansas, first settled in 1877, is representative of the many black communities established during this period. Twenty-five black "colonies" were established in Oklahoma and, as far as the residents and many black leaders, such as Booker T. Washington, were concerned, offered a place where the black man could "prosper and rule supreme in his own community" (Hine, 1980: 196).

Many other freed blacks moved to the urban areas of the South and North. For example, an estimated 15,000 blacks moved to Philadelphia alone between 1870 and 1896 (Johnson and Campbell, 1981). By the end of the era of rural dominance, several states outside the South had received a substantial flow of black migrants, including Indiana, Illinois, Massachusetts, New Jersey, New York, and Pennsylvania.

The size and significance of the westward movement is unparalleled. Between 1850 and 1900, the population of the Upper Midwest and the Central Plains (Iowa, Kansas, Minnesota, Missouri, Nebraska, North Dakota, and South Dakota) increased from 880,000 to 10.3 million. Billington (1949) notes that, between 1870 and 1900, 430 million acres were settled and 225 million acres cultivated in these regions. Hence, a significant segment of the westward movement was essentially a farm-to-farm movement. By the late nineteenth century, the agricultural settlement of most of the land west of the Missouri River was nearly complete (Landis, 1940).

The westward movement substantially altered the regional distribution of the American population (figure 3; appendix table D). During this era, the rate of population growth in the Northeast steadily declined, as did the region's share of the total U.S. population. The South, on the other hand, had a relatively stable rate of population growth, yet, its share of the total population also declined. Clearly, the North Central region captured the major share of population growth during this era, the bulk of which was due to migration.

OTHER MIGRATION STREAMS

Through the mid–1980s, both the movement westward and the movement to larger urban areas nearly "depopulated New England towns and the countryside" (Landis, 1940). These areas faced serious population pressures as well as soil depletion, two "pushes" for potential migrants. Among those who did migrate, the urbanward movement had a higher concentration of young single women, while the westward movement had more single men or family units.

Urban Migration

Although the rural population and rural lifestyles dominated during this era, cities also emerged and thrived. In 1776, less than one in twenty-five Americans lived in cities of 8,000 or more; by 1810, one in twenty Americans lived in these urban places; by 1840, it was one in twelve; and by 1860 nearly one in six Americans lived in cities of 8,000 or more (Schlesinger, 1949). By the end of this era, nearly three out of ten Americans resided in urban places (figure 4). It is remarkable that, by

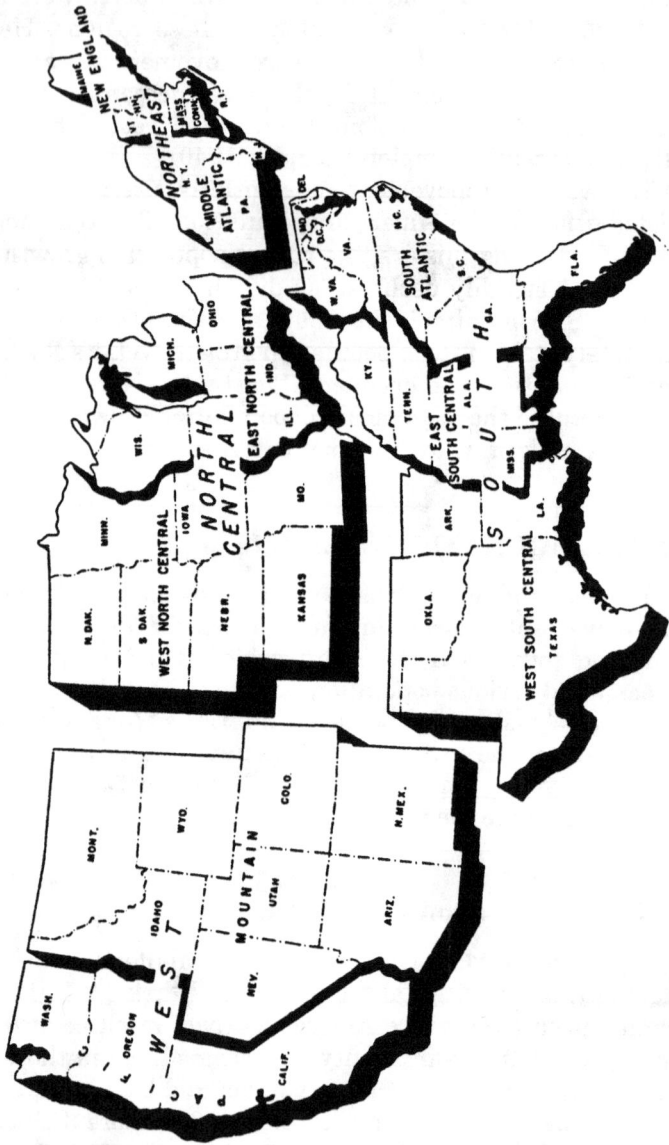

Figure 3
Census Geographic Divisions

Figure 4
Rural-Urban Distribution of U.S. Population, 1790–1880

Decade

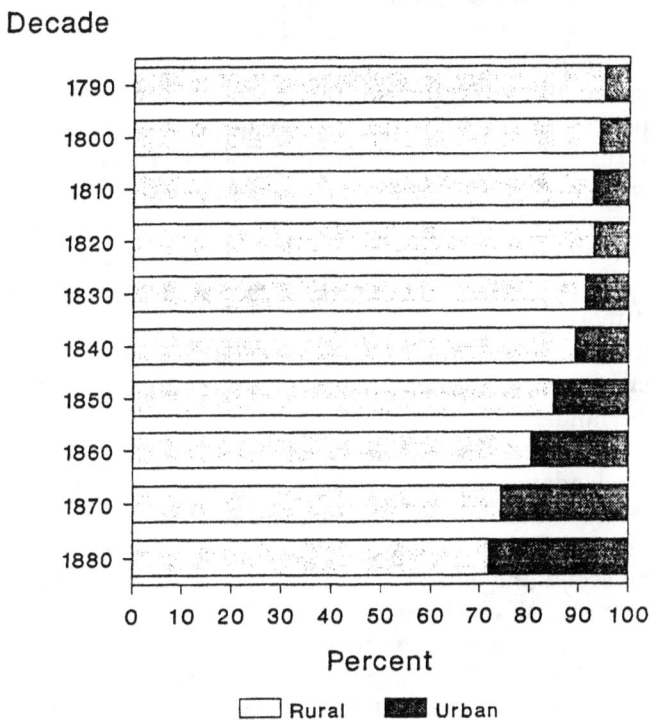

Decade	% Rural	% Urban
1790	94.9	5.1
1800	93.9	6.1
1810	92.7	7.3
1820	92.8	7.2
1830	91.2	8.8
1840	89.2	10.8
1850	84.7	15.3
1860	80.2	19.8
1870	74.3	25.7
1880	71.8	28.2

Source: Adapted from Series A57-72 of Historical Statistics of the United States, Colonial Times to 1970, and the 1985 U.S. Statistical Abstract. U.S. Bureau of the Census, Washington D.C., Government Printing Office.

1880, over half of these urbanites resided in the thirty-five places of 50,000 or more (figure 5).

The growth of urban places during this time reflected an aggressive "boosterism" on the part of city leaders. For example, in the early 1820s Baltimore funded the construction of a turnpike to the eastern edge of the Cumberland Road. New York City business and political leaders secured local and state funding for constructing the Erie Canal which would bring in commercial traffic. Baltimore responded to this competitive threat, and in 1828 began constructing the Baltimore and Ohio railroad. The commercial success of this venture spurred an amazing surge in railroad construction, as cities and towns competed to establish influence over their hinterlands.

These transportation ventures are only one way in which urban leaders sought to attract people and commerce into their sphere of influence. Reducing distance through roads, waterways, and railroads made movement to the cities easier, and commercial and cultural opportunities in the expanding cities attracted both newly arriving immigrants and farm residents alike. So great was the attraction that many rural people feared it as a threat to their lifestyle. Schlesinger (1949) notes that farm journals begged farm sons and daughters not to "sacrifice" their independence to work for others, and many religious leaders claimed that cities were the result of Adams and Eve's fall from grace. Yet, the vitality of the cities continued to attract many.

It is also important to recognize that the westward movement was often an urban, not agricultural, migration. One historian says that towns "were the spearheads of the American frontier" (Wade, 1973: 14). For example, with respect to the period 1860–1900, Jeffrey (1979: 80–81) notes: "The trans-Mississippi West was, in fact, more of an urban place than popular views of the westward movement suggest. Most Western emigrants from outside the cotton belt did not settle on farms, for example; the percentage of the population living in cities nearly corresponded to the average of the nation as a whole.... American frontiersmen were not only farmers but also enthusiastic town builders, planners, and speculators."

Figure 5
Proportion of U.S. Population Living in Places of 10,000+ or 50,000+, 1790–1880

Percent

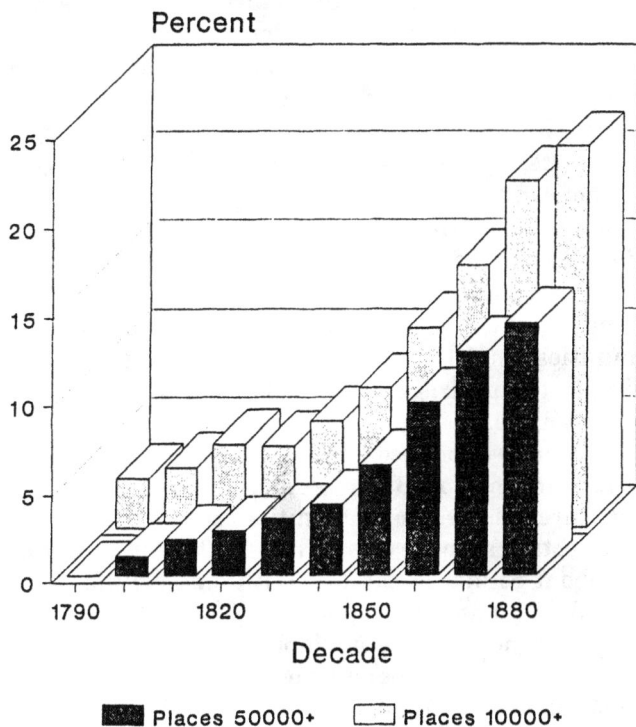

Places 50000+   Places 10000+

Decade	% In Places of 10,000+	% In Places of 50,000+
1790	2.8	0
1800	3.4	1.1
1810	4.7	2.1
1820	4.6	2.6
1830	6.0	3.3
1840	7.9	4.1
1850	11.3	6.3
1860	14.8	9.8
1870	19.5	12.7
1880	21.5	14.3

Source: Adapted from Series A57-72 of Historical Statistics of the United States, Colonial Times to 1970. U.S. Bureau of the Census, Washington D.C., Government Printing Office.

Many of those who traveled westward, including immigrants, settled in towns and cities that seemed to spring up overnight. In 1873, John Beadle described Benton, Nebraska, 700 miles west of Omaha, as a town "located in the middle of absolutely nowhere, where no town should ever have been built because of the hostile climate and terrain.... Yet here had sprung up in two weeks, as if by the touch of Aladdin's Lamp, a city of three thousand people" (as cited in McNall and McNall, 1983: 33). In 1855, the wife of the governor of Kansas reported that fifty-five houses were built in sixty-five days in Lawrence, Kansas (in McNall and McNall, 1983). Yet, most of the towns built during the westward migration were essentially rural communities. In 1870, for example, nine out of ten persons residing in the prairie states lived either in towns of 2,500 or less or on farms.

There were sound economic motivations underlying this westward urban movement besides the obvious ones of jobs and venture business opportunities. It is estimated that by "1860 to establish a farm and live for the first year or so required about $1,000 in capital. With land selling for between $2.50 and $6.00 an acre, plus operating and household costs, farming was not always a viable alternative for newly arrived immigrants or unemployed urban workers." For these reasons, Shannon (1945) estimates that for every urban worker who moved westward to become a farmer, twenty farm-born persons became urban residents, often in established cities east of the Mississippi.

Thus, although the majority of Americans lived in rural areas or small towns and villages, large urban centers emerged and exerted a growing influence over American life. Although natural increase (the excess of births over deaths) contributed to some of this urban growth, by and large cities grew by attracting newly arrived immigrants and young farm persons. The competing attractions of city versus rural life, exhibited by the varied patterns of migration during this era, continue to this day, as do the competing evaluations of the relative merits of urban versus rural living that appear in popular writings of this earlier era. Our national "love-hate" relationship with cities has its roots in this era.

Small Town and Suburban Migration

While the rural-to-urban migration stream was a major, centripetal force acting on the nation's population, there was a small centrifugal force, drawing people from large urban centers to suburban rings and small towns. Between 1815 and 1860, a new kind of community emerged on the outskirts of the largest cities. These "suburbs" were not the residential enclaves of today; they were "a region mingling estates, scattered farms, waste land, dumps, and scrubby artisan hamlets" (Binford, 1985: 1). The residents of these suburbs migrated from the city and surrounding rural areas to "exploit opportunities available at the city's edge—opportunities in suburban land speculation, small business" (Binford, 1985: 2), and innovative services for the growing cities. These suburbs were small, semirural towns adjacent to the larger cities. Economically interdependent with the cities but politically separate, they were the bases from which urban influence eventually extended to the hinterland.

Finally, it is important to understand the extent of internal migration during this era. The histories of the farms and towns and cities of the era of rural dominance are histories of mobility. In the Dakotas in the 1890s, Seth Humphrey, a mortgage collector, found only eight farms out of forty-one still occupied by the original settlers; three were occupied by squatters and the rest had been abandoned (Hine, 1980). "In Wapelo County, Iowa, only 33 percent of the farmers of 1850 remained after ten years. The persistence rate in Kansas in the decade following 1860 was usually under 30 percent and in no cases higher than 42 percent" (Hine, 1980: 97). Comparably low levels of residential stability marked town life. In 1860 and 1870, less than one in eight persons residing in Jacksonville, Illinois, had lived there for ten or more years. In the ethnic settlement of Holland, Michigan, "between 1850 and 1880 the out-migration of labor amounted to 40 percent of the in-migration" (Hine, 1980: 134). In some cases, whole towns simply pulled up stakes and moved to new sites. The numerous streams across the continent during this era both fed the populations in town and urban settlements and established the dominance of the agricultural economy. Farms, towns, and cities, in willy-nilly fashion, attracted new residents and contributed new migrants to these streams.

INTERPRETING MIGRATION DURING THE RURAL DOMINANCE STAGE

If one were to apply the different theoretical perspectives to interpreting migration during the period of rural dominance, it would be clear that both individual and ecological factors contributed to these various migration streams. While it is difficult to impute the nature of a historical decision-making process, the size and uniformity of these migration streams suggest that dominant, underlying perceptions of the desirability of specific residential destinations influenced migration decisions. To clarify the factors associated with these perceptions, let us assume that the perceptions impelling the immigration to America were substantively different from those impelling the migration westward.

Reasons for Immigration to America

During the late eighteenth and nineteenth centuries, several treaties, such as de Tocqueville's *Democracy in America* (Vol. 1, 1835; Vol. 2, 1840), or Crevecoeur's *Letters from an American Farmer* (1782) were published in Europe. These commentaries described the abundant natural resources of the New World, and the enormous economic opportunities for anyone willing to carve out a future. In contrast to the shrinking agricultural opportunities in the British Isles and other countries due to enclosure laws, successions of poor harvests, and growing population pressures, the New World beckoned people to establish independent farmsteads and businesses. Immigration from Ireland illustrates this point. Hundreds of thousands died in Ireland during the great famine (1846–48), and millions more lost their rights to farm their small plots as new agricultural practices led to the consolidation of farm holdings. For thousands of Irishmen, as Handlin (1959: 21) cogently argues, "emigration became the only alternative to death."

The popular European commentaries also noted other unique aspects of American society attractive to potential immigrants, including political and religious freedoms. The opportunity to practice one's religious beliefs free of persecution attracted the Mennonites, the Hutterites, Annabaptists, Shakers, Catholics, Jews, and many other smaller religious sects. For many, religious freedom in America was made even more attractive by the opportunity to establish their own communities and raise their children within their own cultural and religious expectations. Hansen (1940: 8–13) summarizes the extent and motivations underlying this flood of immigration: "To that flood every nation, every province, almost every neighborhood, contributed its stream. . . . It is clear that the cause of so vast an exodus was wider than race or nationality and deeper than legislation or politics. It was not the mania of a single generation, nor of ideas that prevailed for a mere decade or two. The cause was as universal as the movement itself. . . . It touches the stream of human history at many points. It forms part of the agrarian development which revolutionized the European countryside. It is related to the hygienic progress that doubled the [European] population in the course of three generations."

Reasons for the Westward Migration

In America, a host of factors prompted the move westward. First, individual factors, such as restlessness, risk-taking impulses, and the desire for improved status spurred some people to move westward. The excitement, adventure, and economic risks of the gold and silver fields attracted thousands to California, Nevada, and Colorado. For others, "The westward move . . . was the physical expression of a break with the past and a setting out for a new life. The journey occurred when the rhythms of maturity were primed for a change. The determination to go west was either the initial separation from a man's parental family or the second major move, the move 'upward' in the search for economic mobility and success. The adventure took on the color of some 'dramatic right of passage to mastery and adulthood' in the life cycle of frontier men" (Schlissel, 1982: 106). Diaries and letters written by westward migrants during this era suggest that the decision to move was often made on the spur of the moment. Frequently, the decision was made after attending a presentation by someone who had journeyed back east specifically to attract new settlers (Jeffrey, 1979; Schlissel, 1982).

Perceptions of locational alternatives, especially economic opportunity, and the natural increase of the native population also encouraged migration to the frontier. Consider these comments on the settlement of northern Louisiana: "Those pioneers who settled the pine hills 'pitched their tents' in the thousand creek bottoms which divide the hills, and with their own hands worked their way to wealth—their sons and daughters learned to work, and when they married entered lands either 'up' or 'down the creek' " (Smith and Fry, 1936: 7). The diaries of many westward migrants during this time note that the trek west often followed immediately upon marriage, underscoring the symbolic association between geographic mobility and change in life cycle. Landis (1940: 192) comments: "Much of America's history, at least up to about 1890, is a story of man's quest for land; land brought people to the country and land hunger settled the West." While population pressures may have "pushed" young families out of their home communities, the opportunities of open and free land "pulled" these families to the frontier.

This is seen in the movement of many farm residents in the more populated Northeast and, in the mid–1800s, the war-torn South; they moved westward in search of better, cheaper, and larger farmsteads. The desire for farmsteads is often linked to agricultural practices, such as the slash and burn practice in the Carolina delta areas, which limited productivity to about four to six years per parcel and forced farm families to move to new lands. As significant was the deep desire to own land, to build a future, and to participate in the nation-building experience. Stratton (1981: 45) comments: "Beautiful and bountiful, the land was the great lure of Kansas. Some settlers sought freedom, some yearned for prosperity, some craved adventure, but in the end it was the promise of the land that drew them halfway across a continent. Here they could build their own homes, cultivate their own fields and develop their own communities." The removal of the Indian tribes and conscious government policies to maximize the use of material resources in nation building facilitated these individual tendencies.

What role did the growing flood of immigrants play in this westward movement? Hansen (1940) argues that immigrant farmers followed the "pioneer farmers," the native-born settlers who moved into newly opened frontier areas, farmed for a few years, then continued westward. "In the 1820s and 1830s they [immigrants] took over the evacuated lands in western New York, Pennsylvania and Ohio. In the 1840s they swarmed into Missouri, Illinois and southern Wisconsin. In the 1850s they occupied eastern Iowa and Minnesota and consolidated their position in the older states. By the 1870s they had reached the prairies" (Hansen, 1940: 72–76). For Hansen, the population's rapid spread westward was due to pressures from immigrants who "filled in" rural areas and "pushed" native pioneer farmers farther west.

The "push" of immigrant settlers was often more psychological than physical. The sheer abundance of land had psychological and behavioral consequences, producing a predisposition to move onward that marked the American as substantively different from his European counterparts in the eyes of most European observers (Potter, 1954). Schlissel (1982: 20) explains these effects: "In a fashion that men and women of the twentieth century will never fully understand, farmers of the Mississippi Valley and the Plains states had begun to feel 'crowded' (in the 1840s). One farmer said that the reason he had to emigrate from western Illinois was that 'people were settling right under his nose,' although his nearest neighbor was twelve miles away. He moved to Missouri, but that did not satisfy, and soon he abandoned a half-finished clearing and packed his family and household goods onto a wagon and made his way to Oregon where there was only the Pacific Ocean beside him."

In a discussion of the cattle-ranching areas of the Great Plains, Hine (1980) comments on the settlers' great mobility, citing examples of men who lived and worked in three or four different states, and families that moved from one ranching community to another. He concludes: "These men moved as if impelled by steel springs; no economic or social forces can fully explain their restlessness. It stemmed more from what James Malin, the Great Plains historian, assigned to 'group behavior,' the intangible circuits motivated not only by depressions and crises but also by conversations around the wood stove" (Hine, 1980: 163). While the significance of these personality or psychological traits cannot be demonstrated empirically, their consistent appearance in historians' accounts of this era suggest that they not be discounted.

By the late nineteenth century, the "pull" of the western frontier was enhanced by the railroad companies. Railroads actively encouraged westward migration to the Great Plains, advertised cheap land, provided low-cost transportation, and, in some cases, even established the bare bones of communities (Webb, 1931). To make their routes profitable, railroads had to ensure a continuous flow of persons and goods both west and east. This required the establishment of commercially productive farms and town centers of commerce on the Plains, and the railroads had the land to "spend" on these market- and community-building products.

Two basic explanations for the westward movement have been offered. The "safety valve" thesis argues that "eastern wage laborers moved west whenever eastern work conditions became intolerable. A less rigid version of this thesis claims that the urban wage earners moved to the small towns, and the wage earners from these small towns (as well as agricultural tenants) in turn moved west in hopes of rising on the agricultural ladder" (Schaefer, 1985: 563). From this perspective, the westward movement was a mechanism by which labor adjusted to different conditions and opportunities, and, by implication, reduced the likelihood of worker unrest in the eastern urban centers.

Turner (1921) offered a second view, that farmers on marginal lands in the East were more likely to be attracted to the new lands on the frontier. Turner (1921: 215) notes: "Year by year the farmers who lived on soil whose returns were diminished by unrotated crops were offered the virgin soil of the frontier at nominal prices." This view sees the westward movement as inevitable, given the debilitating effects of customary agricultural practices on the productivity of the land. Moreover, "growing families demanded more lands" (Turner, 1921: 215), and only the frontier offered land at a price farm families could afford. Hence, farmers in search of productive and cheap land substituted geographic mobility for improved agriculture.

In one sense, these two interpretations offer similar explanations for the migration of urban and farm people to the western frontier. Migration did serve as a vehicle of social mobility, inasmuch as the western frontier offered opportunities to both urban and farm people. But the nature of these opportunities differed, producing somewhat divergent patterns of geographical mobility. For example, historians argue that agricultural migrants tended to move "westward along lines of equal latitude" (Schaefer, 1985: 564). The explanation for this has been that farmers sought to move to areas where crops, tools, and agricultural practices would be similar, thereby reducing the risks associated with migration (Owsley, 1949). Stoeckel's (1983) study of northern families that moved between 1800 and 1874 confirms that farm families were less likely to deviate from an east-west migration route than nonfarmers.

In a unique multivariate analysis of factors associated with migration to the "frontier" states (Texas and Arkansas) as opposed to the "New South" (Alabama, Louisiana, Mississippi, and Tennessee) between 1850 and 1860, Schaefer (1985: 575) concludes: "The head of household of the frontier migrant family was slightly younger, less likely to own land in 1850 and more likely to be literate than the New South head of household. These last two are quite consistent with historical and economic rationales for migration. It is generally conceded that one of the motives for migration was to acquire land. With the lesser degree of development at the frontier, land acquisition must have been sufficiently easier to motivate the landless families to migrate despite the higher costs imposed by the greater travel distance and dissimilar environment. The migrant to the frontier also benefited from literacy. The greater distance involved in migration to the frontier meant that word of mouth was superseded in importance by the print media (newspapers, agricultural journals, and handbills) as well as written communication from friends and relatives." Schaefer's study, then, supports a view of westward migration as a mechanism of utility maximization implied in economic models of migration.

Reasons for Urban Growth

Given the attraction of the western frontier and the importance of land ownership in the American ethos, why did many persons choose urban destinations? In coastal areas and along the rivers and expanding railroads, urban centers offered unique economic opportunities for immigrants and natives alike. Urban centers served as focal points for commerce, transshipping raw materials from farms to urban and foreign markets, and moving manufactured products back to the hinterland. Some urban areas, such as New York, became financial centers for the rest of the nation. In 1768, business leaders in New York formed the first chamber of commerce in the English-speaking world, signaling an aggressive attitude toward encouraging commercial activity. By the early 1800s, manufacturing flourished to such an extent in many urban centers that citizens complained of sooty skies (Schlesinger, 1949). The economic motives leading some people to seek their fortunes on the frontier led others to the cities. The same quest for adventure, excitement, and change motivating many to test themselves against the frontier led others to test themselves in the cities. The cities tested persons of different ethnic and cultural backgrounds on the frontier of commerce and industry rather than that of agriculture.

POPULATION CONSEQUENCES OF THE MIGRATION STREAMS

Fertility

The patterns of immigration and migration influenced other demographic processes. First, the immigrants brought with them a cultural heritage that, for the most part, emphasized early marriages and high fertility. Historical studies of European fertility during the period of immigration to the United States indicate that, despite the continent's industrialization and urbanization, fertility levels either remained stationary or rose. Fertility norms are often shaped by culture and acquired through the socialization process: hence, they are somewhat resistant to change. Thus, immigrants brought with them fertility norms that may have been temporarily depressed by economic conditions in the old country (e.g., in Ireland during the successive potato famines), but found a socioeconomic setting permitting their full expression. Wilcox (1940: 404) offers this interpretation when he suggests that the rise in the birth rate in the 1850s, as measured by the proportion of children under five years of age to 1,000 women of child-bearing age, was "probably due to the large immigration just before 1850 and to the high birth rate among the immigrants."

During this era, agriculture was a labor-intensive process demanding the labor contributions of all family members, even children. The size of a family farm enterprise and its success was often a function of the number of unpaid family workers contributing to its operation. Moreover, ecological conditions on the Great Plains required parcels much larger than 160 acres to sustain a profitable farm or ranch operation. Hence, during the years of the Homestead Act, when each individual was able to file on a section of land (160 acres), many families filed in the names of spouses and children on multiple parcels.

National data indicates that the median family size for the 1850–80 period ranged from 3.97 to 4.49, while the median number of children per family ranged from 1.91 to 2.35 (Seward, 1978). The fertility ratio—the number of children under 5 years of age per 1,000 women aged 15 to 44—is an appropriate measure of fertility over time, for it takes into account variations in a society's age structure (appendix table A–5). Historical estimates by Graybill et al. (1958) indicate that the fertility ratio steadily declined from 1,281 children under the age of 5 per 1,000 women aged 20 to 44 in 1800 to 754 in 1880. But this ratio masks significant differences in urban and rural rates. In 1800, the urban fertility ratio was 815, while the rural ratio was 1,319. Estimates by residence for 1880 are not available. It is important to remember that the rural fertility ratio represents the joint effects of both rural farm and nonfarm women, and the fertility of farm women has always been significantly higher than the fertility of nonfarm women. Thus, we can assume that the rural farm fertility ratio was even higher than the total rural average.

Also interesting are the regional estimates, which suggest rural farm life contributed to high levels of fertility. The census geographic divisions with high proportions of rural populations had higher fertility ratios than the more urban regions. For example, in 1800 more than 10 percent of New England's population resided in urban areas and had a fertility ratio of 1,098 children under the age of 5 per 1,000 women. During this time in the North Central region, there was virtually no urban population, and the rural fertility ratio was 1,840 children per 1,000 women.

Another way of thinking about the fertility of American women during the period of rural dominance is to consider the distribution of ever-married women by the number of children ever born. Taeuber and Taeuber's (1957) analysis of census data reveals that more than one-third of the ever-married women born between 1835 and 1839 had seven or more children, compared to only one-seventh of one percent of those women born between 1880 and 1884. Furthermore, the number of children ever born to white women was considerably smaller than that for black women. Finally, the median family size declined from 5.4 in 1790 to 4.48 in 1890. Hence, in these years when most people were rural, families were large.

Family Structure

Schlissel's (1982: 152) analysis of the diaries of women who made the westward journey during the 1840s through the 1860s suggests two types of family structure. The first type was "a family that succeeded in producing six or more surviving children." This type of family was usually involved in multiple moves and, "tended to understand its strength as the number of children who could help with the physical labor of clearing the land." The other type of frontier family was considerably smaller and usually more geographically stable. "At the point where they believed they had come to a satisfactory economic condition, a situation that would allow them to develop their opportunities rather than to search out new ones, family size tended to shrink." This analysis implies that family size was influenced by both geographic mobility and the conditions of settlement.

Finally, the effects of the Civil War on family composition and size should be noted. Between 1860 and 1870, "family size, number of children, and male-headed families display a decrease . . . the disruptive effect of the Civil War period upon family structure (especially fertility) seems to be of primary importance here. The increases in the percentage of families that were extended and that included a subfamily also appear related to the war and possibly to the increased rate of urbanization and industrialization spurred on by it" (Seward, 1978: 104). As a result, decennial rates of population increase declined from 35 percent during the 1790–1800 period to 26 percent during the 1870–80 period. These trends are the classic indicators of the demographic transition simultaneously taking place in western Europe. The socioeconomic forces altering the population's residential distribution were also changing the population dynamics of American society.

Age-Sex Structure

The high fertility rate, coupled with the young age composition of the immigration streams, produced an age structure decidedly skewed to the younger ages. In 1800, the median age was 16, similar to that in many Third World nations today. By 1880, the median age had risen to 20.9. Furthermore, in 1800, 11 percent of the nation's population was over the age of 45, rising to 16 percent in 1880, with about 5 percent over the age of 60. The overall pattern of change is one of a substantial proportion (40 percent or more) of the population under the age of twenty, but this very slowly declined throughout the era.

As these figures suggest, the nation experienced a transition in vital rates during the era of rural dominance. Fertility was declining as indicated by the reductions in fertility ratios, the decline in family size, and the rising median age of the popu-

lation. In addition, mortality declined slightly, although acci-
dents and misadventures continued to be a primary cause of
death.

The sex composition of the population during this era was
affected by immigration and natural increase. Typically, men
outnumbered women in the immigrant streams from all places
of origin, as they did in the migration to the western frontier.
On the other hand, young women outnumbered young men in
the migration from farms to cities. As a result of this selectivity
in migration, the rural communities, including those on the
frontier, had a preponderance of males.

COMMUNITY CONSEQUENCES OF MIGRATION

Both immigration and the westward migration had consequences for rural and urban communities. These include effects
on

1. the organization and functioning of communities,
2. the socioeconomic structures of communities, and
3. the nature of social and political life.

Settlement Patterns

Immigrants, representing different ethnic and class backgrounds as well as various reasons for coming to the New
World, established different types of rural settlements throughout the colonies. By the late eighteenth century, the typical
rural settlement in the Northeast was made up of small independent landholders of English, Irish, Scottish, German, and
Dutch extraction, who were mainly from the middle and lower
classes of European society (Smith, 1953: 55). In the southern
colonies, large land grant estates settled by European aristoc-
racy produced a dominant plantation system with a secondary
economy based on small groups of freeholders. This variation
in settlement patterns explains the differentiation in regional
racial composition during the rural dominance period. The labor requirements of the crops of the southern plantation system

(tobacco, rice, and later cotton) led to the expanded slave trade and the concentration of blacks in the southern colonies. Johnson and Campbell (1981) state that by the end of the eighteenth century, the economic system of the South was inextricably tied to the availability of slaves.

The immigrants' settlement pattern was in part a function of whether they arrived as single adults or part of a family group, and in part a function of their ethnic origin. Smith (1890: 51) suggests that German immigrants, drawn from agricultural classes in the old country, tended to migrate in family groups. Their predilection was to settle in farming communities with other German immigrants (Binder-Johnson, 1941). Irish immigrants, on the other hand, were likely to be unmarried young adults of both sexes and to settle in urban areas. One exception to this patterns was the emigration of over 4,000 Catholic families, mostly Irish, to ten frontier settlements between 1875 and 1885. This migration was organized by the Irish Immigration Society and designed to establish economically viable Catholic settlements comparable to the Mormon settlements in Utah (Hine, 1980).

Farm settlement patterns varied among regions. In New England, geography (limited valley lands) and the tendency to make land grants to groups of persons rather than individuals led to the emergence of farm villages. In these villages, homesteads clustered and tillable land radiated outward from the town center. Farm villages were typical in areas settled by groups relatively homogeneous in ethnic, religious, or other ways. However, as the frontier pushed westward, the isolated farmstead became typical in settlement patterns. To a great extent, the rectangular survey mitigated against the settled farm village, since it divided land into a grid of available parcels on which a settler had to establish residence in order to secure a patent (ownership).

Other factors also contributed to the eventual predominance of isolated farmsteads, including the tendency of individuals to settle beyond the Alleghenies and Appalachians, the pace of settlement, and the lack of adequate roads to move people easily from town centers to more distant farmsteads. It is important to recognize that the predominance of the isolated farm-

stead in settling the bulk of the nation's agricultural lands
would have consequences in the future. The geographic location
of this dispersed pattern of settlement translated into a social
isolation. In the decades to come, geography served as a physical barrier, hindering access to technological innovations (electricity, telephones, running water) and the adequate roads
essential for economic development.

Socioeconomic Patterns of Community Life

During the westward migrations, the types of migrants also
influenced the nature of community life. Immigrant groups,
such as the Mennonites in Kansas or the Germans in Illinois,
often settled in the same area where they reproduced their
traditional lifeways. Many of these groups remain today, cel-
ebrating their ethnic heritage in festivals and fairs and, in
some cases, such as the Swedish community of Lindsborg, Kansas, translating their ethnic heritage into a profitable tourist
industry. Several studies of two ethnic communities in Illinois
demonstrate that the ethnic heritage of the early settlers, German immigrants as opposed to "Yankee" settlers from the
Northeast, produced different types of farm enterprises, patterns of inheritance, and attitudes towards family relations
(Rogers and Salamon, 1983; Salamon, 1980; Salamon and
O'Reilly, 1979).

Furthermore, with the exception of the gold and silver rushes
where single men predominated, family units were most common in the westward migrations. Schlissel (1982: 31) notes:
"Whenever possible, families moved west within a kinship network. . . . Once the decision was made, families drew together
from neighboring counties and states so that the extended family with all its households might be transplanted. On the Trail,
families were the natural unit of social order." Families that
had been separated by the marriage and migration of their
children could find themselves united for the trek westward.
Jeffrey (1979) and others (Stratton, 1981) suggest that the
movement of entire family units hastened the transformation
of the frontier into settled communities.

Another influence of immigrants during this era is their contributions to the human and financial capital of the nation. Immigrants brought financial resources that fostered the growth of businesses or fed the national treasury through land purchases. Immigrants built communities and transformed open land into productive agricultural enterprises; their knowledge and skills contributed to the industrial and scientific revolutions that were the basis for the national economy's rapid growth. For example, Russian Mennonites introduced Russian red winter wheat, a crop far more suited to agricultural conditions on the Great Plains than either spring wheat or corn. Today, this variety of wheat still dominates world markets. Hourwich (1922) suggests that an informal division of labor developed, with Americans of native parentage working as farmers, businessmen, or professionals, and immigrants working as industrial wage workers. Without the continuing flow of new arrivals, the national government's efforts to consolidate its control over the continent and to exploit the physical resources would have been greatly retarded or at least significantly different.

Sociopolitical Consequences for Communities

Finally, Handlin argues that the great streams of immigration shaped our social and political life, reducing the likelihood that "rigid class distinctions" would emerge. "Diversity and mobility became characteristic features of life in the United States" (Handlin, 1959: 2). Thus, immigration influenced all aspects of national development, from the rate and composition of population growth, to the nature and speed of economic development, to the structure and functioning of our institutions.

This argument also applies to the effect of the westward migration. On the frontier, class boundaries were flexible and permeable, "people were judged by what they accomplished, not by who their ancestors were" (McNall and McNall, 1983: 40–41). However, this is not to suggest that social and political divisions did not develop in frontier communities. The very diversity of ethnic, religious, and economic enterprises developed on the western frontier ensured that factions would emerge. The practice of democracy, the ideal attracting so many immigrants to America, often produced conflict. For example, the temperance movement had its roots in the cultural traditions of some ethnic groups, and it was most bitterly fought by ethnic Germans.

SUMMARY

Migration was a key descriptive demographic process during the era of rural dominance (1650–1880). The streams of persons spreading across the nation established a rural society of farm and village residents. Agriculture was the primary industry, ownership of one's own farm the primary goal, and migration the primary mechanism for achieving this goal. Yet, there was already evidence of the waning of rural dominance. Jeffrey (1979: 81) states: "Foreigners marveled at the rapidity of urban development in the West. . . . Urban growth was like 'a stroke of magic.' " By the end of this era, the Northeast was essentially an urbanized place, and the urban centers of the North Central and the western regions were attracting ever-larger groups of migrants. The national perception of the relative attractiveness of rural versus urban locations was beginning to shift, and would have consequences for both the decision to move and the selection of a destination for nearly a century to come.

Associated with this changing pattern of migration was the beginning of a fundamental change in the extent and components of the national population. While immigration continued to represent a significant component of population increase, the composition of the immigrant stream changed dramatically throughout this era. Fertility as well as the average size of the family was steadily declining. The socioeconomic characteristics of the nation's population were also changing. The proportion of the nation's labor force engaged in agricultural pursuits declined from three-quarters in 1800 to just under one-half in 1880, and the general standard of living rose steadily. By the end of this era, the nation was poised at a watershed that marked the transition from an essentially rural to a quintessentially urban society.

4

Migration Streams in the Urban Era (1880–1970)

INTRODUCTION

By the last decade of the nineteenth century, the bulk of the land most suitable for agricultural production had been homesteaded. A condition that would plague those desiring to establish their own farms thereafter—high land prices—had begun to trouble the Midwest. A series of devastating depressions (1870–95) struck the farm economy, and farmers found themselves indebted to and foreclosed on by urban bankers and investors. The opportunities for social mobility once found on the agricultural frontier disappeared in the face of growing productivity, declining commodity prices, and mechanization. As a result, "about 1910 the migration cityward in the nation grew to major proportions, marking a radical change in ends sought. No longer was land the goal for migrants; a place in the work world of the urban industrial structure had become the motivating force. Movement shifted toward areas where factories and urban commerce were developing" (Landis, 1940: 194–97). An important signal of this increasing emphasis on urban opportunities is the decline in the proportion of gainful workers in agriculture, fishing, and forestry, from 72.3 percent in 1830 to 35.9 percent in 1900 (Landis and Hatt, 1954).

Political, economic, social, and population changes during the early decades of this era heralded a significant transfor-

mation in rural America. First and foremost, America became
an urban society. Nearly two out of three Americans (65 percent) lived in rural areas in 1890, but by 1920, one-half of all
Americans lived in urban centers (figure 6). Furthermore,
many cities had grown to immense proportions. For example,
Chicago had grown from 4,800 in 1840 to 1.7 million in 1900;
Denver from 4,700 in 1860 to nearly 134,000 in 1900; Kansas
City from 4,400 in 1860 to nearly 164,000 in 1900, and St.
Louis from 1,600 in 1810 to 575,000 in 1900. In 1890, 15 percent
of the nation's population lived in cities of 100,000 or more, by
1920 one-quarter of all Americans resided in these cities. More
striking was the doubling of the proportion of Americans who
resided in cities of 500,000 or more, from seven percent in 1890
to 15.4 percent in 1920.

The proliferation of towns and villages at the smaller end of
the urban continuum also characterized this era, reflecting the
need for service centers in the open countryside for farmers
and their families. The need was grounded in the growing availability of an expanding tide of manufactured consumer goods,
as well as the integration of individual farmers into commercial
and financial markets. Yet, the economic functions of these
small towns were replaced eventually by the rapid growth of
larger urban centers that extended their influence over a geographically distant hinterland, a process facilitated by technological innovations. For example, in 1908, the first Model T
Ford rolled off the assembly line, and by 1914 a car rolled off
the assembly line every ninety-three minutes! Rural delivery,
mail-order catalogues, telephones, improved roads, magazines
(such as *Wallace's Farmer*), newspapers, and, later, radio and
television expanded the boundaries of the urban community,
laying the foundation for a mass consumer society.

Economic disparities between urban and rural places also
contributed to urbanization. The years between 1900 and 1920
were prosperous for farmers, but when World War I ended, so
did the good times. Prices for farm commodities began a re-
lentless decline. A bushel of wheat dropped from $2.15 in 1919
to twenty-five cents by 1931. In the good years, farmers used
their wealth to acquire machinery, land, and household consumer goods, but in the process they also acquired more debt.
When times turned bad, "one out of every 10 farmers lost what

Figure 6
Rural-Urban Distribution of U.S. Population, 1890–1980

Decade

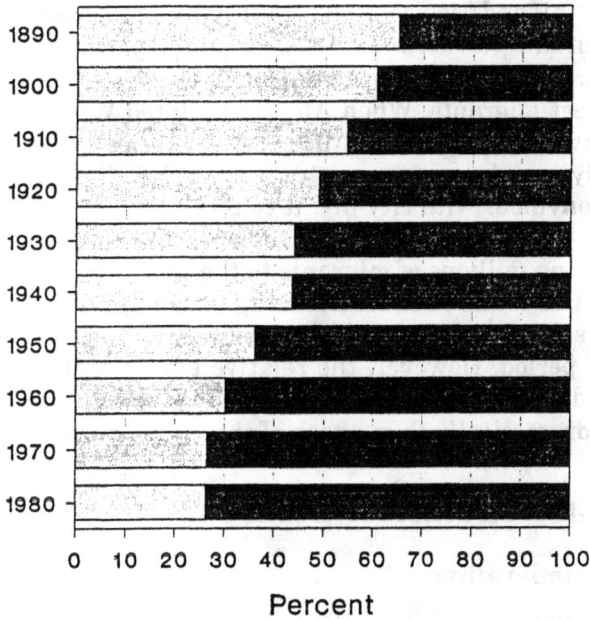

Decade	% Rural	% Urban
1890	64.9	35.1
1900	60.4	39.6
1910	54.4	45.6
1920	48.8	51.2
1930	43.9	56.1
1940	43.5	56.5
1950	36.0	64.0
1960	30.1	69.9
1970	26.5	73.5
1980	26.3	73.7

Source: Adapted from Series A57–72 of Historical Statistics of the United States, Colonial Times to 1970, and the 1985 U.S. Statistical Abstract. U.S. Bureau of the Census, Washington D.C., Government Printing Office.

he had worked for between 1927 and 1932. In the early thirties, almost half of all the farms sold were subject to foreclosure" (McNall and McNall, 1983: 188). While hundreds of thousands of urban workers experienced unemployment during the Depression years, opportunities still existed in the cities to attract migrants. When America entered World War II, manufacturing employment in urban factories exploded. Increasingly, employment opportunities and well-paid jobs became synonymous with city life. It could be argued that, during this stage, the "urban frontier" replaced the western frontier, attracting millions of migrants to the unfolding economic opportunities found in industrializing urban areas.

As in earlier times, several migration streams characterize this period. However, the relative effects of these streams on the distribution and composition of the nation's population differ dramatically from those of the era of rural dominance.

MAJOR MIGRATION STREAMS

Immigration

Between 1880 and 1910, 18 million immigrants came to America. Immigration represented 28 percent of total U.S. population growth in 1890 and 38 percent of that growth between 1900 and 1910 (figure 7). Foreign-born persons represented one in seven Americans (figure 8), while the proportion of Americans with at least one foreign-born parent was even greater. The first few decades of the urban era encompassed the greatest net influx of immigrants to America in our national history. Indeed, it has been argued that the size and composition of the immigrant stream from 1880 to 1910 spurred the first efforts to close the nation's doors to newcomers.

The composition of this stream of immigrants differed from that of the era of rural dominance. Two new European regions began to send immigrants: eastern Europe (Poland, Russia, Latvia, Lithuania, Finland, Austria, and Hungary) and southern Europe (Italy, Greece, and Turkey). Between 1881 and 1890, when the northern and western European nations represented 72 percent of all immigrants to America, the southern and eastern European nations contributed only 18 percent. The proportion of northern and western European nationals immigrating to America slipped to only 22 percent of all immigrants between 1901 and 1910, while southern and eastern European nations sent 71 percent of all newcomers.

To many Americans, even those who were first-generation immigrants themselves, these newcomers seemed to strain the nation's ability to absorb and incorporate their differences. Unlike the yeoman farmers, artisans, and craftsmen from northern European nations, these immigrants were primarily of peasant stock, poor, and illiterate. Moreover, while the earlier immigrants, caught up in the tide of westward migration, spread out to rural and urban areas across the nation, the immigrants of this era clustered in the largest cities. In 1920, the date when more than half of all Americans lived in cities, more than three-quarters of these urban residents were either immigrants or their first-generation sons and daughters. In 1910, the number of eastern European immigrants in New York City alone numbered nearly a million, with the major immigrant groups as follows: 33,000 from Rumania, 77,000 from Hungary, 190,000 from Austria, and 484,000 from Russia (Callow, 1973: 337).

In urban and rural areas, ethnic communities and neighborhoods flourished, stimulated by the swelling tide of new immigrants. These ethnic communities supported ethnic language newspapers, schools, and churches, and created replicas of the homelands they left behind. When World War I began in Europe, the activities of the German-American Alliance on behalf of the German cause, in addition to increasing visibility of ethnic enclaves, crystallized the latent ethnic and racial prejudices that had been simmering since the 1870s.

The "100 percent American" campaign, supported by the proliferation of antiethnic and antiradical movements, provided political muscle for the first restrictive immigration law in 1917, but it was not restrictive enough. In 1921, an emergency quota system permitted the entry of immigrants equal to 3 percent of the number of foreign-born residents of each nation in the United States at the time of the 1910 census. In 1924, the act was revised to place an absolute ceiling of 165,000

Figure 7
Net Immigration as a Proportion of Total Population Growth,
1900–1985

Percent of Total Growth

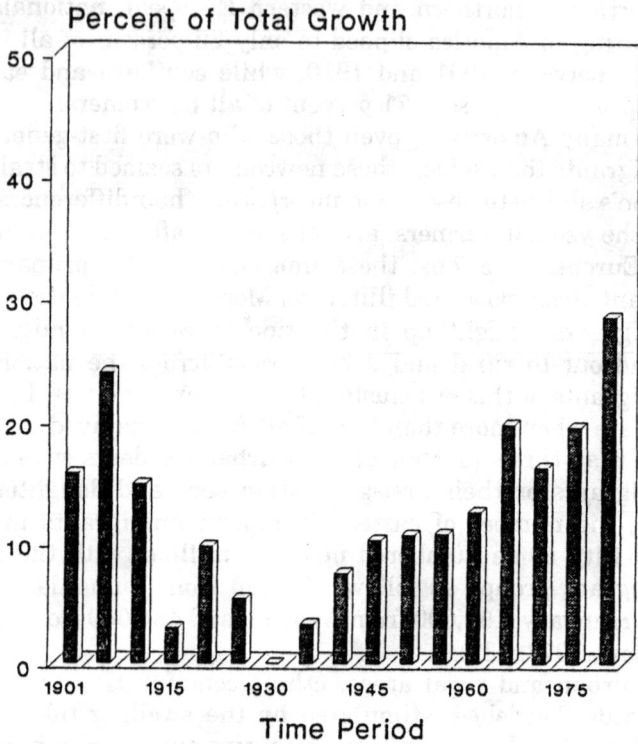

Time Period

Time Period	Proportion of Total Growth
1900 to 1904	15.7%
1905 to 1909	23.9%
1910 to 1914	14.8%
1915 to 1919	2.9%
1920 to 1924	9.7%
1925 to 1929	5.3%
1930 to 1934	-0.1%
1935 to 1939	3.2%

Figure 7 (continued)

1940 to 1944	7.4%
1945 to 1949	10.2%
1950 to 1954	10.6%
1955 to 1959	10.7%
1960 to 1964	12.5%
1965 to 1969	19.7%
1970 to 1974	16.2%
1975 to 1979	19.5%
1980 to 1985	28.4%

Source: Bouvier, Leon F. and Robert W. Gardner. 1986. Immigration to the U.S.: The Unfinished Story. Population Bulletin, Vol. 41(4). Table 6, pg. 20.

immigrants a year from the European nations, and admissions were allocated based on 2 percent of each foreign-born group residing in America in 1890. Asian nations were allocated 1,400 admissions a year, while only 1,200 immigrants from Africa would be admitted. The new quota system meant that of the total 161,446 legal admissions each year from all of Europe, Germany received 51,227 and Great Britain, 34,007, while Italy was allocated only 3,845. Hence, this act and its revision in 1929 effectively stemmed the tide of southern and central Europeans. However, no cap was set on the number of immigrants from the Western Hemisphere (Canada, Mexico, Central and South America), and as a result, the number of immigrants from the Americas increased dramatically.

The passage of these restrictive immigration laws signaled the end of nearly three centuries of "free immigration." Immigration during this period declined from a high average of nearly 9 million a year from 1901 to 1910, to 1 million or less a year from 1930 to 1950. Thus, the great influx of immigrants that had fueled the westward expansion and urban growth ceased to be a major factor during the urban era. The President's Commission on Immigration and Naturalization con-

Figure 8
Foreign-Born as a Proportion of Total U.S. Population, 1850–1980

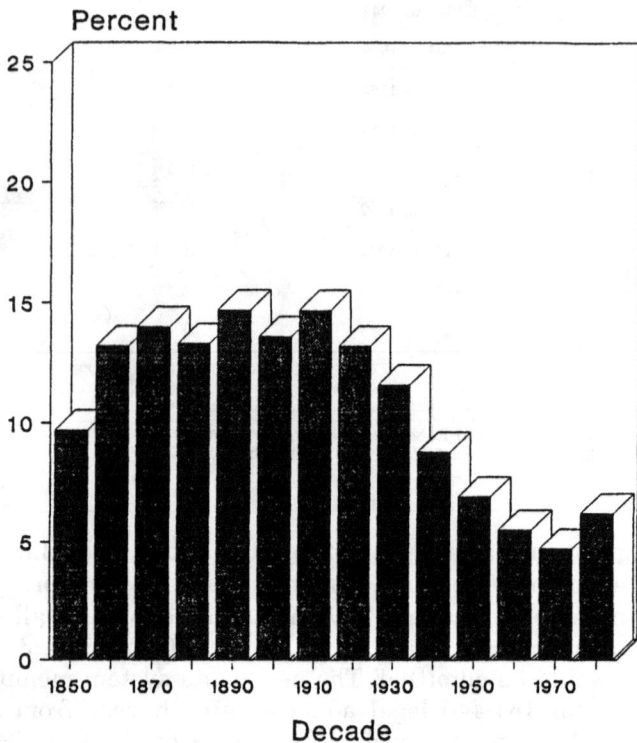

Decade	Foreign Born as % of Total Population
1850	9.7
1860	13.2
1870	14.0
1880	13.3
1890	14.7
1900	13.6
1910	14.7
1920	13.2

Figure 8 (continued)

Decade	Foreign Born as % of Total Population
1930	11.6
1940	8.8
1950	6.9
1960	5.5
1970	4.7
1980	6.2

Source: Leon F. Bouvier and Robert W. Gardner. 1986. Immigration to the U.S.: The Unfinished Story. Population Bulletin, Vol. 41 (4), Table 3.

cluded in 1953 that the substantial reduction in European immigration by the restrictive legislation meant American industries had to look to other sources of labor: "enormous migration" from rural areas; immigration from Puerto Rico, the West Indies, and other countries of the Western Hemisphere; and the passage of special legislation providing for temporary immigration from neighboring countries (such as the braceros program for Mexican laborers) (Handlin, 1959: 204). Each of these reactions had consequences for the populations of rural communities.

Migration to Farms

Migration to farms and farm communities continued during the urban era, but again, to a much smaller extent. The depressed farm economy made this a less attractive proposition than in the era of rural dominance, although it served as a mechanism for social mobility for young farmers and tenants (Anderson, 1937). Federal estimates for the 1920s indicate that while net farm loss through migration was approximately 6.5 million, this reflected the balance of the 19.5 million moving from farms to nonfarm areas and the 13 million moving to farms from nonfarm areas. Landis and Hatt (1954) suggest that farm areas not specializing in commercial agriculture were more likely to attract migrants than did more commercially oriented farm areas.

During the Great Depression (1929–1934), the farm population actually grew, reflecting a greater retentive ability of the farms more than an increase in migration to farms. Taeuber (1938) noted that during the 1930s, the movement to farms in the South was largely to the fringes of urban industrialized areas or to newly opened cut-over areas and swamp lands. These streams were more likely to be composed of entire family groups than those in other agricultural regions, which were composed of single young adults. In the Northeast, where subsistence farms predominated, migration to farms during the Great Depression actually exceeded migration from them, as unemployment forced people to seek a means of support (Hagood, 1950). Landis and Hatt (1954) note that a portion of the growth in the New England farm population during the 1930s represented an increase in the number of part-time farm operators. Following the end of the war in August, 1945, the farm population once again experienced net population gains, primarily among young men between the ages of 20 and 44. However, while there were ebbs and flows in the movement of persons to and from farms during the urban era, the overall pattern was one of substantial population loss due to net out-migration.

Hence, from 1930 to 1950, there were only three years (1932, 1933, 1946) when America's farms experienced a net migration gain. The first two reflect the effects of the Great Depression (McMillan, 1936), and the second the demobilization following the end of World War II. While Taeuber (1938) confirms the existence of a "back to the land" movement, he echoes McMillan's (1936) comments that the new farmers of the Great Depression tended to cluster in those rural areas with the least productive or most marginal farmland. In other words, the movement to the farms during the depression was to some degree an adaptive mechanism to the economic conditions in urban areas, while the surge in the farm population following World War II reflected the temporary relocation of discharged soldiers to a familiar environment prior to re-establishing their civilian lives.

Migration to Rural Places

Other rural areas also attracted migrants during the late nineteenth and early twentieth centuries. The absolute size of the rural population remained remarkably stable, hovering around 54 million for nearly 70 years. "In effect, the growth of the rural nonfarm population has equalled the drop in the farm population" (Beale, 1978: 41). A portion of this growth is attributable to urban-to-rural migration, which continued during this era despite the strong attraction of urban life. For example, the mining areas of Ohio, West Virginia, Tennessee, Alabama, and Pennsylvania had substantial in-migration. Initially, immigrants had worked the mines, but as the American industrial machine demanded ever greater quantities of coal for energy and manufacturing, and restrictive laws limited the flow of immigrants, both rural blacks and whites were recruited to these jobs.

The growth of the rural nonfarm population, like the decline in the farm population, was not evenly distributed throughout the regions of the nation. The Florida peninsula area experienced a 134 percent increase in its rural nonfarm population from 1940 to 1970. The Pacific Coast, Southwest, Lower Great Lakes, and the Northeastern Coastal areas all had population increases of 40 percent or more over the same time period (Beale, 1978). Each of these areas have recreational and climatic amenities that would continue to attract migrants, especially those near retirement age, in the coming decades.

There were also variations in the types of rural nonfarm places experiencing growth. By the end of this era, one out of five rural nonfarm persons lived in incorporated places of less than 2,500 or in unincorporated towns of 1,000 to 2,499 persons. The remainder of the rural nonfarm population resided in the open country or unincorporated hamlets of less than 1,000. While the smallest incorporated rural places (under 500 persons) tended to lose population through the later decades of this era, the general pattern for all towns of less than 2,500 was population increase, often greater than the rate for the nation as a whole (Fuguitt and Beale, 1976; Beale, 1978). A significant proportion of this growth is attributable to net in-migration. Rural towns that were within a metropolitan county but beyond the urbanized area became popular destinations, experiencing a 40 percent gain in population during the 1960s (Beale, 1978).

But the rural nonfarm population outside of incorporated places also displayed a remarkable resiliency during the urban era, especially in its final decades. Overall, Beale (1978: 45) notes, the "rural nonmetropolitan population of the United States outside of incorporated places went from a 0.6 percent loss in the 1950s to a growth of 5.7 percent in the 1960s. Compared to the beginning of that decade, more people today are living in the open country or in villages and commuting to cities for work or for trade and services, even when the city in question is a nonmetropolitan place rather than a large center." Fuguitt and Beale (1976) confirm this decentralizing trend, noting that by the 1960s, in nonmetropolitan counties with an incorporated place of 10,000 or more, population growth was more rapid outside the incorporated places in the county rather than inside.

Westward Migration

The westward movement continued unabated, marked by the shift in the nation's center of population from just west of Cincinnati in 1880, to eight miles northwest of Olney, Illinois, in 1950. The westward movement was especially spurred by drought and agricultural depression in the Great Plains, forcing thousands of displaced farmers to seek new opportunities in the Far West. Tetreau (1938) estimated that two-thirds of the settlers in Arizona's irrigated areas had migrated from the Dust Bowl, while Roberts (1938) linked the only two declines in the Great Plains's open country population to the droughts and depressions of the 1890s and 1930s. The 1930 census indicated that 5 million persons living west of the Mississippi River had been born east of the river (Landis and Hatt, 1954).

The westward migration also included

1. a "filling in" of the open country areas overlooked in the settlement of the trans-Mississippi west,

2. the growth of the midwestern and western urban areas,

3. a movement toward the South, one that steadily increased in strength during this era, and

4. the attraction of a flood of migrants to the Pacific coastal cities (Los Angeles, San Francisco, Santa Barbara, Seattle) with the mobilization for World War II; the stream that continued unabated after the war.

Black Migration

The "Great Migration" to the Northern urban centers by nearly a million southern rural blacks following the outbreak of World War I is another migration stream characteristic of this era. This migration was a swelling of an existing stream, not an emergence of a new one. During the 1880s, more than 30,000 southern blacks migrated to Illinois, New Jersey, New York, and Pennsylvania, but numbers swelled to over 70,000 during the 1890s.

Yet, this post-Civil War migration did not substantially reduce the proportion of blacks residing in the South; in 1910, the South had only a slightly lower proportion of the nation's black population than it had had in 1870 (Johnson and Campbell, 1981: 73). But, between 1910 and 1940, the proportion of blacks residing in the South declined from 89 percent to 77 percent, and by 1970 only one-half (53 percent) of all blacks lived in the South. The Great Migration fundamentally altered the regional distribution of blacks in America (appendix table A–6); first, the Northeast and North Central regions attracted black migrants, and, after the outbreak of World War II, the West began to attract significant numbers of black migrants.

Moreover, the Great Migration is a key factor in the urbanization of the black population. From 1890, when eight out of ten blacks resided in rural areas, to 1960, when less than three out of ten lived in rural areas, the Great Migration was essentially a rural South to urban non-South movement. Most non-South blacks live in urban areas. Indeed, non-South blacks are more likely to reside in urban areas than whites, and they urbanize at a faster rate (figure 9) (Johnson and Campbell, 1983). In the South, blacks were primarily rural residents and

Figure 9
Urban and Rural Distribution of Black and White Population, 1890–1980

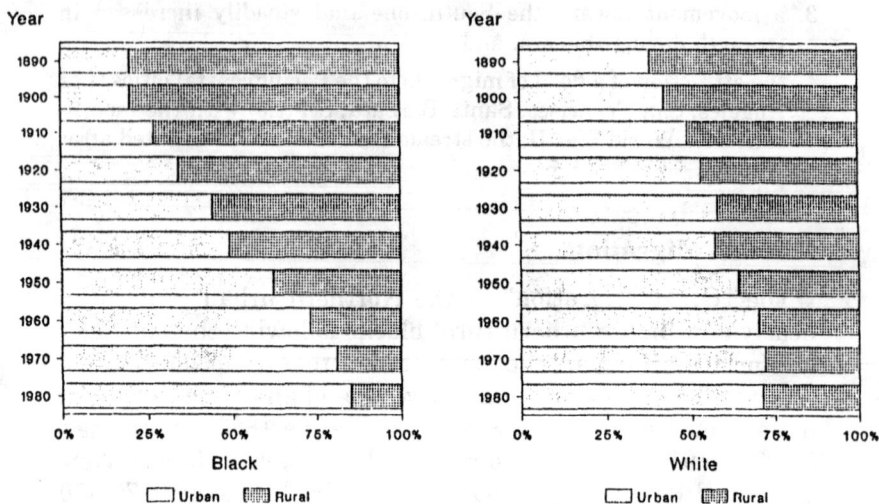

Black

☐ Urban   ▦ Rural   White   ☐ Urban   ▦ Rural

Year	Black Urban	Black Rural	White Urban	White Rural
	Percent Distribution			
1890	20	80	38	62
1900	20	80	42	58
1910	27	73	49	51
1920	34	66	53	47
1930	44	56	58	42
1940	49	51	57	43
1950	62	38	64	36
1960	73	27	70	30
1970	81	19	72	28
1980	85	15	71	29

Source: Adapted from John Reid. 1982. Black America in the 1980s. Population Bulletin, Vol 37 (1), Table 1 and; Series A73-81 in Historical Statistics of the United States, Colonial Times to 1970. U.S. Bureau of the Census, Washington D.C., Government Printing Office.

agricultural workers through the middle of the urban era. While the majority eventually did migrate to urban areas in both the South and the non-South, a substantial number also moved to rural farm and nonfarm destinations. Finally, during this era, an urban-to-urban black migration stream also developed.

URBAN MIGRATION STREAMS

Rural Farm-to-Urban Migration

The most significant migration streams during this era were the rural-to-urban and urban-to-urban movements. The rural farm-to-urban migration is the component of this stream giving the most typical image of the general movement. Based on estimates of the Economic Research Service of the USDA, American farms experienced a net loss of 22.9 million persons between 1920 and 1950 (U.S. Bureau of the Census, 1975: 96). This dramatic loss is illustrated in figure 10, which shows the steady decline of the proportion of the total population represented by farm persons.

Hagood (1950: 242) states: "In four of the five year periods following 1920 the net shift from farms to cities, towns, and villages averaged more than half a million persons a year, and in the most recent period, 1940–1945, it reached more than a million persons a year;... about half of the recent migrants from farms were workers and about half were dependents." Beale (1978) concludes that 1962 was the last year the net migration loss to farms was over 1 million people. After that, while net out-migration from farms continued to average 5 percent a year through the end of this era, the number of farm persons had declined so much that the volume could not approach that of earlier decades.

Yet, while the loss of farm population was nearly universal during this era, not all agricultural regions experienced the same rate of population loss during the same decades. Overall, net out-migration was highest in those agricultural regions with a large number of small farms or unmechanized tenant farms, and increased as these areas mechanized and moved

Figure 10
Farm Population as a Proportion of Total U.S.
Population, 1880–1980

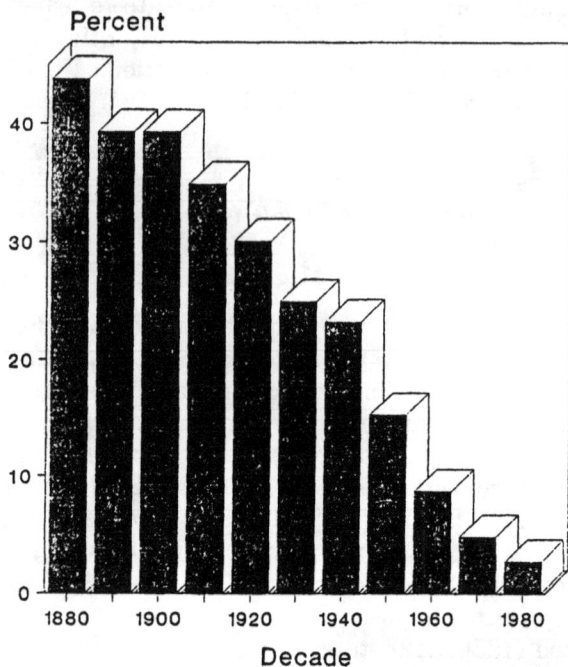

Decade	% Total U.S. Population
1880	43.8
1890	39.3
1900	39.3
1910	34.9
1920	30.1
1930	24.9
1940	23.2
1950	15.3
1960	8.7
1970	4.8
1980	2.7

Source: Adapted from Table 3.2 in Calvin L. Beale. 1978. "People on the Land." pp.37-54 in Thomas R. Ford (editor). Rural USA: Persistence and Change. Ames, IA: Iowa University Press.

toward more intensive commercially oriented production. These characteristics most aptly describe the structure of agriculture in the South (Beale, 1978). While mechanization had rapidly transformed agriculture on the Great Plains and the Midwest, southern agriculture remained characterized by the hoe and mule-drawn plow until the 1940s. During the 1940s, southern agriculture experienced rapid mechanization, substantially reducing the demand for labor, a process intensified by crop reduction programs, soil depletion, and the "transition from tenant farming to day labor" (Johnson and Campbell, 1981: 108). As a result, between 1940 and 1970 "farm population in the south as a whole dropped by a remarkable 77 percent,...with a 90 percent drop among blacks" (Beale, 1978: 40–41).

In the Plains states, population losses due to out-migration were most dramatic during the 1920s and 1930s. In this region, the rising cost of land coupled with the effects of drought, depression, mechanization, and the consolidation of farmland forced thousands off the land in search of new opportunities. While many moved to newly irrigated farmlands in Arizona and California, as did the Joads in *The Grapes of Wrath*, as many moved to cities and towns seeking the jobs and public assistance available in these places.

Rural Nonfarm-to-Urban Migration

A considerable number of persons also moved from rural nonfarm areas to urban destinations. Indeed, Brunner's (1948) study of internal migration during the 1940s indicates that the rural farm population was actually less migratory than the urban or nonfarm population. The gearing up of the industrial economy during World War II recharged migration from rural areas. Gray (1945) estimated that the eastern Kentucky rural nonfarm areas contributed a greater proportion of out-migrants than did the farm sector. Yet, our knowledge of this rural nonfarm-to-urban migration is more limited than our knowledge of its farm-to-urban counterpart, due to the attention paid to the farm exodus by policymakers, the media, and social scientists alike.

Migration to the Urban Fringe

Finally, suburbs—residential communities outside the central city—also attracted migrants. Suburbs and other residential communities outside the central city were a part of the urban landscape even during the era of rural dominance, but their growth skyrocketed from 1940 to 1970. Bogue and Seim (1956) report that during the 1940s, while central cities actually experienced a net migration loss, the suburban rings of metropolitan areas exhibited a 26 percent rate of net migration. By the end of the urban era, nearly 38 percent of the nation's population lived in suburbs, as opposed to 31 percent living in central cities, and a comparable proportion living in nonmetropolitan areas.

Suburbs attracted migrants from both cities and rural areas and, unlike popular media images, represented a broad range of population characteristics, economic activities, and land uses. The 1956 legislation establishing a highway trust fund for constructing the interstate highway system provided an important stimulus for the suburban explosion, but the motivations leading people to choose suburban over city or rural living were the factors guiding people onto these highways to the suburban communities.

Summary of the Various Migration Streams

In summary, the migration streams of the urban era continued population mobility patterns established in the earlier period of national development. However, while westward migration and immigration were the hallmarks of the era of rural dominance, rural-to-urban, urban-to-urban, and suburban migration symbolized the urban era. The migration streams in this era contributed substantially to the regional redistribution of the nation's population (appendix table A–7). The West had the highest rate of population growth during this era, and nearly quadrupled its share of the nation's population at the expense of both the Northeast and the North Central regions, which experienced slowing or stable rates of growth and steady losses in their share of the nation's population. As in the era of rural dominance, the South showed remarkable stability in its share of the nation's population despite significant fluctuations in its rate of growth.

What is often masked by the popular images of rural population change during these years is the great diversity in areas of decline and growth. Rural areas that depended heavily on agriculture, especially the South and the Great Plains, lost substantial proportions of their farm population. However, other rural areas not so dependent on extractive industries and near rapidly growing urban centers actually experienced periods of population growth.

Large urban areas attracted hundreds of thousands of rural migrants, and the structure of urban areas changed even as rural areas changed. As a result, not all migrants to urban areas settled in the central cities; rather, many were attracted to the suburban rings of rural villages and hamlets within the metropolitan boundaries. An urbanizing process was also taking place in nonmetropolitan areas: rural villages and hamlets attracted many of the migrants from farms, and larger villages attracted migrants from smaller villages. The urban era, then, profoundly changed the distribution of the American population, and in the process transformed the nation into a highly urbanized society.

EXPLANATIONS FOR RURAL POPULATION CHANGE

Many factors underlie the migration streams in the urban era. The explanations vary depending on the particular stream, the type of destination community, and the conditions in the larger society. As significant in explaining rural population change is the particular theoretical perspective brought to the analysis.

The Surplus Rural Population

The explanation for the substantial migration from rural to urban areas has often been subsumed under the concept of "surplus population" (Price and Sikes, 1975). A surplus popu-

lation can be the result of a high rate of natural increase, a
condition typical of rural areas throughout most of the first
half of this century, or of a change in the demand for labor. To
some degree, these two conditions are related; over time, high
fertility will swell the working age population and, if the economic structure does not provide an ever-expanding supply of
new job opportunities, the excess labor supply must leave in
search of alternatives. However, technological changes that
displace labor through mechanization, or a restructured mar-
ketplace that reduces the number of firms or production units,
in the process reduces the demand for labor, creating a labor
surplus.

Both of these situations appear in rural areas. In fact, it is
difficult to find a study of rural migration that does not note
the declining demand for agricultural labor as a causal factor
in the migration of the farm population. Heilbroner (1977: 150)
illustrates this effect: "It took twenty manhours to bring in an
acre of wheat in 1880; less than ten by 1930. As a result, the
proportion of the total work force needed on the farm dropped
from over half in the 1860s to less than a quarter in the 1920s."
Table 2 shows the increases in labor productivity compared
with the average net out-migration of the farm population.
Clearly, labor productivity gains came first in the major field
crops of corn and wheat typical of the farming system of the
North Central region, while productivity gains came much
later to the cotton system of the South. Furthermore, the largest losses to the farm population through out-migration occur
in those periods with the greatest gains in labor productivity.

While most studies point to the impact of mechanization on
this declining labor demand, it should also be noted that the
restructuring of agriculture—the shift toward fewer but larger
firms—as well as other technological innovations, such as the
use of fertilizers, pesticides, and herbicides, also affected labor
productivity and, hence, the demand for agricultural labor
(Hamilton, 1939 and 1964). The significance of these factors is
demonstrated by the areas that experienced the highest rates
of net out-migration. The South and the North Central regions
contributed the bulk of the rural-to-urban migrants. In the
South, black agricultural laborers were displaced at a far

Table 2
Increases in Labor Productivity and Out-migration of the Farm Population

| Period | Labor Productivity in Farming | | | Period | Annual average net out-migration from the farm population | |
	Corn (for grain) (Hrs. per 100 bushels*)	Wheat (Hrs. per 100 bushels*)	Cotton (Hrs. per bale*)		Thousands	Percent
About 1800	344	373	601			
About 1840	276	233	439			
About 1880	180	152	304			
1910-1914	135	106	276			
				1920-25	666	2.1
1925-1929	115	74	286	1925-30	593	1.9
				1930-35	58	0.2
1935-1939	108	67	209	1935-40	708	2.3
				1940-45	1,602	5.8
1945-1949	53	34	146	1945-50	677	2.8
				1950-55	1,115	5.4
1955-1959	20	17	74	1955-60	910	5.2
				1960-65	794	5.7
1965-1969	7	11	30	1965-70	594	5.5
1970-1972	6	9	25	1970-73	113	1.2

Source: Productivity estimates from Wayne Rasmussen, "The Impact of Technological Change on American Agriculture, 1862-1962", Journal of Economic History 1962; and U.S. Department of Agriculture, Agricultural Statistics, 1973, Table 651. Migration data from Vera J. Banks and Calvin L. Beale, Farm Population Estimates, 1910-1970, U.S. Department of Agriculture, Rural Development Service, Washington, D.C.: Government Printing Office.
*Man hours per unit of production.

higher rate than whites due to their concentration in cotton and, to a lesser extent, peanut production.

In the North Central states, the structural reorganization of agriculture served both as a major factor contributing to rural farm migration, as well as a factor in the eventual economic decline of agriculturally dependent rural communities. The declining demand for farm labor "pushed" displaced farm workers out of rural areas, and the search for new opportunities began. The structural reorganization of agriculture also led to a concentration of farmland into fewer but larger landholdings, displacing farm families as well as farm laborers. As the number of farm workers and farms declined, the demand for the agricultural services of nearby communities declined, retail sales diminished, as did the tax base, and the cycle of small town decline began.

Differential Opportunities

These comments suggest that the rural-to-urban migration resulted from a "push" from rural areas. Yet, while rural communities were generating a surplus population, urban areas, especially the large metropolitan areas of the Northeast and North Central regions, experienced major economic expansions that also "pulled" rural residents. Industrial production, first fueled by the demands of World Wars I and II, and then stimulated by the general economic prosperity of the "baby boom" years (1947–65), rapidly widened the employment differentials between rural and urban areas. These new job opportunities, coupled with changes in the agricultural sector, the lack of competition from immigrants, and a general rising of quality of life expectations, exerted a strong pull on persons to move to urban areas. Moreover, during the early decades of the urban era (1880–1930), there were marked economic contrasts between rural and urban areas. For example, "in 1910 an average farmer's income had been about 40 percent of an average urban worker's income. By 1930 it had fallen to less than 30 percent" (Heilbroner, 1977: 175). This gap in farm and nonfarm family income and a similar gap between rural and urban family income persists.

Thus, the primary explanation for the aggregate flow of persons between rural and urban areas can be subsumed by economic perspectives. Differences in the opportunity structures of rural and urban areas directed the net flow of persons toward those areas of greater economic advantage (Tarver and Gurley, 1965; Rutman, 1970; Lansing and Mueller, 1967), and urban places captured the lion's share of this net flow. Economic motivations have also been used to explain migration at the individual level. Individuals with high occupational aspirations, or those seeking greater opportunities for social mobility moved to areas providing the chance to fulfill these aspirations. Even when alternative explanatory frameworks for the study of rural-to-urban migration are presented, they are usually in the context of how these alternatives extend our understanding of the operationalization of economic motivations in the individual decision-making process.

A wider variety of factors both pushed people from rural areas and pulled them to urban areas. For example, cultural amenities (museums, libraries, theaters, concert halls) and the emerging popular culture (motion pictures, big bands, radio) were centered in the cities. Furthermore, the urban standard of living exceeded that of rural areas. Medical services (hospitals, doctors, dentists) and public services (running water, sewers, professional police and fire departments) available to urban residents, were often only distant wonders for rural residents. But, besides these amenities, other forces were at work.

For example, southern blacks were often recruited as strike breakers in the iron, coal, and steel industries in the late 1800s and early 1900s. This recruitment provided a vehicle for northward migration that guaranteed a job at the end of the line (Farley, 1970). Labor agents, the media (newspapers such as the *Chicago Defender*), handbills, and correspondence from family and friends spurred movement out of the South by noting the existence of job opportunities and offering assistance in moving. Some labor agents, for example, advanced the cost of transportation North. During the Depression, the out-migration from rural to urban areas and from the South continued. While general unemployment was high, blacks experienced even higher levels, and black sharecroppers suffered extreme poverty (Shannon, 1965). Moreover, during the Depression public relief programs were more common in urban areas, and unemployed or displaced rural blacks often found assistance only by moving to the cities.

The research of Schwarzweller, Brown, and Mangalam (1971) on Appalachian migrants also illustrates these other motivations. Their research uses LePlay's concept of the "stem family" to examine the social system linking an origin and a destination. The stem family, located at an origin, has branch families in one or more potential destinations. Branch families send information on employment, housing, and a variety of other issues back to the stem family. They also may provide temporary housing, money, or simply social emotional support to family newcomers arriving in their area. The stem family provides a kin network for distributing information to family members and assistance for those who are interested in moving. These supportive activities help overcome what Lee (1966) calls "intervening obstacles" (e.g., geography, distance, information, resources) that may deter migration and ease the migrant's adjustment to a new environment. This is, then, an established kinship network within which individuals can obtain information about other places, receive assistance in relocation, and find a safe haven if economic circumstances deteriorate. Thus, this strand of research explains how objective economic conditions in different areas are translated into individual motivations and communicated to potential migrants.

Structural Transformations

Any explanation of migration patterns during this era must also take into account the structural transformations occurring in American society. Wardwell's (1980) theory of urban-rural migration in the developed world, although developed to explain migration patterns in the post–1970 decades, highlights critical changes in society's structure that also help account for the patterns of migration during the urbanization era. First, infrastructure improvements in smaller urban places provide industries with greater locational choices. The massive federal expenditures on the interstate highway system, and comparable expenditures by state governments for intrastate highways and more complete secondary road systems represent one type of infrastructure improvement by the end of this era. Other types include public water and sewer systems, and the expansion of and innovations in communication systems. Second, economies of scale and agglomeration may occur in smaller urban places, not just the largest cities. Factors such as the cost of transportation, the availability and quality of the work force, and access to complementary firms led to the concentration of population and economic activities in the larger urban places. However, infrastructure improvements reduced, to a certain extent, the comparative advantages of the largest urban places. Moreover, certain diseconomies, such as rapidly increasing taxes, wages rates, and traffic congestion, began to accumulate in the largest urban places. These diseconomies did not afflict smaller urban places. Thus, structural changes in society as a whole slowly began to reduce relative advantages once enjoyed by the largest urban centers, such that size of place was no longer directly associated with desirable amenities.

Applying the Cognitive-Behavioral Model

If we were to summarize these various explanations of the patterns of migration during the urban era, the cognitive-behavioral model would offer a parsimonious theoretical framework. A variety of economic and demographic factors—employment opportunity, occupational diversity, and standard of living—gave urban locations an objective advantage over rural areas. Furthermore, the obstacles that had once hampered migration diminished during the urban era. For example, information is a key factor in migration decision-making. With the diffusion of telecommunications (national news magazines, telephones, radio, television) throughout America, even persons in the most remote areas could obtain information about employment opportunities elsewhere. Additionally, federal and state investments in all-weather roads, and the intra- and interstate highway systems alleviated the physical and psychological barriers of distance, for now one could move to a distant place in search of greater opportunities while still maintaining contact with loved ones. Literally millions of individuals perceived the relative advantages of urban locations vis-à-vis rural ones, and migrated from rural areas to urban destinations of various sizes. But, many did not. The advantage of the cognitive-behavioral model is that it also offers an explanation for why millions did not perceive these objective differences between rural and urban areas, or, if they perceived them, did not act on their perceptions.

Uhlenberg's (1973) study of three groups of people that did not migrate from areas with clear disadvantages vis-à-vis alternative locations illustrates the utility of this perspective.

Uhlenberg argues that an examination of the living conditions of southern blacks from 1860 to 1920, of Japanese-Americans in internment camps during World War II, and of Appalachian residents from 1930 to 1960, would disclose severely negative environments that should have spurred a high level of out-migration. Yet, this did not occur. Uhlenberg suggests that a major determinant of the motivation for migration is the relative balance between perceptions of conditions at the place of origin and at alternative destinations. Information is a key factor in developing perceptions of alternative destinations, and it is the weighting of these perceptions in the decision-making process that determines whether motivation is translated into actual migration. Uhlenberg then suggests economic factors (direct cost of move and level of investments in origin) and noneconomic factors (extent of integration into and dependence on the local community, or perception of the adjustment to a new location) influence the relative importance of locational perceptions. In offering an explanation for why certain groups did not migrate to urban areas during this era, Uhlenberg supports the cognitive-behavioral approach to understanding migration.

An Example of Episodic Migration

Finally, the effect of the mobilization for World War II illustrates the influence of a sociohistorical episode on migration patterns. It is estimated that between 1940 and 1942 migration increased fivefold. Landis and Hatt (1954) report that during 1940 alone more than 1.5 million persons migrated as part of the defense mobilization. Typical cities with migration gains include Seattle, which gained approximately 110,000 persons in a twenty-seven-month period from 1940 to 1942; Detroit, with 336,000 new residents; and Norfolk, Portsmouth, and Newport News, with 107,000 new residents. Included in this defense migration were over 1 million young males mobilized for the armed forces and transferred to military bases (e.g., Oakland, Calif.); hundreds of thousands who moved to industrial urban areas where existing industries converted their operations to meet the demands of new defense contracts (e.g.,

Detroit); and, thousands of others who moved to smaller cities where manufacturing industries developed or converted to capture their share of the defense production. But Landis and Hatt (1954: 411) also note that between 1940 and 1942 nearly 30,000 farm families were "displaced through the purchase of lands for military purposes." Finally, in 1943, the federal government began to subsidize the migration of persons from isolated rural areas in the Appalachian and Ozark regions to industrial centers.

The effects of the wartime migration were dramatic. The Plains states lost more people from 1940 to 1942 than they had during the previous decade. The U.S. Department of Agriculture estimated that from September 1941 to September 1942 American farms lost nearly 1.6 million farm workers and operators. Just over four in ten of these farm persons entered the armed forces, and the remainder took nonfarm jobs (Landis and Hatt, 1954). Moreover, many of these persons never returned to their rural communities; indeed, their presence in the urban industrial centers attracted others. Landis and Hatt conclude that more people moved in this short period of time than at any other moment in our history. Significantly, rural peoples composed the bulk of this wartime migration.

SUMMARY

The urban era began with the absolute predominance of persons living in rural places and ended with the waning of the rural majority. Massive out-migration from rural areas, especially the nation's farms, provided a steady stream of new residents for urban areas. This migration stream was particularly critical for continued urban growth—both economic and demographic—following the restriction of immigration in 1921. Throughout this era, then, "rural America [was] the seed-bed of the nation" (Kolb and desBrunner, 1952: 55), furnishing the human resources that served continued economic expansion in urban centers.

There was also increasing diversity in the ecological structure of rural and urban communities as migration contributed to the growth of rural villages and hamlets as well as suburban enclaves and urban places of various sizes. Migration, then, was the basis for both centripetal and centrifugal population movements, concentrating population in urban centers and dispersing population to suburban rings and more distant rural towns. The next chapter explores some of the consequences of these changing patterns of migration.

5

Consequences of Migration During the Urban Era

INTRODUCTION

In the previous chapter we examined the size and direction of the migration streams of the urban era, and saw that during this era millions of persons left their rural residences for new destinations in urban centers, suburban rings, and rural villages and towns. Since the turn of the century, when the rural population represented more than one-half of the American population, the proportion living in rural areas declined to around one in four Americans.

The size, composition, and direction of migration streams during the urban era affected the population structure and processes and socioeconomic characteristics of rural communities. A critical question in rural community change is: Who moved during this era? Studies of migration selectivity give us the composition of this mass movement and indicate the consequences for rural communities.

CHARACTERISTICS OF MIGRANTS

Educational Selectivity

One of the most persistent areas of research on the selectivity of migration concerns educational aspirations and attainment.

Rural youth who intend to move to urban areas and those who actually do move have higher educational aspirations and attainments than those who remain behind (Martinson, 1955; Landis, 1946). The extensive research on this topic suggests that educational aspirations develop first, followed by occupational aspirations. In other words, a decision concerning future residence is made based on those locations offering the greatest opportunity for employment in a preferred occupation (Payne, 1956).

In addition, migrants to urban areas have higher levels of educational attainment than those who move to other rural areas or those who remain behind (Landis, 1946; Beers, 1947; Brunner, 1948). Educational selectivity is most pronounced for males and for blacks. In other words, among these groups, higher levels of educational attainment are associated with higher rates of migration.

The relationship between educational aspirations and attainment and migration is modified, for males, by an intention to farm. If the young man plans to become a farmer and has the opportunity to do so, he is less likely to express an intention to move or to actually migrate (Bohlen and Wakely, 1950). Martinson (1955) develops this theme by noting that the development of "urban-oriented" interests has been strongly associated with the migration of rural males. Then, as now, young men raised on farms are less likely to migrate to cities if they have a strong commitment to farming or can reasonably expect assistance in establishing themselves as farmers.

The sociological meaning of these relationships is not clear. Is it the additive effect of the educational process that leads to migration? In other words, as one spends more time within the formal educational system, is one more likely to acquire a desire to move? Are highly motivated individuals likely to acquire greater amounts of formal education and see migration as a way to satisfy strong motivations in other areas, such as occupational aspirations? Or, is it that rural areas offer fewer opportunities for advanced education, and, thus, individuals must leave if they want postsecondary education (Schultze, et al., 1963)? The interactions between educational and occupational aspirations and migration are still not clearly understood. Yet, overwhelming evidence demonstrates that these aspirations enter the decision-making process, influencing the utility of urban versus rural locations. Moreover, Long (1973) notes a strong relationship between education and interstate moves, suggesting that as education increases, individuals expand the geographic range of their employment searches.

The educational selectivity of migration strongly affected black migration, producing a marked depression in educational attainment for the South, which lost the better educated but gained the poorly educated through migration interchanges during this era (Johnson and Campbell, 1983). Indeed, as the distance moved increased, the educational attainment of black migrants increased. Johnson and Campbell (1983: 136) conclude: "The heavy out-migration of blacks from the South, combined with the educational selectivity, resulted in a 'brain drain' for the region. The South was disadvantaged in at least two respects: one, the public investment in education for the out-migrants was lost to the region; two, the region was left with blacks of lower educational achievement, who were less able to make positive economic contributions."

The selectivity of migration streams for high educational aspirations as well as educational attainment "fits" the expectations of economic models of migration. As we have seen, labor force models assume rational individuals will attempt to maximize utilities; that is, all things being equal, they will choose to move to those areas of greater economic opportunity. Numerous studies (Murdock et al., 1984; Tarver and Gurley, 1965; Williams, 1981) have documented the economic advantages offered by urban settings, including greater diversity in employment opportunities, higher wages, and better employment benefits. Thus, persons with high aspirations and the educational skills to act on them would more likely move to urban areas or greater distances (Lipset, 1955: Long, 1973).

Age Selectivity

Migration streams during this era can also be differentiated by the age composition of the streams. A wide variety of studies conducted in different areas of the country confirm that the rural-to-urban migration was essentially a movement of the young.

For example, Baker (1935) estimated that during the 1920s about one-third of those moving from farms to cities and towns were under the age of 15, another third were between 15 and 25, and about a tenth were aged 25 to 35. During the 1940s, the rates of out-migration were highest for young persons, lowest for children and persons aged 25–44, and intermediate for those over the age of 45 (Bowles, 1957). This pattern was confirmed using retrospective residential histories collected in 1958 from cohorts aged 18, 24, 34, and 44 at that time. Taeuber (1967) found that among each cohort, off-farm movement began around age 18 and continued at a decreasing rate as the cohorts aged. Another study of rural farm migrants from eastern Kentucky indicated that 40 percent of the men aged 15–34 left the area between 1940 and 1942 (Larson, 1943), while Brunner (1948) found that during the late 1930s, the highest rate of migration was for persons aged 25 to 29. Black migrants mirrored this age selectivity with young adults (20 to 25 years old) predominating in most streams from the South. However, those who moved to the South were more likely to be teenagers (14 to 19 years old) or adults of retirement age (65 and older) (Johnson and Campbell, 1983). Hence, the rural-to-urban migration is essentially a movement of the young, but there appears to be some variability in this age selection by race and region.

Selectivity by Sex and Family Composition

The rural-to-urban migration was also selective for sex, and, as a function of the age and sex composition of these streams, it is also true that the streams were composed primarily of single persons rather than family groups.

Young women, more than young men, were likely to be rural-to-urban migrants (Bowles, 1957). Women were also more likely than males to migrate at an earlier age (Lively and Taeuber, 1939). Bernert (1944) confirms this higher rate of migration for younger farm women, but also notes a higher net out-migration of older women, many of them widows. Others also confirm these general patterns (Baker, 1935; Melvin and Smith, 1938; Smith, 1953). The over-representation of young women among rural farm-to-urban migrants may be related to the marriage market. Women tend to marry men who are somewhat older than they are, and who have higher socioeconomic status. The several decades of out-migration of young males with higher levels of educational attainment may have limited the selection of mates, thus producing a "push" toward urban areas, where marriage opportunities were greater.

Other Types of Selectivity

Whether migration selects for other factors is somewhat uncertain. For example, does rural-to-urban migration select for persons with higher occupational status? There has been less research on the occupational selectivity of migration, perhaps reflecting the fact that so many of the rural-to-urban migrants have been younger and therefore at the beginning of their occupational careers.

The evidence as to selectivity by income is mixed. Limited research suggests that, for blacks, higher family incomes are associated with a greater likelihood of migration to urban areas (Price and Sikes, 1975), but the reverse is true for whites. Again, the age of the migrants and their labor force status may affect these findings.

Family influence on occupational aspirations and hence intentions to move and actual migration also serves as an explanatory factor. In a study of eighth and twelfth grade boys in Georgia, Payne (1956: 117) found: "Boys were aware of the prestige value of occupations and choosing above their parents, and were choosing more 'urban' occupations than their parents, and were expecting to leave their home communities to live and work as adults." In a longitudinal study of a rural Appalachian community, Schwarzweller and Brown (1967: 5) found "a migrant's social class origin influenced not only when he left the mountains, where he moved, and with whom, but also his subsequent level of living in the urban area."

Thus, the great migration of persons from rural to urban

areas siphoned off the young more than the old, single persons more than family units, women more than men, and those with high educational and occupational aspirations. While the tendency might be to assume that the population redistribution of the urban era siphoned off the best and the brightest from rural communities, this is not the reality. After reviewing all the literature on this topic, Thomas (1938a) concluded that the city attracted the extremes, both those with high and those with limited abilities. The "selection does operate positively, negatively, and randomly, at different times, depending on a variety of factors that, up to the present, have not been adequately investigated" (Thomas, 1938a: 407).

Selectivity in the Counterstream to Rural Areas

One strand of research on the selectivity of migration during the urban era has focused on the counterstream of migrants from urban to rural areas and considered whether these individuals were moving to rural areas for the first time or were return migrants. The concept of return migration has been operationalized in several ways. Some have defined it very broadly, using the concept to imply a move to a state or a region of birth. Others have operationalized the concept more narrowly as a move to a particular place, usually a community or a county of prior residence.

Eldridge (1965) embraces the broader definition of the concept, postulating that return migrants constitute a disproportionate share of the counterstream, and that returnees tend to be older than original migrants to the cities. The 1967 Survey of Economic Opportunity indicates that whites are more likely to move to rural areas than blacks, and those who move to rural areas are younger than those who move to urban areas (Bowles, Bacon, and Ritchey, 1973 and 1974). The authors explain these age differentials as reflecting a movement to suburban or rural nonfarm areas.

Much of our knowledge about return migration using the narrower definition is based on case studies. Several studies of migration to Appalachia have examined return migration to

particular communities. A study of West Virginian Appalachian return migrants found that return migrants were older,
had smaller households, and were drawn from the extremes of
the occupational spectrum, as compared to persons who moved
to the area for the first time or to long-term residents (Photidias, 1970).

A variety of other studies touch on the characteristics of
persons who moved to rural areas during the urban era, without
taking into account whether they were return or first-time
movers to rural places. For example, the streams of migration
to rural communities from other rural places or from urban
areas tended to have an older age composition. The two exceptions to this were migration to college and, to a lesser degree,
military communities. However, while these in-migrants
tended to be older than those moving from rural to urban areas,
many were in the early stages of family formation. Hence,
many destination rural communities experienced sharp gains
in school-age children, especially in the 1960s (Dailey and
Campbell, 1980).

Educational selectivity also appears among migrants to different types of rural communities near the end of this era. Older
migrants attracted to retirement and recreation communities,
while having lower educational attainment than those moving
to government services or college communities, still represented a net gain to the educational level of their destination
communities. Hence, the various types of rural economic bases
attracted migrants of different educational attainment and, in
the case of college communities, attracted migrants with high
educational aspirations.

Finally, some evidence as to the occupational composition of
the rural-to-urban migration stream appears in one study of a
remote rural district from 1900 to 1930. Reuss (1937) found
that rural places adjacent to urban centers lost a higher proportion of business and professional people, while rural places
adjacent to industrial centers most frequently lost skilled and
unskillled workers. Migrant streams to rural communities appear to select for those occupations that best fit the particular
community's economic base. Unskilled blue-collar workers and,
to a lesser extent, white-collar professionals and managers tend

to dominate these streams in response to the demand for services from new residents.

DEMOGRAPHIC CONSEQUENCES OF MIGRATION

The consequences of migration streams for rural communities during this era fall into two categories: demographic and socioeconomic. This division is somewhat arbitrary, since the demographic characteristics of a community's population affect its socioeconomic structure and opportunities. Yet, this division provides a convenient way of thinking about the important community changes of the urban era.

CHANGING AGE STRUCTURE

Migration profoundly altered the age-sex structure of rural America. At the beginning of this era, well over one-half of the rural population was under the age of twenty, but a substantial porportion was also of working age. However, by 1950, as Smith (1953: 76) notes: "The nation's children are concentrated on the farms, its persons of productive ages in the cities, and its elderly folk in the villages, small towns, and suburban areas." During the 1950s, it was the completely or predominantly rural counties that lost, through net out-migration, "40 percent of their youth who reached twenty years of age during that decade. Losses were even higher in some areas—50 percent in the Southern coal-field area and 60 percent of Negroes in the poorest Southern counties" (Beale, 1974: 45). Mills County, Texas, illustrates the effects of the net migration loss of young persons: the average age of the population in this county rose from 25 in 1940 to 35 in 1950, to 45 in 1960, and nearly 49 in 1970 (Beale, 1974).

In many rural counties, the age structure has been so distorted that a condition of natural decrease occurs. These counties, about 500 during the 1960s, lost so many young persons through out-migration that the number of adults of childbearing age who remained was insufficient to offset the deaths in the elderly population. Throughout this era, natural decrease was essentially a condition of rural rather than urban areas, and can be attributed to the rural-to-urban migration stream (Beale, 1974).

Sex Ratio

Despite the changing sex structure, the sex ratio in rural areas underwent only minor changes; specifically, the excess of males over females declined somewhat, but rural areas—especially rural farm areas—retained their surplus of males (Thompson and Whelpton, 1933; Smith, 1953). The rural-to-urban migration stream did contain a higher proportion of females than males throughout this period. Yet, the shifting distribution of the rural population and the balance of rural nonfarm and farm populations, in conjunction with the concentration of women, especially widows in the rural village population, meant that sex ratios for the total rural population remained somewhat stable (Smith, 1942). Indeed, Belcher (1946) found no fundamental difference between the sex structure of rural villages and that of the urban population.

However, migration patterns in the era of rural dominance contributed to highly distorted sex ratios in the West that did not approach those of other regions until the 1940s. For example, in 1850 there were nearly three men for every woman in the West, but this declined to approximately 1.1 males for every woman by 1930. The Northeast, on the other hand, had nearly equal proportions of males and females throughout this period, in all likelihood reflecting the migration drain to the West throughout this era.

Fertility

The changing age structure in rural communties is one factor associated with the substantial decline in rural fertility. The rural population maintained exceptionally high birth rates during the bulk of this era, and without the "safety valve" of urbanward migration the rural population would have experienced an explosive natural increase. For example, the National Resources Committee estimated that, "expressed as percentages of the ratio necessary to maintain a stationary population, in 1930, the urban native white population met only 86 percent of replacement needs, the rural population 154 percent, and the rural farm 170 percent" (Smith, 1953: 133). The National Resources Committee estimates, then, that without migration, the urban population in the 1950s would have declined 1.8 percent, and during the 1960s it would have declined by 3 percent.

Graybill et al. (1958) demonstrate that between 1910 and 1950 rural farm residents had larger completed family sizes than urban residents, regardless of the husband's occupation. These differences in completed family size were greatest for rural farm families where the husband was employed in white-collar occupations. There were, however, considerable regional variations in rural fertility. For example, the Midwestern Cornbelt had higher rates while the Southern Cottonbelt had lower rates, but, overall, the general pattern of higher rural fertility persisted throughout this era, albeit to a declining degree (Woofter, 1948; Hagood, 1948; Hill and Tarver, 1951; Beegle, 1966). Overall, the fertility ratio of urban women (the number of children under 5 years of age per 1,000 women aged 20 to 44), continued to be lower than that of rural women, regardless of region (appendix table A–8).

At the end of World War II, Rindfuss and Sweet (1977) estimated that total fertility rates reflected 2.7 live births for rural white women and 1.8 for urban white women. This gap narrowed in the next decade, in part because urban fertility increased more rapidly than rural fertility, and high fertility persisted longer in urban rather than rural areas. The decline is also explained, in part, by the continued loss of young adults who would have established families and borne children in rural communities (Woofter, 1948; Beegle, 1966). Finally, the urbanization process, more specifically, the territorial expansion of urban areas and the growth of urban-like villages in rural areas, affected fertility through the extension of urban values and fertility preferences to the rural population.

The gradient principle of ecological theory provides a framework for interpreting this effect (Tarver, 1969). Its underlying assumption is that distance represents a surrogate measure for the influence of urban norms, mores, or lifestyles of the rural population. It has been argued that the location of the farm population with respect to urban centers helps explain fertility differentials within the farm population. Beegle (1966: 415) suggests: "The location of the farm population with respect to large urban centers helps to determine interaction, participation and internalization of the urban-industrial system." As the geographic territory encompassed by metropolitan or urban centers expanded, increasing proportions of the rural population were brought into closer proximity with urban influences, enhancing the depressing effects of urban norms and preferences.

Moreover urban-to-rural migrants brought with them urban-based fertility preferences and behavior. Such migrants had lower fertility than the resident native population and "serve[d] to lower the growth rate in rural areas" (Ritchey, 1973: 26). But rural village growth was also fueled by intra-area mobility, the migration of rural persons who did not bring urban-based fertility preferences. This suggests that the more critical factor in lowering rural fertility during this era was the extension of urbanlike influences into rural areas through the mass media and consumer expectations.

The selectivity of the migration from rural areas, then, contributed to a reduction of the historically high rate of rural population growth. As young people poured into the cities, the pool of potential parents declined dramatically. The counter-stream of urbanites to rural communities in association with the emergence of a mass, urban-based culture served to depress traditionally high fertility expectations, also contributing to declining rural rates of natural increase.

There were, however, exceptions to this pattern of declining fertility. In some rural areas of the South, especially those with high concentrations of blacks, fertility remained high. In the rural Southwest, enclaves of Hispanics persisted in high fertility rates. And, in the mountainous regions of the Appalachians and the Ozarks, cultural traditions sustained early marriage and childbearing, producing exceptionally high fertility rates through the end of this era.

Changing Ethnic Structure

The decades of the Great Migration profoundly affected the racial composition of the rural South. In 1890, eight out of ten blacks resided in rural areas, more than nine out of ten in the South, but in 1970 less than two in ten blacks were rural residents and only 53 percent lived in the South. As noted earlier, blacks (73 percent) were more likely than whites (70 percent) to live in urban areas by 1970. Southern agricultural areas suffered the greatest losses of black population as both tenants and owners moved to the cities. In 1920, black farm operators numbered 926,000 and represented one in seven American farmers, but by 1978 there were only 57,271 black farmers, representing just above 2 percent of all farmers. Yet, most rural blacks continue to reside in the South, where many rural counties have significant black populations.

In the Southwest, rural clusters of persons of Mexican or Asian origin plummeted during the urban era, although this region retained the largest share of residents in these ethnic groups. Indeed, by 1970 both groups were more likely to be urban residents than whites. In certain states of the Southwest, such as New Mexico and Texas, persons of Mexican origin also cluster in rural towns and villages. However, the overall effect of migration during this era has been to reduce the racial and ethnic diversity of rural areas.

The Emergence of Metropolitan Areas

Any consideration of the demographic consequences of migration during the urban era must address the emergence of metropolitan areas. As early as 1933, R. D. McKenzie wrote about the emergence of the metropolitan community. McKenzie (1933) notes that, in 1930, a quarter of the nation's population resided in 27 of the nation's 3,072 counties, and fully three-quarters resided in only 862 counties. In fact, between 1890 and 1970 the proportion of the population residing in places of 50,000 or more persons increased from less than one in five Americans to more than one in three. Furthermore, during the same time period the proportion of Americans residing in places of 1 million or more persons nearly doubled.

McKenzie also notes the tendency of these metropolitan populations to settle in the outlying fringes rather than in the central cities. In the decades that followed, this pattern of overall metropolitan growth, with decline or stability in the centers and growth on the fringes, persisted. The diffusion of automobile ownership, improved highways, and a latent desire to live in rural or small town environments facilitated this pattern of metropolitan growth. The introduction of the SMA in 1950 acknowledged the increasing economic and social integration of counties. The SMA brought to light that "a city's effective population is no longer the number of persons who happen to live within its corporate limits" (Peterson, 1975: 471).

However, urban places of all sizes experienced substantial population growth (appendix table A–9), and by the middle of this era the smaller urban places were posting rates of population increase substantially higher than those of the largest urban places. Clearly, the lines between rural and urban living blurred as the migration streams reduced the geographic isolation of rural towns and expanded the geographic boundaries of the cities.

SOCIOECONOMIC CONSEQUENCES OF MIGRATION

Opinions on the socioeconomic consequences of the migration from rural areas during this era have run the gamut, from declarations that this represented the only solution to the depressed living conditions in these places, to warnings of the imminent collapse of small town America. The reality shifted between these two extremes, often depending on the economic base of the rural area and economic conditions in the larger society.

Dependency Burdens

The dependency ratio (the proportion of persons under 18 or over 65 to those aged 18–64) in rural areas underwent signif-

icant changes. The out-migration of young persons just entering the labor force and the in-migration of persons at or near
retirement age significantly raised the dependency ratios in
many rural communities. The reduction in the working-age
population coupled with the other socioeconomic processes of
change meant that less fiscal resources were available to support community services. The will to support educational services was often diminished as community leaders and residents
saw the cream of their youth skimmed off to the benefit of the
cities.

Moreover, the high dependency ratio meant communities had
limited human resources available to attract new industries,
which could provide jobs to curb the tide of out-migration. In
this sense, the great out-migration from rural places during
this era began a cycle of economic decline. Few educated young
persons remained to serve as a labor force for new industries,
few industries located in rural places because of the relative
advantage of urban centers, resulting in few reasons for young
persons to stay in rural communities, and so on. Finally, the
loss of these young persons also meant that the pool of candidates for the next generation of political and economic leaders
had been depleted, some would argue, of those persons with
the greatest motivation and personal resources to serve as leaders.

Loss of Human and Economic Capital

Others have estimated the economic consequences of the
rural-to-urban migration using a different measuring stick.
The great majority of the migrants were young persons who
had recently completed their education, at which time they
promptly took their educational skills to the cities. The monetary loss to rural areas from the out-migration of farm youth
during the 1920s has been estimated at about $1.4 billion,
which had been spent in education, medical services, food, and
clothing (Baker, 1933). Kolb and Brunner (1946) estimate that
the cost of the migration of farm-born youth was approximately
20 percent of the annual net farm income between 1920 and

1930. As Folsom (1937: 17) notes: "During the decade, 1920–1929, about 40 percent of the youth who started to work in factories, offices, and stores of the cities came from the farms—for probably two decades on the average, they had been fed, clothed, and educated by the farming people, and were then provided practically free of cost, to the cities, ready for life's work." Thus, many argued that the massive migration of farm-born youth to the cities made the poorer farm areas bear the cost of rearing and training these youth with few prospects for recouping their investments through the economically productive contributions of these young adults.

Moreover, an additional $300 to $400 million was transfered to farm-born city residents in the settlement of estates (Baker, 1935), representing a transfer of real farm wealth through inheritances. Yoder and Smick (1935) studied farm inheritance patterns in Whitman County, Washington, and determined that over 80 percent of the inheritances went to heirs in towns and cities. A similar study in Ohio and Arizona confirmed that more wealth from rural estates flowed into cities than city inheritances moved into rural areas (Tetreau, 1940). Thus, the massive out-migration from farm communities during the urban era was costly not only in terms of human capital but also in terms of real wealth.

Changing Commercial Structure

Finally, while economic specialization enabled many rural villages and towns to grow in population during this era, the "number of individually-owned small stores in villages and hamlets" decreased, replaced by rural affiliates of urban-based firms (Brunner, 1968). The generalized retail stores of many rural villages were slowly being replaced by more specialized ones, changing the retail character of these communities. And, some rural villages suffered general losses of retail business, especially the agriculturally dependent ones in areas of farm consolidation and decline (Brunner, 1952; Hassinger, 1957). Johansen (1974) estimates that between 1950 and 1970 nonmetro towns of less than 2,500 lost nearly a third of their consumer business establishments. In an analysis of the relationship between population change and business activity in nonmetropolitan areas from 1930 to 1970, Johnson (1985:51) concludes: "In general, [retail] establishment shifts were similar in magnitude to those in population. Establishment change was in the same direction as population change but was less than proportionate, suggesting organizational resistance to change."

Ecological Diversity

Yet, there developed during the urban era a remarkable diversity among rural communities due to the changing ecological structure of rural communities. More specifically, the territorial expansion of urban areas, the growth of urbanlike villages and towns, and specialization in rural economic bases produced increasing diversity among rural communities. These changes were both a consequence and a cause of the migration streams during this era.

Villages and towns either grew or declined in size, depending, in part, on their proximity to larger urban centers. Another factor producing change in the ecological structure of rural communities after 1940 was the growing specialization of rural service centers. Retirement, recreational, government service, college, military, regional trade, agricultural, and mining communities increasingly provided employment or residential and commercial services to particular segments of rural America. The specialization derived from the fortunate presence of natural resources, favorable climate, military bases, or state colleges, and the attraction of these physical amenities or economic opportunities for migrants and residents. The type of community economic base influenced the numbers and types of migrants attracted to the community and the ability of the community to retain its residents (Kirschenbaum, 1971).

For example, while retirement communities tended to attract substantial numbers of migrants at or near retirement age, college communities tended to attract migrants in their late teens or early career stages. In both cases, the demand for commercial and other services stimulated the local business climate, providing more economic opportunities for residents as well as other migrants. Alternatively, agricultural communities experienced a nearly steady loss of population, and many mining communities experienced cycles of population growth and decline in response to the demand for their particular resource base. Hence, the great diversity in economic bases among rural communities both produced and resulted from differential patterns of migration.

Alternatively, a study of a multicounty development district in rural Kentucky found that a high proportion of new plant jobs were taken by return migrants who had left higher paying jobs in the cities to come "home" (Mueller and Barth, 1964). Similar results appear in a multicounty study in the Ozarks. Bender et al. (1971) conclude that return migrants may actually deepen rural poverty because they are more competitive for new jobs than unemployed or underemployed rural residents. Research on rural industrialization confirms that new jobs are often taken by migrants rather than unemployed residents. Finally, in a study of Butler County, Kentucky, Price and Sikes (1975) report that nearly two-thirds of white adult residents had at one time or another lived in urban areas. These return migrants preferred rural living and had left employment in the cities to take jobs, often at lower wages, in rural industries.

Summary of Socioeconomic Consequences

The effects of out-migration on communities left behind can be summarized as follows: "Effects of rural out-migration may also be seen in the physical deterioration of many rural communities. One needs only to drive the back roads through the Great Plains or Corn Belt to see the deterioration in small towns that has been associated with out-migration. Empty buildings often dot the main street of the towns, which no longer can support the businesses and services of yesterday. In the countryside, numerous abandoned farmsteads attest to the changes in agricultural technology that have caused many people to leave farming. Many larger towns are struggling as the population of their hinterland shrinks and it becomes more difficult to finance services, schools, and other institutions" (Beale, 1974: 49).

But this description does not fit all rural areas, for, as we have seen, many rural villages and towns experienced population growth during this era. Towns of 2,500 or more adjacent to metropolitan areas tended to experience population growth during this era (Johansen and Fuguitt, 1973). Moreover, counties with significant proportions of their labor forces employed in manufacturing also experienced extended periods of population growth. Thus, the effects of the patterns of migration on rural communities during this era are as varied as the diverse types of rural communities both contributing and attracting migrants.

SUMMARY

Hence, during the urban era, the rural-to-urban migration seems to have had serious negative consequences for rural communities. The out-migration drained the young working-age population from rural communities, leaving behind a population of younger and older dependents. The out-migration cost rural areas an enormous investment in the development of human capital—its youth—who then moved to the cities to generate wealth for them rather than their home communities. The out-migration seems to have drained the best and the brightest from rural communities, leaving behind a main street of closed businesses, a population of older persons at the end of their work careers, and younger persons simply awaiting their turn to leave for the cities.

Yet, as Beale (1974) suggests, the population picture in rural areas was mixed; while some areas lost considerable population, some experienced population stability, and others experienced growth. The ability of many rural communities to retain their population or attract in-migrants during this era is a harbinger of the changes in coming decades.

6

The Era of Residential Diversity (1960–?)

INTRODUCTION

A centripetal force continued to attract and concentrate population in centralized, predominantly urban locations, a continuation of the historical pattern of rural population loss due to net out-migration and urban population growth due to net in-migration. Yet, in isolated rural areas such as the Ozarks and the Upper Great Lakes, stirred a countervailing centrifugal force—a slowing and, in some cases, a reversal of rural population losses due to net out-migration.

By the mid–1970s, it was apparent from the Current Population Survey and other population estimates that "hundreds of previously declining rural counties were showing population and net migration gains" (Wardwell, 1982: 26). The 1980 census confirmed that the nation's nonmetropolitan (nonmetro) areas had experienced a rate of population growth exceeding that of the metropolitan (metro) areas (15.9% vs. 9.8%). The growth in nonmetro population was widespread, from the most remote nonmetro counties to those contiguous to metro areas, from those in the West to those in the Northeast. Finally, Vining and Kontuly (1978) reported that this phenomenon was not unique to America. Rather, in twelve other northern and western European nations, as well as in Japan, major metropolitan areas experienced reduced growth or population decline.

The growth of the nonmetro population can be attributed to two demographic factors: natural increase and net in-migration. It is not that the rate of nonmetro natural increase rose during the 1970s, rather, the excess population that natural increase contributed to the nonmetro population was no longer being lost, as in the past, through out-migration. The traditional pattern of migration exchange between nonmetro and metro areas also changed during the 1970s. First, fewer nonmetro residents left for metropolitan destinations; in other words, nonmetro areas experienced an enhanced ability to retain their natives. Second, metro residents moved to nonmetro destinations in greater numbers than they had in the past; in other words, nonmetro areas demonstrated an enhanced ability to attract new residents.

Economic and social diversity exemplify this era. Economic transformations dramatically altered the industrial structure and the composition of the labor force, and these changes provided a foundation for residential diversity. Goods production as a percentage of the Gross National Product and as an employing sector gave way to services production. Manufacturing firms became "foot-loose," that is, they were no longer tied to rail or water transportation due to inter- and intrastate highway systems. Hence, towns and small cities that even in the early 1960s could not hope to attract industry could now compete with Chicago, Pittsburgh, or Indianapolis.

Despite a serious recession in the early 1980s, national wealth and family incomes rose rapidly, and governmental programs (Social Security, Aid to Families with Dependent Children, Food Stamps, Medicare, and Medicaid) provided a "safety net" for low-income persons. Gradually, the income gap between rural and urban areas diminished, although poverty remained disproportionately a rural problem.

This was also a time of social turmoil. Civil rights became a national movement, with sweeping changes in the social and political position of blacks—voting rights, desegregated housing, education, public transportation and accommodations, and, most critically, equal employment opportunities. During the 1960s and early 1970s, the marked differences that had once distinguished living conditions for blacks in the North and in the South gradually blurred. While improvements in opportunities and race relations in the South accounted for closing part of this gap, the deterioration in race relations and de facto segregation in many northern urban areas also played a role. The central cities of major urban areas housed more racial and ethnic minorities, and the poor as well as the white middle class left the cities for the suburbs. Violent crime, illegal drugs, social turmoil, and deteriorating public services captured the urban experience, especially during the 1960s and the 1970s.

Throughout this chapter both rural and nonmetropolitan population trends will be considered. The reasons are threefold:

1. the enormous amount of data available for nonmetro and metro areas through the census and other federal statistical agencies,
2. the nearly universal adoption of the nonmetro and metro concepts by social scientists conducting social demographic research, and
3. the diminishing amount of research focused exclusively on rural and urban areas.

Despite the reservations expressed earlier as to the theoretical problems with assuming that nonmetro and metro areas are interchangeable with rural and urban areas, the overwhelming tendency in social demographic research in recent years has been in this direction.

STREAMS OF MIGRATION

The major migration streams of earlier years persisted during this era. But, once again, important differences in size, composition, and direction developed, altering the relative contributions of these various migration streams to rural population change.

Immigration

Immigration continued, accounting for 16 percent of population growth from 1970 to 1974, nearly 20 percent from 1975 to 1979, and rising to 28 percent during the early 1980s (figure 7). The increasing importance of immigration as a factor in national growth is as much a function of the declining rates of natural increase as the level of immigration. The composition of the stream of legal immigration changed dramatically with new legislation in 1965. While Europe had accounted for well over half of the immigration between 1920 and 1965, their share of the post–1965 legal immigration declined to less than 17 percent. Nearly 75 percent of the legal immigrants now come from Asia (40%) or Latin America (37%) (Bouvier and Gardner, 1986). Yet, as in the urban era, recent immigrants tend to settle in urban rather than rural areas.

Westward Migration

The westward movement continued, swelling to such proportions that by 1980, for the first time in American history, more than half of the American people resided in the South or West. This movement is symbolized by the increasing southerly shift in the geographic center of the nation's population. In earlier times, the West and, to a lesser extent, the Southwest attracted migrants from all regions. But by the 1960s, migrants literally flocked to Southeastern and Southwestern states. Between 1975 and 1980, when the Northeast lost nearly 1.8 million persons and the North Central region nearly 1.4 million, the South gained nearly 2 million and the West nearly 1.2 million. During these years, then, the South reversed its traditional role as a net exporter of persons and began to attract migrants from the Northeast and North Central states. This pattern persists into the 1980s, with both the Northeast and North Central regions continuing to post net migration losses and the South and West to post net gains (U.S. Bureau of the Census, 1984).

Black Migration

A significant aspect of interregional migration during this era was the growth in the counterstream of black migrants to the South. Although a minor counterstream had existed since the post-Civil War period, it was not until the 1970 to 1973 period that the counterstream increased to 150 percent of the

South-to-non-South stream. Interestingly, while the bulk of South-to-non-South stream has historically been a rural-to-urban migration, the counterstream primarily has been a metropolitan-to-metropolitan (64 percent) or a metropolitan-to-small towns and cities movement (10 percent) (Campbell et al., 1974). Yet, nearly 25 percent of black migrants to the South moved from urban to rural destinations. Given black migrants' historical preference for urban destinations, the fact that a quarter of the counterstream migrants moved to rural destinations signals some important shifts in the dynamics of migration during this era.

RURAL AND URBAN MIGRATION INTERCHANGES

Migration was an important factor in the continuation of the population's urban concentration as well as its changing character (appendix table A–10). Although most metropolitan areas experienced net migration gains over the course of the 1960s and most nonmetropolitan areas continued to experience net migration losses, from 1965 to 1970 there was actually a net out-migration of 352,000 persons from all metropolitan areas. This net movement from metro to nonmetro areas at the end of the 1960s was a precursor to the migration patterns of the 1970s. Between 1970 and 1975, the total net out-migration from metro to nonmetro areas was nearly 1.6 million persons, and from 1975 to 1980 it was just over 1.3 million persons.

Although metropolitan counties have once again begun to exhibit significant migration gains since 1980, many nonmetro counties have shown a resiliency in their population growth, albeit to a lesser degree than in the 1970s. Hence, the primary demographic differences between the urban era and the era of residential diversity are the relative balance between the migration streams producing population concentration or deconcentration, and how the nation's different regions have expressed these particular patterns. To interpret the remarkable diversity in rural and urban migration interchanges since 1960, we must begin with an analysis of the specific patterns of population interchange.

Urban and Metropolitan Growth

In 1960, 69.9 percent of the population were urban residents, in 1970, 73.5 percent, and in 1980, 73.7 percent. However, the distribution by types of urban places was changing (figure 11). The largest urban centers, those with populations of 1 million or more, steadily declined in their share of the national population. This decline suggests that the centrifugal forces drawing people to the very largest cities were diminishing.

This possibility is confirmed by considering the distribution of the population by type of urban place (appendix table A–11). In 1960, 32.3 percent of the total population resided in the central cities of urbanized areas, but by 1980 it had declined to 29.6 percent. In 1960, 21.1 percent of the total population resided in the urban fringe of urbanized areas; in 1980 it had risen to 31.8 percent. In 1960, 16.4 percent of the total population resided in urban places outside of urbanized areas; in 1980 it was 12.3 percent. Thus, while the concentration of the population in urban areas continues throughout this era, this increase reflects some important shifts in the distribution of the total population in urban places. The population in central cities declined as did the population residing in urban places outside of urbanized areas, but the urban fringe population increased.

If we use the convention of metropolitan and nonmetropolitan residence, the same pattern appears. In 1960, nearly 67 percent of the nation's population were metropolitan residents, rising to 74.8 percent in 1980 and 76 percent in 1983. Yet, both urban and rural areas inside these metropolitan areas experienced population growth, again emphasizing the tendency of people to disperse their residences within metropolitan areas. But not all metropolitan areas experienced net migration gains or similar rates of growth.

In the 1960s, the metropolitan areas of 500,000 or more had the highest rates of annual net migration. But during the 1970s, the largest metro areas, with populations over 1 million, actually experienced net migration losses, while the annual rates of net migration for other metropolitan areas were indirectly related to their size. To illustrate, metropolitan areas of 1 million or more grew by 7.3 percent; SMAs of 250,000 to

Figure 11
Proportion of U.S. Population in Places of 50,000+
and 1 Million+, 1890–1980

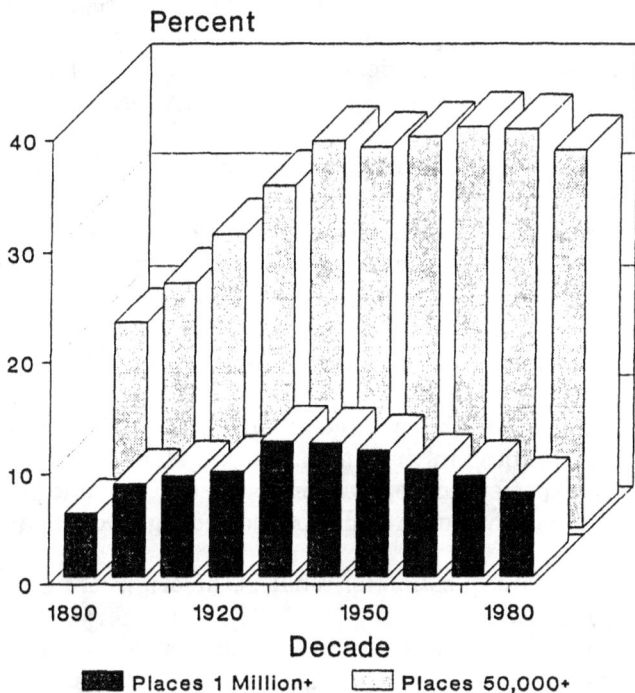

Decade	Places of 50,000 or more	Places of 1 million
1890	18.6	5.8
1900	22.2	8.5
1910	26.6	9.2
1920	30.9	9.6
1930	34.9	12.3
1940	34.4	12.1
1950	35.3	11.5
1960	36.2	9.8
1970	36.0	9.2
1980	34.1	7.7

Source: Adapted from Series A57-72 of Historical Statistics of the United States, Colonial Times to 1970 and, 1985 U.S. Statistical Abstract. U.S. Bureau of the Census, Washington D.C., Government Printing Office.

1 million persons grew by 13.1 percent; SMAs of 100,000 to 249,000 persons grew by 16.4 percent; and metropolitan areas of 50,000 to 100,000 persons grew by 13.3 percent. The smaller metropolitan areas experienced the highest rates of population growth and net migration gains during the era of residential diversity.

Important regional variations in the growth of metropolitan areas also appeared (appendix table A–12). During the 1970s, metropolitan areas in the Northeast experienced a 1.8 percent decline in population, while the North Central metropolitan areas had an increase of only 2.2 percent. In contrast, the metro areas of the South and West grew by roughly 22 percent. The importance of these regional differences is apparent when we consider the growth of the central cities of metropolitan areas. During the 1970s, the average growth rate of all cities was 0.2 percent, but those in the Northeast and North Central states actually experienced population losses (1.0 percent per year) while those of the South and West posted significant gains (1.3 percent a year).

An important question is: What is the origin of migrants to metropolitan areas? During the 1965 to 1980 period, more persons left metro areas for nonmetro destinations than moved from nonmetro origins to metro destinations. Wardwell (1977: 157) estimates that approximately 1 million "fewer people moved into SMAs from nonmetropolitan counties, despite the slight (1.0 percent) increase in the total volume of movement." Similarly, Tucker (1976: 442) estimates that migration out of nonmetropolitan counties declined by about 12 percent during the early 1970s.

Hence, the volume of migration from nonmetropolitan to metropolitan areas declined significantly during the 1970s, accounting for the small metro gains through net in-migration. The differences in rates of metropolitan gains through net migration for various-sized metro areas during this decade more appropriately reflect variations in the interchange of metropolitan population among these areas rather than dissimilar abilities to attract nonmetro migrants. In other words, the metro-to-metro interchange of migrants accounts for a significant portion of the change in population growth in metro areas since 1970.

Urban Fringe and Nonmetropolitan Growth

Concomitantly, deconcentration was at work. By the 1950s, rural areas in America had actually begun to post modest net population losses, a phenomenon that continued into the 1960s. However, the 1970s witnessed a tremendous rebound of rural population growth (Morrison and Wheeler, 1976) (figure 12). The rural population grew by nearly 6 million persons in this decade, a level of growth not seen in rural America since the end of the era of rural dominance in the 1880s. Given the pattern of diminishing rates of population growth in rural areas throughout the twentieth century, this return to substantial levels of population growth was remarkable and unexpected.

Using the metropolitan area as the unit of analysis, population growth as well as net migration was concentrated in the metropolis's suburban rings during this era. This process began in the urban era when, by 1920, "the suburban territories of all cities of 50,000 or more population were in the aggregate growing at rates three times as high as the growth rates of the central cities" (Hawley and Mazie, 1981: 4). Moreover, throughout the 1970s and early 1980s, over 60 percent of the nonmetropolitan counties were deconcentrating, that is, growth in the rural parts of these counties exceeded that of urban places (Fuguitt et al., 1987). This pattern of deconcentration in nonmetro counties has been marked in those adjacent to metropolitan areas and those with larger (greater than 10,000) urban places (Fuguitt et al., 1987).

Nonmetro growth varied significantly among regions (appendix table A–12). For example, in the Northeast, adjacent nonmetro areas suffered persistent population losses not occurring in any other region, except the North Central region, since 1980 (Fuguitt et al., 1987). On the other hand, both adjacent and nonadjacent nonmetro places in the South and West posted typically strong population gains throughout this era. Wardwell and Gilchrist (1987: 3) comment on these regional

Figure 12
Change in Rural Population in the United States, 1890–1980

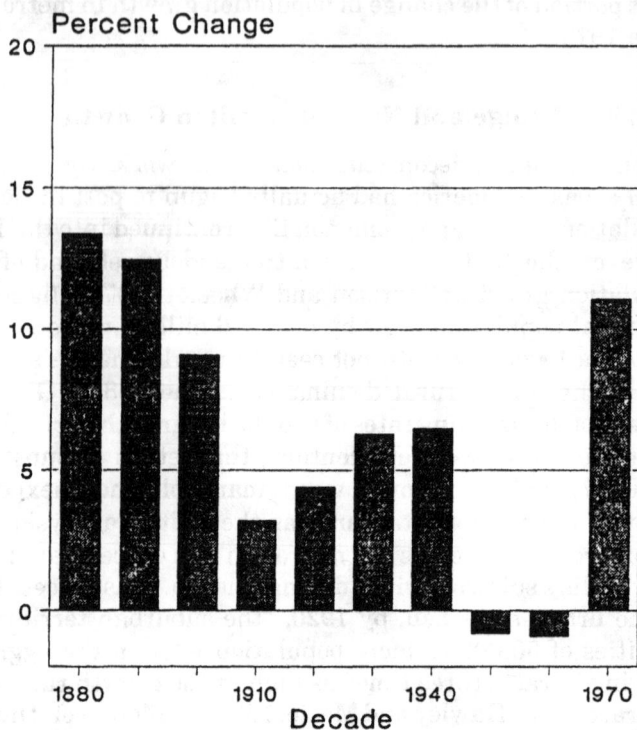

Percent Change

Decade	Population Change (millions)	% Change
1880 to 1890	4.8	13.4
1890 to 1900	5.1	12.5
1900 to 1910	4.2	9.1
1910 to 1920	1.6	3.2
1920 to 1930	2.3	4.4
1930 to 1940	3.4	6.3
1940 to 1950	3.7	6.5
1950 to 1960	-.4	-.8
1960 to 1970	-.5	-.9
1970 to 1980	5.9	11.1

Source: Adapted from U.S.Bureau of the Census, Current Population Reports Series, P-20 No. 374. Population Profile of the United STates: 1981. Washington D.C., Government Printing Office, 1982.

differences: "While overall U.S. nonmetropolitan growth rates are only 82 percent of metropolitan (less than the 187 percent of the 1970s, but well above the 54 percent of the 1960s), these nonmetropolitan rates remain above metropolitan growth rates in the Northeast and Midwest (208 and 144 percent, respectively), and are essentially identical in the West. Only in the South have these rates fallen far below the metropolitan, and in the South in the 1970s the rates were nearly equal. In all regions except the South, metro and nonmetro growth rates are both lower, and more nearly equal, in the 1980s than in the 1970s."

Did migration account for the bulk of this growth in nonmetropolitan areas during the 1970s? Lichter et al. (1985) examined the components of nonmetro population change during the 1970s, highlighting the importance of differences between absolute (total) and relative (proportional among areas) population changes. First, they note that while nonmetro areas experienced a higher rate of growth during this period, two-thirds of the absolute population increase during the 1970s actually occurred in metropolitan areas. Second, they note that 75 percent of the absolute growth in the 1970s occurred in areas outside of incorporated urban places with populations greater than 2,500. Third, 80 percent of absolute nonmetropolitan growth occurred in rural areas, accounting for 30 percent of the total absolute growth in the U.S. population. Fourth, in all regions, rural growth represents the major component of nonmetropolitan growth in both adjacent and nonadjacent counties. Deconcentration of the population within both metro and nonmetro areas is apparent from this analysis. "It represents a fundamental alteration in the character of aggregate nonmetropolitan population growth. That is, nonmetropolitan population change is now largely rural population change, a pattern quite different from the past when nonmetropolitan population growth was fueled largely by growth in urban places" (Lichter et al., 1985: 96).

These conclusions are echoed by Ballard and Fuguitt (1985) upon examining the structure of small towns in nonmetropolitan areas. During the 1970s they found a convergence in the growth of large (10,000–49,999), medium (2,500–9,999) and small (less than 2,500) nonmetro places, producing "a growth advantage for small (and to a lesser extent, medium) places over large" (Ballard and Fuguitt, 1985: 109). This signals what these authors call an era of deconcentration and village revival.

The importance of migration in the growth of the nonmetropolitan population, especially during the 1970s, cannot be overstated. In the 1950s, only 12 percent of all nonmetropolitan counties gained population through net migration, which increased to 22 percent during the 1960s. But, during the 1970s, nearly 66 percent of nonmetropolitan counties experienced net migration gains (De Jong and Sell, 1977). During the 1970s, nonmetro counties exhibited the unexpected ability to not only retain their native populations but to attract migrants from metro areas. The significance of this pattern of migration can be illustrated as follows: "Of the 1,896 counties and county-equivalents in the U.S. that lost population through net migration between 1960–1970, 1073 'turned around' between 1970 and 1978 and gained population through net migration" (Poston and Coleman, 1983: 437). Hawley and Mazie (1981: 6) further emphasize the novelty of this reversal. "The reversal of the trend was most notable in the nonmetro counties that are not adjacent to metro areas, for those had the longest histories of decline. Nine out of ten nonadjacent nonmetro counties, or 979 counties, had been losing population through migration prior to 1970. After 1970 that declined to four of ten, or 438 counties."

Two other aspects of the migration streams during this era need to be noted. First, rural-to-rural migrants represented both a component of rural population growth during this era and a factor in the redistribution of the rural population. Sofranko and Fliegel (1983: 43) note that between 1965 and 1970, "migrants originating in rural areas outnumbered migrants originating in urban areas by a ratio of 1.1 to 1." There is a need to continue assessing the importance of the migration interchange among nonmetropolitan areas as a component of net nonmetro migration gains.

The other component of the nonmetropolitan or rural migration streams that must be noted is the movement to America's farms. Our knowledge of this component is based on case studies and inference. In a study of seventy-five North Central nonmetropolitan counties experiencing net in-migration of at least 10 percent between 1970 and 1975, nearly 30 percent of the migrants from metropolitan origins had settled on farms (Sofranko and Williams, 1980). Moreover, trends in farm size evidenced by recent agricultural censuses indicate a proliferation of small farms. For example, between 1964 and 1974 there was an increase in the number of farms of less than fifty acres in all regions except the South (Coughenour and Wimberley, 1982). The terms "part-time farmer" and "hobby farm" signal the appearance of a new type of agricultural enterprise in which one or both spouses are employed off the farm and farm sales account for a very small proportion of total family income. It seems likely that some of these farms are occupied by urban-to-rural migrants. However, it is important to remember that despite the emergence of small farms and part-time farm enterprises, the farm population, as a proportion of the rural population, has continued to decline throughout this century (figure 13). Furthermore, the decline has been most precipitous since 1950. Clearly, if a portion of the nonmetropolitan growth during the era of residential diversity did lead to the establishment of farm operations, it was insufficient to offset the continuing loss of farm families in the agricultural sector.

Summary of Rural-Urban Migration Interchanges

During the era of residential diversity, then, both concentration and deconcentration of the population occurred as a result of migration. There was a slight increase in the proportion of the nation's population living in urban places, and yet a slight decline in the proportion residing in metropolitan places. Nevertheless, urban and metropolitan growth was likely to occur in the smaller places, especially during the 1970s. Additionally, the rural territory of metropolitan areas and the most rural counties of nonmetropolitan areas captured the largest share of both relative and absolute growth. Long and DeAre (1982) summarize the changes of this era of unprecedented deconcentration by noting the first decline ever in

Figure 13
Farm Population as a Proportion of the Rural Population, 1880–1980

Percent

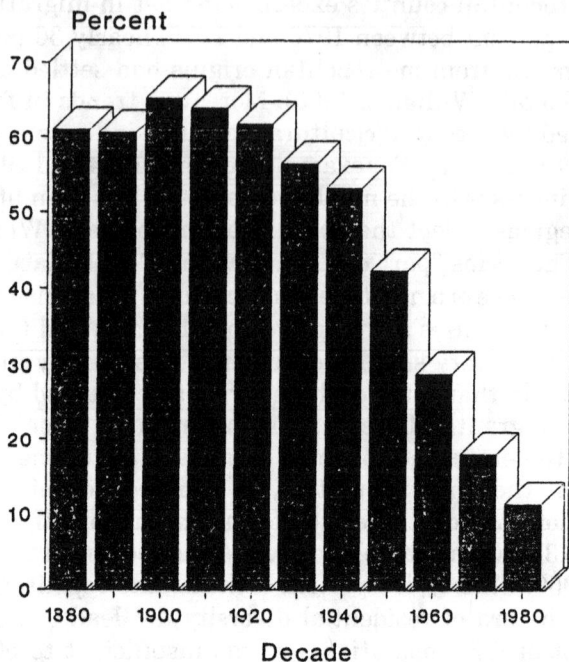

Decade

Decade	% Rural Population
1880	61.0
1890	60.6
1900	65.2
1910	63.9
1920	61.8
1930	56.5
1940	53.2
1950	42.3
1960	28.9
1970	18.0
1980	11.3

Source: Adapted from Table 3.2 in Calvin L. Beale. 1978. "People on the Land." pp.37–54 in Thomas R. Ford (editor). Rural USA: Persistence and Change. Ames, IA: Iowa University Press.

county population density, and the highest increase ever in the rural population.

EXPLANATIONS FOR RESIDENTIAL DIVERSITY

To understand the population trends of the era of residential diversity, we will use the approach of Hawley and Mazie (1981) and think in terms of the necessary and sufficient conditions that facilitate these population trends.

Explanatory Preconditions

The processes of modernization have altered the social and economic conditions of life in all geographic areas of society. By the 1970s, all things once associated with urban industrial life were diffused to even the most remote areas of the nation (Wardwell, 1980). Physical space has been transcended: distance is no longer a barrier to interpersonal relations. Communications networks connect the different areas of the society through a national system of mail delivery, telephone service, and the mass media. Between 1950 and 1980, the proportion of American households with telephone service increased from 62 to 96 percent; the proportion with radios increased from 93 to 99 percent; and the proportion with television sets from 9 to 98 percent. In 1952, seventy cable television systems serviced 14,000 subscribers, but by 1983 there were 5,600 systems serving 25 million subscribers. Finally, rapid developments in land-based satellite receivers meant that even the most remote households could, for the right price, choose from over 120 channels (U.S. Bureau of the Census, 1983).

The completion of many all-weather surfaced roads, an interstate highway system, and an intrastate road system provided the infrastructure for rapid transportation. For example, between 1950 and 1981 the proportion of surfaced rural roads increased from 56 to 86 percent. But it was the rapid and nearly universal access to motor vehicles that transformed this infrastructure into a reality. Between 1960 and 1982, the number of registered motor vehicles (cars, trucks, and buses) in America increased from 73.9 million to 160.4 million. This meant there were 539 automobiles for every 1000 persons in this country!

The final necessary condition for the residential diversity of this era is a function of the changing ecological structure of rural areas driven by population trends in earlier decades. The number of towns, villages, and hamlets in nonmetropolitan counties has been steadily increasing, especially since 1950, and over half of all places in all size categories (except those under 500) experienced population growth over the same period (Fuguitt and Beale, 1976). Moreover, two general types of "trade centers" appeared over the years: "a large group of small centers serving local needs, and a small group of centers serving specialized shopping needs over large areas" (Hodge, 1966: 185; Hassinger, 1957; Johansen and Fuguitt, 1973; Tarver and Beale, 1968; Yoesting and Marshall, 1969).

Bender (1980) suggests that structural changes in rural economies are strongly related to patterns of population change and migration. Structural change includes not only industry composition and the size and characteristics of the local labor force, but also "implies a set of behavioral relationships in an economy" (Bender, 1980: 137). Thus, the attraction of rural places as residences and places to do business, or the willingness of firms to relocate to rural areas, is also part of the structural change occurring in America. Bender's (1980: 158) model of economic and population change suggests that "changes in basic employment generate symbiotic service employment and population increases," and this process becomes reinforcing.

The combined effects of these changes have been the diffusion of urban influences and lifestyles into rural and nonmetropolitan areas. The increasing diversity of nonmetropolitan trade centers, including the development of regional shopping malls, has increased access to specialized consumer services and products in the hinterland. Franchise fast food restaurants are now as common a sight in many small towns as family-style restaurants. Improved highways bridge the physical distance once separating rural residents from the amenities associated with large urban centers. "In short, as living conditions in nonmetro territories have become increasingly urbanized the distance restraints on the general centrifugal drift of the urban population have been relaxed and the movement has accelerated" (Hawley and Mazie, 1981: 7).

But, these transformations, which had been developing for several decades, did not halt the net loss of persons through out-migration or the decline in the rural or nonmetropolitan proportion of the population. Between 1940 and 1970, nonmetropolitan areas experienced a net migration loss of 9 million persons (De Jong and Sell, 1977), yet this net flow reversed during the 1970s. So, while the necessary conditions for retaining residents and attracting new ones to nonmetropolitan or rural areas existed prior to the 1970s, what produced the "quantum leap in the deconcentration movement" (Hawley and Mazie, 1981: 7) at this time?

Explanatory Precipitating Conditions

The theories of migration presented earlier identify a set of sufficient conditions that could explain the timing of the migration turnaround. The most consistent explanations for migration differentials have been given by the economic models focusing on variations in labor market opportunities and wages among alternative destinations. Until the 1970s these economic factors favored urban or metropolitan places as destinations for migrants. Yet, the 1970s ushered in an era of industrial deconcentration, and, as Wardwell (1982: 24) concludes, "one of the most important reasons for the change has been growth of employment opportunities in nonmetro counties." In Wardwell and Gilchrist's (1987: 7) terms, there developed a convergence in the "material standards of living and social infrastructure" of urban and rural places, and "migrants now stood to gain less in a move to a large city, or lose less in a move to a smaller-sized place." Thus, a dynamic equilibrium in the characteristics of places was established, reducing the competitive advantage of urban places in attracting migrants. Do changes in the economic conditions in metro and nonmetro areas during this era substantiate this conclusion?

During the 1970s, employment in goods-producing industries increased by 23.8 percent in nonmetro counties as op-

posed to 3.9 percent in metro counties. Employment in
service-producing industries increased by 42.4 percent in nonmetro counties and 33.2 percent in metro counties (Population
Reference Bureau, 1981). Till (1981) found that the growth in
manufacturing job opportunities represented plant expansions
and the development of new industries, rather than simply
relocations of existing ones. Furthermore, unlike existing
heavy industries, new manufacturing firms have more flexibility in determining location, maximizing labor costs, and
other political-economic considerations, such as tax advantages. Menchik (1981) has demonstrated that the service industries sector grew at least 65 percent faster than the goods-
producing sector, and accounted for 74 percent of the gains in
nonmetro employment.

Thus, the relative growth of employment opportunities during the 1970s favored nonmetro counties, although metro counties retained their advantage in absolute terms (Till, 1981;
Menchik, 1981; Tweeten, 1981). Moreover, metro areas retained an advantage in terms of the types of employment available, especially with respect to managerial, administrative,
and sales occupations, and, to a lesser degree, professional,
clerical, and crafts occupations. The explanatory power of these
shifts in employment opportunities increases if we place these
employment changes in the context of the transportation improvements in nonmetro areas. Commuting to and from place
of employment—over longer distances than in the past, yet
within shorter periods of time—became an increasingly viable
option for nonmetro residents during this decade (Bowles and
Beale, 1980; Brown and Beale, 1981).

Another set of economic factors often associated with migration is wage and income differentials among areas (Tarver and
Gurley, 1965). As employment differentials between nonmetro
and metro areas have diminished, and, as a result of the general
growth of real income, family income differentials between
these areas have also been reduced. Zuiches and Brown (1978)
demonstrate that nonmetro family income was 66 percent of
metro income in 1950, 75 percent by 1970, and 77 percent by
1981. The reduction of these income differentials contributes

to the diminution of the economic advantages of metro residence.

Noneconomic Factors in Migration

The changing employment structure and income characteristics of metropolitan and nonmetropolitan places give credence to the explanation of migration offered by economic models, especially since 75 percent of the metro-to-nonmetro migrants are in the labor force (Bowles, 1978), and employment-related factors remain primary reasons for moving (Long and Hansen, 1979; Long and DeAre, 1980). In fact, research indicates that labor force models retain their explanatory power, with certain constraints for some groups (Williams, 1981; Murdock et al., 1984; Brown and Wardwell, 1980).

But reduced explanatory power of the labor force models, as well as the exceptions to their utility, has forced a search for alternative perspectives. As Zelinsky (1977: 176) so aptly states, the utility of economic models is in jeopardy "when we confront those hundreds of remote, thinly settled, and emphatically bucolic counties for whose recent demographic resurgence there is no half-way plausible economic rationale." There is one cautionary note on the utility of a purely economic analysis: "The most notable changes between the 1950s and 1960s are not in the realm of determinants of migration but rather the determinants of employment growth. . . . It would seem advisable to direct more attention to . . . the relatively new nonmetropolitan expansion of the recreation industry, and the role which retirement-age migration may play in generating subsequent employment growth" (Williams, 1981: 198).

Ecological models examining migration as a way to adjust the population to changes in technology, social organization, and the environment help explain the identified variations in migration among nonmetropolitan counties. This line of analysis examines variations in the sustenance organization of nonmetropolitan areas (Frisbie and Poston, 1976 and 1978; Brown and Beale, 1981; Poindexter and Clifford, 1983).

One analysis of the relationship between sustenance organization and nonmetropolitan population change during the 1970s found that "those counties dependent on 'personal and recreational services' and/or 'commercial agriculture' typically experienced higher rates of growth than those dependent on 'general agriculture' and/or 'retail and wholesale trade'" (Poindexter and Clifford, 1983: 433). The relative influence of these different sustenance activities represents a shift from earlier decades. The authors conclude that differential rates of growth represent a "response to the need for particular types of labor" (Poindexter and Clifford, 1983: 431).

But, another factor is necessary to fully explain the migration and population trends of this era. "At the ecological level, job growth is certainly causal to migration patterns. At the individual level, except in the case of transfers, perhaps we should see jobs as facilitators of migration rather than as causal. Thus, given employment possibilities, those who move to nonmetropolitan areas may be 'selected' on a predilection for the types of amenities found in more rural locations, and report such reasons in surveys. Without the minimum condition of jobs, fewer would be there" (Williams, 1981: 199). This brings our attention to the issue of noneconomic factors in migration trends.

Noneconomic factors are important to individual approaches to the study of migration focusing on decision making. Such an approach is critical to interpreting migration trends in this era because it identifies the sufficient conditions underlying the trends. It is clear that employment differentials between metro and nonmetro areas diminished during the 1970s. Why, then, did so many more persons choose nonmetro as opposed to metro destinations? The cognitive-behavioral approach to locational theory provides an explanation by focusing on subjective evaluations of the attractiveness or desirability of alternative locations. This approach assumes that an individual decides to leave or stay and selects a destination in order to "maximize some personal preference or satisfaction function defined by his dispositions or attitudes" (De Jong and Fawcett, 1981: 33).

Residential Preferences

The factor most strongly associated with this perspective on migration decision making is residential preferences (Zuiches and Reiger, 1978; Zuiches and Fuguitt, 1971; De Jong and Sell, 1977; Zuiches, 1981). In 1972, the President's Commission on Population Growth and the American Future published a series of reports that included one of the first analyses of residential preferences. The study disclosed that the great majority of Americans preferred to live in small towns or open county communities rather than in large metropolitan areas. Further, if most Americans acted on their residential preferences, the population of the nation's great metropolitan areas would decline as people sought the rural lifestyle they desired (Zuiches annd Fuguitt, 1972). Thus, it could be argued that there has existed a long-standing preference for the quality of life associated with smaller places. During this era, it has been argued, either migrants shifted their decision making to emphasize these noneconomic characteristics over economic considerations, or structural changes reduced the economic variation, allowing noneconomic motives to be expressed (Wardwell and Gilchrist, 1987).

What does the evidence suggest as to the use of these explanations? Other studies have further specified the nature of residential preferences. For example, Zuiches and Fuguitt (1976) found that preferences for smaller places were conditional upon proximity to larger places, especially a city with a population under 50,000. In a comprehensive review of the residential preferences literature, Zuiches (1981: 101) identified several factors associated with residential preferences and migration to nonmetropolitan areas. Two of the most significant of these include location-specific capital or community attachment and experience, and quality-of-life considerations. These are significant because they help us understand why migrants choose a particular nonmetro destination.

Location-Specific Capital

Location-specific capital can be accumulated in many ways (DaVanzo and Morrison, 1981). The presence of family and/or

friends in a particular area represents a form of prior attachment to a place. In the case of "return" migrants, those moving
to a place or general area of prior residence, these attachments
are based on previous experience with a community. In a study
of migrants to nonmetropolitan Midwestern counties experiencing high rates of in-migration, nearly six out of ten older
and nearly four out of ten younger in-migrants had ties to their
destinations (Stuart, 1980). Williams and McMillen (1983) note
that prior residence is not a precondition for building ties to a
community, for the presence of family and/or friends in a destination community is considered in the decision making of
both primary (first-time move to area) and return migrants.
The presence of family and/or friends in a particular nonmetro
community may increase the attraction of rural living in general, and the preference for a specific destination.

Location-specific capital can also be acquired through va-
cations to an area. In a study of migrants to Maine, Ploch (1978)
found that one in five persons had vacationed in the area. Vacation homes have also figured in selections of nonmetropolitan
destinations in studies of the Ozarks (Campbell et al., 1977),
Midwest (Sofranko and Williams, 1980), and Upper Great
Lakes. This form of location-specific capital is linked to quality-
of-life considerations.

One aspect of residential preference is environment amenities, which usually define recreational areas, a type of nonmetro place experiencing high net in-migration during the
1970s. Research (Fuguitt and Zuiches, 1975; McCarthy and
Morrison, 1979; Brown and Wardwell, 1980) suggests that
migrants attribute to rural or nonmetropolitan areas such
quality-of-life characteristics as low crime, more desirable for
rearing children, lower cost of living, friendlier residents, and
greater community pride. Whether these are viewed as evidence of antiurbanism (a push from urban areas) or prorur-
alism (a pull to rural areas), evidence shows these sentiments
are linked to migration (Blackwood and Carpenter, 1978; Ilvento and Luloff, 1982; Christenson and Garkovich, 1985).

Zuiches (1981: 105) comments: "Underlying much of this discussion is the implicit notion that individuals are trading off
income for quality-of-life attributes and psychological and so-

cial benefits associated with rural and small town residents."
Yet, if we take into account the differentiation in the nonmetropolitan ecological structure, the trade-offs may not be so great
as to offset the advantages of satisfying preferences for rural
living. If this is true, it suggests that Mazek and Laird's model
(1974) might explain post–1970 population trends: "Preexist-
ing preferences for smaller-sized places are acquiring a greater
causal role in influencing residential locations as structural
changes permit a greater locational flexibility. . . . [It can be
argued] that for the mover who prefers a smaller-sized place,
there is an unavoidable trade-off between income and quality
of life. Population distribution patterns accurately reflect city-
size preferences only when income differentials do not exist,
under conditions of economy-wide full employment. Under
other conditions, population movements reflect a search for the
optimum trade-off between income and city-size" (Wardwell,
1977: 173).

Some residential preference studies added conditionals of distance to a larger urban place, as well as potential effects on
income from moving. These studies indicate a decline in the
proportion of persons willing to move to smaller places within
a thirty-minute drive of a metropolitan center. Yet, Ploch's
(1978) study of migrants to Maine, as well as Sofranko and
Williams's (1980) study of migrants to Midwestern nonmetropolitan counties, indicate that over half of the migrants experienced a net decline in income after migrating. This
suggests that traditional economic assumptions of the explanatory power of labor force and income differentials in accounting for migration trends must incorporate the importance of
noneconomic factors in the decision to move and the selection
of a destination.

Labor force and income models assume that people act on
the basis of economic rationality, yet the place of economic
factors in an individual's hierarchy of values determines the
kinds of trade-offs they are willing to make. Hence, the
cognitive-behavioral model suggests the desirability of nonmetro as opposed to metro destinations is a result of objective
conditions in metro and nonmetro places, subjective perceptions of these conditions, and evaluations of the opportunities

for satisfying preferred goals. Finally, as Williams and Mc-
Millen (1980: 208) note, it is important to recognize that areas
that had in the past experienced substantial migration outflows
are prime candidates to receive major inflows due to the "return
generating effects of prior residence." This suggests that, as
the population ages, rural areas will attract a substantial proportion of the retirement migration stream.

Metropolitan Expansion

Finally, any discussion of the explanations for migration patterns in the era of residential diversity must acknowledge those
who argue that these streams do not represent a marked divergence from earlier patterns. Rather, the migration streams
of this era represent a continuation of a historical pattern of
metropolitan expansion, "a rather long and uninterrupted period of metro agglomeration [that] characterized the pre–1970
period" (Steahr and Luloff, 1985: 166). From this perspective,
the migration events of this era are a function of the geographic
expansion of the area "inextricably linked to the central city
by transportation and communication networks and via labor
force and consumer demand" (Steahr and Luloff, 1985: 166).
The significant size of migration streams to the nonmetro counties adjacent to metro areas, or to those nonmetro counties
where 20 percent or more of the work force commute to a metro
area for employment, substantiates this interpretation.

Furthermore, if one broadens the "metro expansion" explanation to include the possibility that metropolitan expansion
is one manifestation of a more general process of urbanization,
then this interpretation becomes more persuasive. There is
some evidence to support this interpretation. For example, during the 1970s nonmetro counties not adjacent to metropolitan
areas but containing a city of 10,000 or more experienced a
larger population increase than similar counties without a city
of 10,000 or more. This interpretation follows Wardwell's
(1980) suggestion that economies of scale and agglomeration
are now occurring in smaller urban places, and when linked
to certain internal constraints on urban growth in the largest

urban places (e.g., high tax rates, land prices), tend to encourage population growth across the urban continuum.

However, the Lichter et al. (1985) decomposition of nonmetropolitan population change during the 1970s demonstrates that the rural parts of nonmetro nonadjacent counties accounted for three-quarters of the total population change in these counties. Thus, the argument that the "rural turnaround" of the 1970s represents simply an expansion of metropolitan areas to more distant hinterlands cannot explain the substantial growth, both proportionate and absolute, in the most rural of nonmetropolitan counties.

CONSEQUENCES OF MIGRATION FOR RURAL COMMUNITIES

As in earlier eras, the consequences of migration changes during the era of residential diversity are a result of the size and composition of migration streams. We have seen that, during this era, the rate of growth in nonmetro counties exceeded that of metro counties for the first time in history. Moreover, this change in growth rate can be attributed primarily to an important shift in historical patterns of migration, because natural increase had now declined to near or below replacement level. Migration played a key role in nonmetro population growth in two ways: it increased the flow of persons to nonmetro areas from metro areas, and it decreased the outflow of persons from nonmetro to metro areas.

Composition of the Migration Streams

To evaluate the consequences of the migration streams during this era, we must decompose these streams into three groups of migrants: metro-to-nonmetro, nonmetro-to-nonmetro, and nonmetro-to-metro. The bulk of the research during this era focused on the metro-to-nonmetro migration stream, since it showed the most remarkable departure from past trends. During the early 1970s, national studies indicated that metro-to-nonmetro migrants were younger and better educated than nonmetro nonmovers, disproportionately white, from higher status occupations, from families with higher incomes, and were less likely to be over 65 years of age (Zuiches and Brown, 1978). Moreover, the metro-to-nonmetro migrants were more likely to be intact family units (De Jong and Sell, 1975).

Yet, there seem to be regional variations in the characteristics of the metro-to-nonmetro stream. For example, Sofranko and Williams's (1980) study of migrants to Midwestern nonmetro counties found a higher proportion of the metro migrants in the 55 and older age group than nonmetro residents. Moreover, Clifford et al. (1983: 468) point to the "significance of elderly migration in fueling the aging of the nonmetropolitan populations. The influx of the elderly to retirement areas in Florida, the Southwest, the Upper Great Lakes area, and the Ozarks contributed to the relatively rapid aging found in amenity areas of the United States." Thus, in certain rural areas with environmental amenities or pre-existing retirement-age populations, the composition of the metro-to-nonmetro stream differed from those directed at rural areas with other types of characteristics (e.g., major energy development projects).

Nonmetro-to-nonmetro migrants, or intra-area migrants, were twice as likely as residents to be under the age of 30, slightly more likely to be in the labor force and in skilled blue-collar occupations, and more likely to have one or more children in their households. In all other characteristics, the intra-area movers resembled the nonmetro residents (Zuiches and Brown, 1978; Sofranko and Williams, 1980).

When compared with the metro-to-nonmetro migrants, the intra-area migrants were more likely to be black, have less college education, and have lower occupational statuses resulting in lower incomes (Zuiches and Brown, 1978). A similar comparison for migrants in the Midwest suggest that intra-area movers were far more likely to be younger than the metro-to-nonmetro migrants, yet, as Sofranko and Williams (1980: 23) point out, "from the residents' point of view, however, both groups of in-migrants are much younger.... Retirement-related migration is certainly in evidence, but it is considerably offset by gains in population at younger ages." Sofranko and Fliegel (1983) state that "in many respects, rural-origin newcomers to Midwestern rural growth counties resemble compositionally, former rural-to-urban migrants. One is thus left with the impression that rural growth areas are attracting migrants who under other circumstances might have formed a part of the rural-to-urban stream" (Sofranko and Fliegel, 1983: 48).

Finally, who left nonmetro areas during this era? The non-metro-to-metro migrants were younger and considerably better educated than the residents who remained behind. They were also more likely to be in the labor force and to have higher occupational statuses (Zuiches and Brown, 1978). When compared to those persons who moved to or within nonmetro areas, those who left were younger and had substantially more education and occupational status.

What has been the net effect of this migration interchange? Zuiches and Brown (1978) argue the net effect is that nonmetro areas continue to lose a disproportionate share of their younger and better educated persons while attracting a disproportionate share of retirement-age persons. Furthermore, nonmetro areas are attracting more young families while losing single persons. Clifford et al. (1983) conclude, after examining various demographic factors contributing to the aging of the nonmetro population, that migration was primarily responsible for "spatial variation in relative age compositional changes across nonmetropolitan counties," especially in the proportion of the population over 65 years of age. Brown and Beale (1981) note that while only 17 percent of the net migration to nonmetro counties was of persons aged 65 and older, this group is only 12 percent of the nation's total population. Thus, while there were many similarities among the persons in these different streams, it is also true that the net effect for nonmetro areas has been the continued loss of younger and better educated persons, and the simultaneous gain of older persons.

Demographic Consequences

What have been the consequences of these migration streams on the rural or nonmetropolitan population? The demographic composition of a nonmetropolitan area is the cumulative result of both migration and natural increase or decrease. That many nonmetro areas have a high concentration of older persons reflects the combined effects of "aging in place," the out-migration of younger persons, the in-migration of older persons, and natural increase (the difference between the number of births, and sum of deaths plus those who live to 65) of those under 65 (Lichter et al., 1985; Clifford et al., 1983). In certain areas of the Midwest and the Great Plains, decades of out-migration by young persons in conjunction with the aging in place of the remaining residents have produced a dispropor-tionately older population structure. In many counties, a sixth or more of the population is over 65 (Brown and Beale, 1981). In many other nonmetro counties, the in-migration of persons at or near retirement age have pushed the median age upward and created rural retirement communities. Finally, some non-metro areas have a higher than average proportion of persons both 65 and older and 18 and younger. Yet, Brown and Beale (1981) conclude that, overall, the age disparity between the metro and nonmetro populations increased during this era.

The aging nonmetro population demands particular kinds of public services as well as a community able to generate the resources to pay for these services. For the elderly, a higher proportion of nonmetro residents as opposed to metro residents have incomes below poverty level, and the nonmetro elderly are more likely to be in poor health (Lee and Lassey, 1982). Yet, the migration of older persons to nonmetro areas has been facilitated by the overall improvement in older persons' in-comes, due to private pension plans and Social Security pay-ments. Older persons have more discretionary incomes than younger persons, who have the costs of maintaining families. Hence, the counties experiencing high proportions of elderly in migration do not necessarily suffer serious economic dis-ruptions.

Fertility levels in the coming decades are another demo-graphic consequence of migration to rural areas and their en-hanced ability to retain residents. Since nonmetro counties have increased the proportion of their population in the family formation stage, fertility levels are likely to increase. Thus, in the long run, even though migration to nonmetro areas may diminish, the legacy of the 1970s will be population growth due to natural increase.

Socioeconomic and Political Consequences

Other consequences of the reversal in rural and nonmetropolitan growth are public services, land values, and sociopolitical conflicts between residents and newcomers. Initially, there was great concern about the ability of small communities to provide the financial resources necessary for public services (police and fire protection, water and sewage treatment systems, health and education services) to growing populations. The problems confronting these communities have been as much a result of the composition of growth as the sheer numbers. For example, the service needs of a community growing due to the in-migration of those near retirement are fundamentally different from those of a community growing due to the in-migration of families with young children (Wardwell, 1982). Yet, as Dailey and Campbell (1980) note with respect to migration to the Ozarks, the sheer numbers of new arrivals overwhelmed the rudimentary infrastructure of many communities.

In a study of three Pennsylvania counties, Luloff (1978) found fewer complaints about community services in a turnaround county (one that experienced population decline in the 1960s and growth in the 1970s) as compared to a county experiencing continuous population decline, and to one experiencing a continuous level of moderate growth. To a certain extent, this indicates that many rural communities had underused capacity in their physical plants (water and sewage treatment systems and schools). Thus, population growth enabled these communities to operate their facilities more efficiently. In other cases, rural communities captured economic benefits from the industrial deconcentration accompanying population growth, or controlled the costs of service delivery through land-use planning and zoning. But, for many communities, there is a time lag between when demands for services are made due to the arrival of newcomers and when the revenues for supporting services can be generated. Moreover, if people move to an area because of its low tax rate, local leaders' efforts to improve services by raising taxes can meet great resistance (Dailey and Campbell, 1980).

This may explain why Price and Clay (1980) found a relationship between nonmetro growth and dissatisfaction with services. As is apparent, former metro residents bring with them expectations for a certain level and quality of public services. These expectations often collide with the sheer physical difficulty of delivering such services to the more dispersed population in rural areas (Stinner and Toney, 1980). Yet, the weight of evidence suggests that metro-to-nonmetro migrants are more likely to state their satisfaction with the quality of life in their new nonmetro residences than to demand additional services (Blackwood and Carpenter, 1978; Baldassare, 1981).

Land-use issues reflect the competition for land between agricultural, commercial, and residential users. Those characteristics that make a parcel of land ideal for agricultural use (slope, drainage, soil, etc.) also make it ideal for urban use. There was great concern that in-migrants could leverage higher prices for residential land, while commercial firms could easily offer agricultural landowners a higher return for their land than could an agricultural producer. Clawson (1981) acknowledges these pressures but notes they have been most severe in those nonmetropolitan communities adjacent to metropolitan counties. Yet, as Hawley and Mazie (1981) note, the cumulative effect of these various land conversions represents a significant transformation in nonmetro land uses.

The final area of concern is social relations between newcomers and residents. Again, the research leaves no clear answer to the effects of nonmetro growth. Ploch (1978) found that in-migrants to rural areas of Maine often assumed leadership positions on school boards, generating conflicts with local residents over school policies. Ploch (1978) and Graber (1974) both found conflict over continued growth and land-use planning between new and old residents, but studies in other areas, such as Pennsylvania (Luloff, 1978) and Michigan (Price and Clay,

1980), found no significant loss of community solidarity in rapidly growing rural communities. Baldassare (1981: 136) concludes, after an extensive review of the literature, "there is no convincing support for the contention that net migration to nonmetro areas has adverse effects on community residents. The research evidence is contradictory and at times even points to higher evaluations of residential amenities and some aspects of personal life in growing areas." Growth may bring new strains, yet it can also generate the new economic resources necessary to respond to the new demands. Hence, growth has been a double-edged sword for nonmetro communities bringing both problems and opportunities.

SUMMARY

Nonmetropolitan population growth and, in particular, the concentration of growth in rural areas of both metro and nonmetro counties during this era mark a significant departure from the population trends of previous decades. Yet, it is important to recognize that what happened was essentially a "holding of the line" against the significant declines in the proportion of the total U.S. population residing in rural areas. In other words, the rural proportion of the total population declined from 36.9 percent in 1950 to 26.4 percent in 1970. But, during the 1970s, the rural proportion of the U.S. population held constant. Accompanying this stabilization in the rural population was the continued movement of the nation's residents to the South and West. The growth of rural and nonmetro areas can be attributed to both the in-migration of metro residents and the ability of these places to hold onto residents who, in earlier decades, would have left for urban destinations. The migration stream from metro-to-nonmetro areas encompasses persons of all ages, family types, and socioeconomic backgrounds. Moreover, all types of nonmetro counties, from the most remote to those adjacent to large metropolitan places, participate in the population resurgence.

The convergence in the economic opportunity structures of metro and nonmetro areas was an important factor in nonmetro growth, and improvements in transportation and communications extend urban amenities to most nonmetro areas. Widespread access to private pension programs, as well as Social Security retirement benefits, increase the standard of living for older Americans. These factors facilitated the expression of residential preferences for smaller places and enable people to consider noneconomic factors in their migration decision making. People continue to make trade-offs in their decisions as to place of work and place of residence, but personal values and preferences now have freer expression.

The growth of the nonmetro population provides both challenges and opportunities to rural residents and local leaders. The challenge has been to reverse a long-standing acceptance of community decline and begin planning for growth. Newcomers bring with them expectations for a certain level of services, a desire to preserve the quality of life they found in the rural communities, and financial and human resources allowing them to make substantial contributions to their new communities.

While post–1980 population trends indicate a slowing of nonmetropolitan growth, it is unlikely that we will ever again see a situation of massive rural depopulation as in earlier decades. Yet, this is not to say that some rural areas may not experience continued population losses. There remains considerable diversity in rural socioeconomic structures. Agriculturally dependent and mining dependent rural counties may suffer population losses due to economic depression in their primary industries. This in fact happened in many midwestern farming communities following the financial crisis of the early 1980s. Other rural communities may experience natural decreases due to high proportions of older persons. Finally, rural communities that fail to diversify their economic bases and find a niche in the economy of the twenty-first century may face major population declines as people continue the trek to urban opportunities begun decades ago.

The era of residential diversity is one where social economic differences between rural and urban places have been blurred but not eliminated. Furthermore, Americans have more opportunities to express, through their migration decision making, underlying preferences for living in different types of areas. The choices inherent in the era of residential diversity will continue to have consequences for rural population dynamics.

7

Institutional and Scientific Forces Influencing Rural Population Studies

INTRODUCTION

Scientific research does not occur in a social vacuum. Scientists bring to their research activities culturally based values, normative expectations, professionally derived ideologies, and discipline-bound empirical methods. Further, these factors are expressed in a particular institutional setting at a particular sociohistorical moment. Sewell (1965: 430) states: "In any social science field there tends to be a number of shifts in interest over time as social conditions change, as new sources of support arise, as changes take place in the occupational milieu, and as the discipline itself evolves because of methodological and theoretical advances and recruitment and training policies." This chapter examines some of the scientific and institutional forces that have driven and shaped rural population studies.

SOCIAL SCIENTISTS AND RURAL POPULATION STUDIES

Bealer (1975) comments that value judgments made by sociologists about what we do influence the content of the discipline. These value judgments, it can be argued, reflect the disciplinary training and orientations brought to the research process. In the beginning, rural population studies were often conducted by persons who were not trained sociologists, but were agricultural economists or sociologists with positions in agricultural economics departments (Duncan, 1954). The professional backgrounds of these individuals influenced the kinds of research questions they asked, the kinds of theoretical paradigms they employed, and their selection of research strategies.

Conceptual Orientation

In the early years of rural population research, a "social problems" orientation toward the study of rural America reflected the influence of church-based social activists and social practitioners in the emergence of rural sociology. For example, many point to Sir Horace Plunkett's efforts to encourage the establishment of a commission to study rural life as the beginning of rural social studies (Nelson, 1965). Plunkett, concerned with the exodus from the land, told President Roosevelt: "The town is draining the country.... A social life must be built up in the country which will stop the exodus of all the best elements in the rural population" (Nelson, 1965: 422). The Country Life Commission, staffed with representatives of rural churches, rural social workers, and academics from the liberal arts, conducted studies and heard testimony on the quality of rural life. The report of the Country Life Commission in 1911 highlighted many social and economic problems confronting rural America, key among which was the persistent loss of population through out-migration. This report, it has been argued, was the stimulus for the establishment of the Division of Farm Life Studies within the Bureau of Agricultural Economics, U.S. Department of Agriculture (USDA), under the direction of Charles Galpin.

The bulk of the early rural population research was conducted by scientists in the Division of Farm Life Studies. To a great extent, the scientists in the division had been trained as economists, and this influenced their approach to the study of farm life. Hoffer (1961: 2) comments: "There was a general belief in the early decades of the present century that if the economic well-being of farmers and other rural dwellers could be improved, the social problems confronting rural people would be, or could be solved." Many early rural population studies documented the economic causes and costs of the urbanward migration in a search for mechanisms to improve farm life so as to reduce the migration stream to urban areas (e.g., Baker, 1935). This "social problems" orientation guided the research toward identifying the negative factors "pushing" rural people from their homes. It also led to an interpretation of rural-to-urban migration emphasizing its negative consequences, rather than viewing migration as a positive adjustment by individuals to differential economic opportunities among areas.

Most theoretical explanations of rural migration have rested on the assumptions and propositions of economics. Differences in the economic conditions of places have been viewed as prompting mobility by persons with specific levels of investments in human capital. Individual motives, when they have entered into analyses, have been couched in terms of utility maximization. With few exceptions (e.g., De Jong and Gardner, 1981; Schwarzweller, Brown, and Mangalam, 1971), the influence of values and beliefs in structuring decision making has been overlooked. This is one reason why, when researchers "discovered" the importance of noneconomic motivations in the rural turnaround of the 1970s, there was no empirical basis for determining whether these noneconomic motivations had always existed, waiting to be acted on when conditions were right, or reflected a fundamental shift in the value hierarchy underlying migration decision making.

Methodological Approaches

These early roots in agricultural economics influenced the selection of research methods and data sources. The dominant methodological approach has been the use of aggregate level data in the study of area or group characteristics. This approach fits the theoretical paradigms used in the early rural population studies that emphasized the influence of market conditions, economic structure, or, in some cases, social structure on individual behavior. The aggregate approach, then, asserts that one can associate characteristics of a group with macro level conditions in order to identify and define underlying demographic trends. This methodological approach has meant a heavy reliance on census data in the analysis of both economic and population trends, and the most frequently used source of demographic and economic data on rural areas continues to be the decennial census.

Little has changed through the years despite evolutions in theory, methods, and professionalization of the discipline of rural sociology. This in part reflects the continued dominance of economic models in the study of migration, fertility, and the general process of population change (Price and Sikes, 1975). It also reflects the continuing reliance on census and other macro level government-generated data sources (e.g., Social Security Continuous Work History Records, Current Population Surveys), as the development of the profession focused on empirical, quantitative, and complex multivariate analyses (Stokes and Miller, 1985). But, another factor has shaped both the direction and content of rural population studies, and this is the institutional context within which the research occurs.

THE INSTITUTIONAL CONTEXT OF RURAL POPULATION STUDIES

Sewell (1965) notes that most departments of rural sociology are located in land-grant colleges as either a small independent department or part of a department of agricultural economics. "Its location in the land-grant college system has given rural sociology access to limited federal and state funds for research support, but at the same time has meant that rural sociology has been subject to organizational pressures and institutional interests which emphasize research designed to solve the practical problems of agriculture and rural people. Moreover, because of its minority status in its organizational setting, rural sociological research may often reflect the interests of the administration which controls the research funds" (Sewell, 1965: 430). The institutional context, then, influences the kinds of issues studied, the resources available for research, and often the methods of analysis.

A considerable proportion of demographic research by rural sociologists has been conducted within two institutional settings: the land-grant college system and the USDA. These institutions have a clearly defined mission as presented in the legislation that established them. This mission includes the generation of scientific research to improve the quality of life of rural persons and those engaged in agricultural production, the delivery of such research findings in a form useful to the clients of these institutional systems, and the training of persons in the use or application of these research findings within their own situations. The mission orientation of these institutions has meant that research issues are often defined by the social problems of the time.

As noted earlier, the roots of a rural sociological perspective on American population studies can be traced to the appointment in 1919 of Charles J. Galpin as chief of the Division of Farm Life Studies in the Bureau of Agricultural Economics, USDA. The formation of this division within the federal government provided institutional legitimacy for demographic studies focusing specifically on the farm population. The passage of the Purnell Act in 1925 gave rural sociology, and, by extension, rural population studies, a home within the land-grant college system. The Purnell Act specifically calls for an annual allocation of funds through the Agricultural Experiment Station system to provide for "such economic and sociological investigations as have for their purpose the development and improvement of the rural home and rural life." This expanded the scope of rural population studies beyond the farm population and agricultural labor issues to encompass a broader range of traditional social demographic concerns.

During these early years, it could be argued that sponsoring population studies as the primary focus of rural social science research best fit the interests and concerns of the Agricultural Experiment Stations. Demography had its roots in the natural science disciplines, and, thus, its methods and scientific approaches mirrored those of the other agricultural sciences (Duncan, 1954; Notestein, 1982). Rural population studies appeared more concrete or "scientific" than the kind of "inexact and often questionable procedures" of general sociological research (Landis, 1940: 574). The heavy reliance on demographic methods in the insurance industry underscored the practical "value" of such a science. As a result, deS Brunner (1957: 5) argues that these early rural social scientists "were under heavy pressure to demonstrate the utility of their offering, since they were judged by the same concept of utility held by the dominant physical scientists of the experiment stations."

Several examples illustrate the interaction among the institutional context of research, the nature of current social problems, and the focus of research efforts. First, the Great Depression stimulated considerable population research under the auspices of the Federal Emergency Relief Administration and the Works Progress Administration. In addition, there were cooperative agreements with state Agricultural Experiment Stations (Notestein, 1982). This work tended to focus on the characteristics of the rural relief population, the relationship between the rural relief problem and rural human capital, farm labor problems, and the migration of rural problems. In general, much of this research was oriented toward describing social problems and suggesting methods of ameliorating them. The institutional basis of the research did influence the topics studied (e.g., Lively and Taeuber, 1939), but without this support little research would have been conducted during this time of economic crisis.

Second, the migration of the farm-born has been a persistent research issue; this is understandable given that the farm population represents the primary clientele of the Agricultural Experiment Stations and the USDA. The analysis of the size, age-sex composition, and characteristics of the farm population has been the driving force for a considerable portion of rural population studies. The evaluation of the characteristics and adjustment of the farm-born population in urban areas represented some of the first research on the selectivity of migration and its consequences for both sending and receiving communities. Analyses of the size of the farm population and the characteristics of the agricultural labor force provided some of the first evidence of the population consequences of technological and structural change. Comparative studies of the attitudes and behaviors of the farm-born and other population subgroups illustrated the importance of childhood socialization in the formation of attitudes and values. Thus, although instigated by a pragmatic concern for a declining client population, the considerable body of research on the migration of the farm population made substantive contributions to the general field of demographic studies.

Third, villages and hamlets have been a focus of research conducted in both institutions due to their importance in the "fabric of rural settlement" (Trewartha, 1941). Villages and hamlets have been of enduring interest because they represent what appears to be an intermediate point in the urbanization process. Defining and documenting the function of villages and hamlets in rural society provided a vehicle for understanding the consequences of the urban-industrial transformation of society. For example, while some speculated that the steady decline in the rural farm population would be the death knell of specialized agricultural trade center villages, it became obvious that this was not always the case. The broadening of service functions in some of these villages and the decline in others demonstrated that population change in villages is, to a great extent, a response to national, social, economic, and political changes that alter their function in society's ecological framework.

Fourth, research on the rural turnaround of the 1970s is an exemplary illustration of institutional influence on rural population studies. Calvin Beale (1975) a researcher with the Economic Research Service (USDA), was the first to note the shift in migration trends. Furthermore, it can be argued that, through his persistent efforts to document this phenomenon, the broader scientific community came to acknowledge the emergence of a different pattern of migration. By far, the largest portion of the research on this topic was conducted by rural sociologists in the USDA or the Agricultural Experiment Stations. Why? The turnaround followed an era of public policy concern for "the places left behind," an era that had produced a variety of Great Society programs designed to stimulate economic development in rural communities. As research on the turnaround moved from simply documenting the extent of the phenomenon, to analyzing migrants' characteristics, and to considering the turnaround's consequences, these rural development programs, funded through the USDA and the Agricultural Experiment Stations, shifted from assisting rural communities in coping with population decline to helping them deal with growth.

Thus, the research on migration trends of the 1970s made important contributions to our substantive knowledge of the migration process by explicating in greater detail factors entering the decision-making process. It is also true that public attention focused on migration to rural communities, as exemplified by stories in *Newsweek* and *Time* and on national evening news programs, and justified continued public expenditures for rural development.

A fifth example of the influence of the institutional setting on rural population research is the relationship between the Agricultural Experiment Station and the Agricultural Extension Service. Extension specialists often have strong backgrounds in demographic research and analysis, for community development is an important facet of their work. Community development often involves providing training and technical assistance in planning and program evaluation, both of which rely extensively on descriptive demographic data and population estimates and projections. A considerable portion of rural population research in the Agricultural Experiment Station is directed toward providing state population data either through case studies or analyses of the decennial census. This information is used by other extension service personnel in program planning and development, by local and state public officials in service planning and program evaluation, and by private firms for site location and marketing. State and local users of such population data rely on the cooperative efforts of researchers and extension specialists not only to provide the demographic information, but also to translate it for their particular uses.

Sixth, the selection of research methods or strategies has been influenced by the institutional context. The mission orientation of these institutions has meant a focus on research questions having relevance to the pressing social needs of the institution's clientele. Therefore, research that uses methods permitting generalizations to the entire population represented by the supporting institution is usually preferred. Data from censuses, vital statistics, and other records are primary sources of data for a large proportion of rural population studies, especially since midcentury. Case studies of single communities or even a single substate region have become noticeable by their near absence from the professional literature. Within the Agricultural Experiment Stations, the need to provide state level demographic data for a variety of users has encouraged analysis at this level, while the USDA focuses on national or regional analyses. Of course, this tendency not only reflects institutional pressures, but also professional standards for publication (Stokes and Miller, 1985).

The final influence of the institutional context is on the publication outlet. While rural population studies have represented a relatively constant proportion of the articles in the professional journal *Rural Sociology* (Christenson and Garkovich, 1985), this outlet represents only a very small proportion of all scholarly publications in rural population studies. Several thousand reports, bulletins, working papers, and other types of publications have been published under the auspices of the Agricultural Experiment Stations and the various divisions of the USDA. The majority of these are descriptive analyses of population trends or the components of population change, or population estimates or forecasts for the geographic unit represented by the publishing institution. Within this publishing outlet, research is most often based on case studies, small geographic units, or other analytic techniques. Because sponsoring institutions are mission-oriented, a considerable amount of professional activity is devoted to these publications, given their utility in responding to client needs and interests.

The institutional settings of the land-grant college systems and the different divisions of the USDA define a focus for rural population studies, identify problem areas, and provide sources of funding and publication outlets. The influence of these institutional settings on the kinds of research questions asked, the kinds of research methodologies used, and the methods of reporting research findings cannot be overestimated. The need to monitor the agricultural labor force and to document the farm population's changing characteristics provided the initial impetus for federal support of rural population studies. But, early studies by Galpin and others took up the issues of rural-to-urban migration and the demographic relationship between rural and urban areas. As social conditions changed and new social problems emerged, the scope of rural population studies supported within these institutional settings expanded appropriately. Moreover, through their connections with these institutions, researchers in the area of rural population studies often had opportunities to identify significant sociopolitical and economic trends, such as the growth of isolated rural communities through in-migration during the 1970s.

THE INSTITUTIONAL SIGNIFICANCE OF MIGRATION

Disciplinary perspectives and institutional forces have shaped the character of rural population research over the last half century, yet, why has migration been the focus of such a substantial proportion of this population research, as indicated by the fifty-year review of *Rural Sociology* (Christenson and Garkovich, 1985)? The answer lies in the meaning and uses of migration research from the perspective of supporting institutions.

The massive migration of the farm-born has reduced the farm population, a condition with political and economic consequences for the Agricultural Experiment Stations and the USDA. As Powers and Moe (1982) note, both of these institutions have tended to define their primary constituency as the agricultural population, and, as its size has declined due to out-migration, the demographic base for their ability to influence policies, programs, and funding at national and state levels has shrunk accordingly. The focus of early migration research on identifying causal factors in the out-migration of the farm-born and assessing the consequences for the continued expansion of agricultural productivity reflects this concern with a shrinking power base.

However, increasing mechanization of agriculture reduced the labor demands of agricultural production. Productivity became dependent on investments in capital rather than the availability of labor. Migration, properly interpreted, is a visible and politically neutral explanation for the decline of the agricultural population. As we have seen, a significant proportion of migration research has assumed that migration is motivated primarily by different economic opportunities among places. Migration in this context serves as a mechanism for the adjustment of human capital among areas with different levels of opportunities and wages. In other words, this perspective presumes that migration is a voluntary response to positive factors attracting individuals to greater economic opportunities. The dominance of this theoretical emphasis on the "pull factors" associated with migration precluded, for many years, consideration of the effects of mechanization and structural concentration in agriculture on the forced displacement of farm persons—the "push factors." In other words, the social consequences of research and innovation promulgated by agricultural institutions could be dismissed as subsidiary to the individual economic motivations underlying migration.

Another reason for interest in migration is its importance in the dynamics of general rural population change. Inasmuch as the missions of both the USDA and the land-grant colleges have included the general welfare of rural peoples, rural population decline has placed another constituency at risk. Migration has been seen as a key factor in shifts in the fertility of the rural population. High levels of out-migration from rural areas siphoned off the reproductive population, and migration interchanges with urban areas depressed rural fertility preferences and behaviors. The increased ability of rural areas to retain their populations and attract urban residents during the 1970s underscored the importance of migration as a factor in rural population change, and highlighted the need to support migration research.

The other major type of rural population study during the last half century has focused on general population trends. Again, as already noted, such research has been aptly suited to the mission orientation of the supporting institutions. General demographic data on the size, composition, and characteristics of rural, farm, and nonmetropolitan populations provide an important service to a variety of clients, and such descriptive research has often been the primary service activity of rural sociologists in these institutional contexts.

These comments are not to suggest that other types of rural population research did not occur over the last half century. Professional training and developments in a discipline can stimulate research questions. For example, studies of the dynamics of fertility have been a continuous thread throughout the last half century reflecting its strong emphasis in mainstream demography (Notestein, 1982). Furthermore, because agricultural institutions are so closely linked to clientele demands, rural population researchers have often been able to respond to significant socioeconomic events more quickly than to those funded by or operating in other institutional contexts. For example, as the economic repercussions of the farm crisis of the 1980s spread to rural communities, studies of the population consequences were initiated. Such efforts have examined the out-migration and adjustment of farm families forced out of business through foreclosures, and the population effects of the crisis on dependent agricultural communities (e.g., Bultena et al., 1986).

CONSEQUENCES OF THE INSTITUTIONAL CONTEXT FOR RURAL POPULATION RESEARCH

The institutional context has influenced the direction and content of a significant proportion of rural population studies. The questions we focus on, the units of analysis, the methodological approaches, the perspectives we employ to interpret our results, and the audiences to whom we direct our conclusions all reflect the institutional environment within which we function. The institutional context has also provided funds for research—funds that, at certain times, such as the Depression, would not otherwise have been available. Finally, the institutional context has provided a certain legitimacy for rural sociology and rural population research.

However, these advantages have not been without costs. Rural sociology and rural population studies have, from their early years, been accused of pursuing raw empiricism at the expense of theoretical development (Busch and Lacy, 1983). Until recently, this accusation had merit. For decades, rural population research has relied on relatively simplistic economic models to interpret the causes and consequences of population change. The tendency for rural population research to be published in specialized journals or institutional publications has meant limited pressure to integrate mainstream sociological and demographic theoretical perspectives into our research efforts. Population trends during the era of residential diversity have modified this situation. Rural population trends have become of interest to social scientists and demographers outside the agricultural institutional system, producing a cross-fertilization of conceptual frameworks and methods.

Another cost has been the avoidance of politically and economically tough or sensitive issues, especially after the 1930s (Busch and Lacy, 1983). While the depression years produced a host of studies examining the relationships among rural population trends and social welfare, community processes and structures, and agricultural change, the following decades narrowed the focus of rural population studies to more descriptive accounts. Illustrative of this is the limited amount of research on the effects of structural change in agriculture on rural population and community processes, or the virtual absence of research on the relationship between the environmental effects of agricultural chemicals and the biophysical bases of fertility and morbidity in agriculturally dependent communities, or the relationship between the population dynamics of rural minorities and community stratification systems. Each of these issues can potentially challenge the interests of major clientele groups of the agricultural institutions, and, whether consciously or not, have been avoided as topics of research.

How one weighs the relative costs and benefits of the long-term association between rural population research and agricultural institutions depends on one's values and ideological perspective. What is important is recognizing that the institutional setting for the bulk of the rural population research by American scholars has had a profound influence on the research process. Given these comments on the institutional and scientific forces influencing rural population studies, what will and should be its future course? The answers are the focus of the final chapter.

8

Research Challenges for the Future

INTRODUCTION

Hobbs and Dillman (1982: 5) quote a former president of the Rural Sociological Society in their article on research for the rural United States: "The problem is not one of knowing how to do research. Neither is it one of whether we will do research. Our dilemma is, do we know enough to ask the right questions?" To this might be added, "Do we know enough to select the most creative method of answering these questions?" To a certain degree, the research agenda for the next fifty years will be shaped by many of the same forces that shaped research in the last fifty years.

It can be stated with a high degree of certainty that most rural population studies will continue to be conducted by rural sociologists located within either the land-grant system or the USDA. From its inception, the growth of the discipline in terms of academic and nonacademic positions, research funding, and key publication outlets has been integrally linked to these institutions. As Bertrand (1982: *xiii*) points out: "In a very real sense, the impact of the Purnell Act was to provide the support needed to launch rural sociology as a viable independent discipline." It is unlikely that this situation will change in the future. Thus, the institutional pressures discussed previously will continue to be factors in future research efforts.

Yet, this does not preclude agenda setting, for, as Hobbs and Dillman (1982: 9) comment, "unless we think ahead to what research is needed, we will likely end up doing more of the same." The purpose here is not to identify specific research questions that ought to be addressed, for others have done this (for example, see Hobbs and Dillman, 1982). Rather, the purpose is to highlight some general research problems that must be addressed if rural population studies are to achieve their potential contribution to the substantive knowledge base of the discipline and to the "future development and well-being of the rural segment of American society" (Bertrand, 1982).

A RESEARCH AGENDA

Concept Clarification

The most pressing problem confronting rural population studies is not specific to this area, but affects all rural sociology. Concept clarification—the development of a theoretical understanding of the relationships among rural, urban, nonmetropolitan, and metropolitan—is a research issue that must be confronted.

Since 1950 these concepts have been used interchangeably, yet it is clear they are not identical. Metropolitan and nonmetropolitan are administrative concepts with potent political overtones. Shryock and Siegel (1973: 129) describe the definitional process in this way: "The local pride and financial interests result in pressures for creating new areas that do not meet the given criteria, adding additional counties, or splitting off independent areas. In these Brobdingnagian clashes, the demographer has a relatively feeble voice." These comments suggest that the delineation of metropolitan areas and, by extension, nonmetropolitan areas is more than simply the application of objective statistical criteria as the originators envisioned. Rather, the definition of metropolitan areas is the battleground of economic and political interest groups, each jockeying for a coveted designation that statistically bestows a prestigious reality. It is a reality that brings with it access to targeted federal funds, special attention from businesses and industries, and, perhaps as important, a cornucopia of additional detailed census data.

While urban sociologists and geographers have developed ecological theories designed to address the conceptual relationships among various-sized cities within the context of urban hierarchies, rural sociologists have not brought a similar theoretical rigor to our subject. At this time, "nonmetro counties are a residual category comprised of varied geographic units marked by social, economic, and demographic heterogeneity.... When nonmetro areas are treated as a unitary category, it is not surprising that apparently contradictory explanations appear in the literature. What is needed in such discussions is at least a recognition of the ecological position of the nonmetro areas relative to SMAs and the urban/rural nature of nonmetro areas themselves" (Steahr and Luloff, 1985: 39). While these comments are directed at the problematic nature of the various explanations for the migration patterns of the era of residential diversity, they illustrate why it is critical to begin developing a theoretical understanding of the sociological significance of metropolitan and nonmetropolitan areas. The intermingling of urban places in nonmetropolitan counties, and the presence of rural farm and nonfarm residents in metropolitan counties demands theoretical explanation. To fail to do so will mean that, as a discipline, we will not be able to account for the sociological significance of the phenomenon we study.

One place to begin is to consider the relationship between size of place and proximity to place. This would require thinking about the theoretical relationship among these concepts in terms of the interaction between the size of an urban place and the proximity of residence to these different-sized places. Moreover, it would imply that demographic and other social processes that have been associated with rural life are a function of, at a minimum, size, density, and social heterogeneity of place, economic structure, functional interdependency, and the spatial characteristics of the environment, including proximity to other-sized places (Sorokin and Zimmerman, 1929; Smith, 1953; Hawley and Mazie, 1981). Finally, this would focus theoretical attention on why demographic characteristics have served as effective identifiers of *rural* and *urban*. What is needed, then, is to once again address the fundamental questions underlying the rural sociological discipline: What is rural? and, How does it differ from what is urban?

Assessing the Components of the Rural/ Nonmetropolitan Population

This theoretical activity could be facilitated by demographic research on a neglected component of the rural and nonmetropolitan population, the open country residents. Although not directly addressed in this review, the bulk of rural population studies have examined demographic characteristics of the farm population or persons in towns, villages, and hamlets, or the population has been defined as rural without specifying the nature of the rural residence. Open country areas or the rural nonfarm population captured the bulk of the population growth during the 1970s (Lichter et al., 1985), yet we know remarkably little about the demographic, economic, and social characteristics of the persons residing in these rural nonfarm areas. The first question to ask is: What characteristics distinguish persons residing in nonmetropolitan urban places, open country, and metropolitan open country areas?

An associated issue is the relationship between the growth of the open country or rural nonfarm population and town or village growth and change. While there has been a considerable body of research on the relationship between changes in the size of a village and its proximity to a larger urban place (Fuguitt and Beale, 1976; Johansen and Fuguitt, 1984), the influence of the size and composition of the open country population on changes in America's villages is basically unknown. The investigation of this issue could shed light on the first problem posed, the theoretical relationship among these various place identifiers.

Theory Construction

Another issue on the future's research agenda must be the development of migration theory, as well as further improvements in the integration of migration theory and our methods of analysis. Perhaps the most productive theoretical focus would be further development in the cognitive-behavioral model. This approach offers a mechanism for integrating both the aggregate and individual levels of explanation for migration behavior, thereby acknowledging the objective and subjective bases of migration decision making. The approach amplifies the utility of the "value-expectancy model" recently proposed by De Jong and Fawcett (1981) by providing an explanation for how opportunity differentials between areas can enter the decision-making process.

The utility of this approach will depend, however, on our ability to develop aggregate measures of "subjective evaluations of residential desirability [as well as] ... the conditions of areas that contribute to their perceived attractiveness" (Ritchey, 1976: 398). Additionally, we must strive to link the conceptualization of migration to appropriate measures and analytic techniques.

Methodological Improvements

Methodological improvements are especially critical; we have tended to use aggregate level data to determine individual motivations for migration. Stokes and Miller (1985: 553) comment: "Many sociologists move between individual and aggregate levels of analysis with minimal concern over whether the same theory fits both phenomena. Failure to address this basic theoretical issue has contributed to the situation in which method appears to be dictating substance." To this can be added, with respect to rural population studies, that the availability of census and other government-generated records has focused research on national trends with an implicit assumption that national trends in the timing and volume of migration, for example, reflect conditions at the regional and subregional levels. However, this review demonstrates that this is not always an appropriate assumption.

Related to this is the preponderance of research using county level data. In some states, the county is not only a meaningful political unit but also a sociologically significant unit. In other words, counties are relatively small geographic areas encompassing a population that shares similar socioeconomic characteristics and a sense of common identity. To illustrate, if you ask someone in Kentucky where he or she lives, he or she will respond with a county name, not a place name, with the exception of the major metropolitan areas of Louisville, Lexington, Ashland, Bowling Green, and Paducah; but in other states, especially those west of the Mississippi, counties are large geographic areas encompassing a great diversity of towns and cities, and, as a result, a diversity of economic bases and population characteristics (Steahr and Luloff, 1985). In these states, variations in the population dynamics within a county may be more significant than those between counties. Hence, county-level data may mask demographically and sociologically significant differences.

The overwhelming tendency to rely on net migration to interpret the mobility relationships among places continues to mask important variations in gross migration flows. For example, a focus only on the net migration of nonmetropolitan areas during the 1970s would have missed the considerable diversity in nonmetro migration gains by type (e.g., adjacent or nonadjacent to metro areas) and regional location. Furthermore, migration stream analysis—examining the gross interchanges between particular places—has the potential to enhance our ability to test the role of area differences in attracting migrants. Yet, both of these methodological approaches suffer from a lack of data. Although gross migration data is available from the U.S. Census, publication of this data in the past has depended on private efforts. Moreover, because migration stream analysis by its very nature tends to focus on specific origins and destinations, most of this research has been at state or regional levels. However, this does not diminish the potential value of these approaches.

Therefore, we must ask if we are willing to find creative ways of using the most important sources of migration data. We must also ask if we are using the full range of research methods in our arsenal. Consider, for example, a research strategy that once predominated in the literature—the case study. The application of social anthropology's research methods once offered insights into population dynamics not possible from more contemporary methods. Consider, for example, the Beech Creek studies (Brown, Schwarzweller, and Mangalam, 1963; Schwarzweller, Brown, and Mangalam, 1971) that highlighted the importance of kinship networks in both the decision to move and the choice of a destination, or the case studies that initially addressed the consequences of the 1970s in-migration (Graber, 1974; Rank and Voss, 1982). While such a method may not produce data sets permitting generalizations to the universe of rural communities or complex multivariate analyses, their contributions to our understanding of the dynamics of rural population change are critical. Often, such case studies provide the substance for the hypothesis development guiding further research.

Future Population Trends

A final question for future research concerns the role of population change in a "postindustrial" or "information" society. The economic structure of American society has undergone profound transformations over the last quarter century. The manufacturing sector no longer employs the bulk of workers, and its character has changed as durable goods industries have lost their dominance to nondurable goods manufacturing. Service industries now employ the greatest proportion of American workers, and will continue to capture the largest share of new jobs in the future. Industrial location is no longer bound to the geographic attributes of a site, rather, factors such as the availability and cost of labor, the cost of a site, and other economic considerations are more likely to determine the location of a new firm or plant. Interarea differentials in employment opportunities have been mitigated by these transformations, as well as by economic measures of standards of living.

The assumption underlying most population studies is that population change is a mechanism for adjusting population to resources or labor market needs. If differentials in these factors are reduced by general socioeconomic trends, what is the function of population change, and what drives it? The rural population studies of the last quarter century have laid the foundation for a reconceptualization of the meaning of population change, but more theoretical work must be done.

Thus, a research agenda for future rural population studies includes the honing of theoretical paradigms, concept development, and the refinement of our measurement and analytic techniques. All are essential to fully develop our understanding of the people and communities comprising rural America, and the nature of the relationship between the rural and urban segments of society. While many other research questions could be proposed, these provide an appropriate starting point.

SUMMARY

The history of rural population studies in America is a remarkable record of achievement. Our substantive knowledge of the dynamics of population change has been immeasurably increased by a combination of case studies of small communities, state and regional research, and aggregate national analyses. While the relative importance of these procedures has changed over time, each has made an important contribution to our understanding of how rural population change occurs, and why it occurs in the way that it does. Our theoretical frameworks for interpreting rural population change have matured to take into account the results of these research efforts, yet there remains much theoretical and conceptual development to be done.

The profound changes in the socioeconomic character of both rural and urban America, and the accompanying flux in historical patterns of population interchange and growth, offer an important challenge to our traditional interpretations. To continue the historical record of both substantive and applied research contributions requires that we be willing to question the assumptions and methods driving this research engine. That is the challenge of the future.

Appendix

Table A–1
Definitions of Rural and Urban in Successive U.S. Censuses

Date of Definition	Period for which Used	Definition of Urban	Definition of Rural
1874	1790-1920	8,000+	Residue
1880	1880-1900	4,000+	Residue
1890[a]			Residue and compact bodies of <1,000
1900	1900	Places of +4,000; semi-urban incorporated; or places <4,000	Unincorporated and <4,000
1906	1900-1910	Cities of 25,000+ or urban places of 2,500+	County Districts Residue
1910	1880-1970	2,500+ and incorporated	<2,500 or unincorporated
1920	1920-1970		Rural nonfarm and farm
1930	1930-1950	Population of 10,000+, and density of 1,000/ sq. mi.	
1940	1940	Metropolitan District: City of 50,000+ with contiguous areas	
1950	1950-1970	New Definition of urban[b], Urbanized area[c], and SMA[d]	1,000 to 2,5000 or <1,000
1960	1960-1970	Standard Consolidated Area[e] SMSA	
1983	1990-?	Metropolitan Statistical Area[f] Primary Metropolitan Statistical Area[g] Consolidated Metropolitan Statistical Area[h]	

Table A–1 *(Continued)*

[a]In 1890 the rural population was subdivided into compact bodies of 1,000 or more and the remainder, but this division was not included in the census, apparently inadvertently.

[b]The new definition of urban included all persons living in (a)incorporated places of 2,500 or more (except in New England and other states where towns are subdivisions of counties); (b)the urban fringe, whether incorporated or not; and (c)unincorporated places of 2,500 or more outside an urban fringe. The remaining population was classified as rural.

[c]An Urbanized Area is composed of at least one city (or a pair of contiguous cities) of 50,000 or more pluse the surrounding densely settled, closely spaced, urban fringe.

[d]A Standard Metropolitan Area is the original name of the Standard Metropolitan St/tistical Area. Except in the New England States, a Standard Metropolitan Statistical Area is a county or group of contiguous counties which contains at least one city of 50,000 or "twin cities" with a combined population of at least 50,000. In addition to the county, or counties, containing such a city or cities, contiguoug counties are included if, according to certain criteria, they are socially and economically integrated with the central city. In the New England States, SMSA's consist of towns and cities instead of counties.

[e]A Standard Consolidated Area is composed of two or more contiguous SMSA's and additional counties that do not appear to meet the formal integration criteria dut do have strong interrelationships of other kinds. SCSA's initially involved the metropolitan complexes around New York and Chicago but many others have since been designated.

[f]A Metropolitan Statistical Area is relatively freestanding and not closely associated with other MSA's. These areas are typically surrounded by nonmetropolitan counties. Areas qualifying for this designation have either a city with a population of at least 50,000 or a Bureau of the Census urbanized area of at least 50,000 and a total metropolitan statistical area population of at least 100,000. Each MSA has one or more central counties containing the area's main population. It may also include outlying counties which have close economic and social relationships with the central county(ies). There are four levels of MSAs. Level A are those with populations of 1 million or more; Level B are those with populations of 250,000 to one million; Level C are those with populations of 100,000 to 250,000; and Level D are those with populations less than 100,000. Only MSAs in Level A can be further designated at Primary Metropolitan Statistical Areas or Consolidated Metropolitan Statistical Areas.

[g]Primary Metropolitan Statistical Areas are those in areas with over 1 million population. These areas consist of a large urbanized county, or cluster of counties, that demonstrates very strong internal economic and social links, in addition to close ties to neighboring areas.

[h]When Primary Metropolitan Statistical Areas are defined, the large area of which they are component parts is designated a Consolidtated Metropolitan Statistical Area.

Sources: Adapted from Table 13-1 in Peterson, William. Population. Third Edition. New York: Macmillan, Inc., 1975. Definitions from Peterson (1975) and "The Metropolitan Statistical Area Classification" in the Statistical Reporter, December, 1979.

Table A–2
Geographic Expansion of U.S. Land Area

Year	Area in Nation (square miles)	Other Territory Under U.S. Control (square miles)	Acquisitions (square miles)
1790	867,980	318,167 (Northwest of Ohio River)	
1800	867,980	25,855 (Northwest of Ohio River) 5,290 (South of Tennessee)	
1803			827,192 (Louisiana Purchase)
1810	1,685,865	777,940 (Missouri Territory)	
1819			72,003 (Treaty with Spain)
1820	1,753,588	608,565 (Missouri Territory)	
1830	1,753,588	608,565 (Missouri Territory) 52,750 (Indian Territory)	
1840	1,753,588	511,967 (Indian Territory)	
1845			390,144 (Texas)
1846			285,580 (Oregon)
1848			529,017 (Mexican Cession)
1850	2,944,337	535,003 (Indian Territory)	
1853			29,640 (Gasden Purchase)
1860	2,973,965	69,414 (Indian Territory 312,094 (Dakota Territory)	
1870	2,973,965	69,414 (Indian Territory) 147,687 (Dakota Territory)	
1880	2,973,965	69,414 (Indian Territory) 147,687 (Dakota Territory)	
1890	2,973,965	30,790 (Indian Territory)	
1900	2,974,159	30,790 (Indian Territory)	

Source: Adapted from Series B 24-25 in Historical Statistics of the United States, 1789-1945. U.S. Bureau of the Census, Washington, D.C.: Government Printing Office.

Table A–3
Rural and Urban Population and Intercensal Change, 1790–1980[a]

Decade	Total U.S. Population (millions)	Rural as % of U.S. Population	Rural Total (1000s)	Rural Intercensal Net Change (1000s)	Rural Intercensal Percent Change	Urban Total (1000s)	Urban Intercensal Net Change (1000s)	Urban Intercensal Percent Change
1790	3.9	94.9	3,728			202		
				1,258	33.8		120	59.4
1800	5.3	93.9	4,986			322		
				1,728	34.7		203	63.0
1810	7.2	92.7	6,714			525		
				2,231	33.2		168	32.0
1820	9.6	92.8	8,945			693		
				2,794	31.2		434	62.6
1830	12.9	91.2	11,739			1,127		
				3,485	29.7		718	63.7
1840	17.1	89.2	15,224			1,845		
				4,424	29.1		1,699	92.1
1850	23.2	84.7	19,648			3,544		
				5,578	28.4		2,673	75.4
1860	31.4	80.2	25,226			6,217		
				3,430	18.6		3,685	59.3
1870	38.6	74.3	28,656			9,902		
				7,370	20.5		4,228	46.7
1880	50.2	71.8	36,026			14,130		
				4,815	13.4		7,976	56.4
1890	63.0	64.9	40,841			22,106		
				4,994	12.5		8,054	36.4
1900	76.2	60.4	45,835			30,160		
				4,138	9.1		11,839	39.3
1910	92.2	54.4	49,973			41,999		
				1,580	3.2		12,159	29.0
1920	106.0	48.8	51,553			54,158		
				2,267	4.4		14,797	27.3
1930	123.2	43.9	53,820			68,955		
				3,426	6.3		5,469	07.9
1940	132.2	43.5	57,246			74,424		
				-3,016	-6.5		22,044	29.6
1950	151.3	36.0	54,230			96,468		
				-176	-.08		28,801	29.9
1960	179.3	30.1	54,054			125,269		
				-167	-.09		24,056	19.2
1970	203.2	26.5	53,887			149,325		
				5,608	10.4		17,726	11.9
1980	226.5	26.3	59,495			167,051		

Source: Adapted from Series A 57-72 of Historical Statistics of the United States, Colonial Times to 1970. U.S. Bureau of the Census, Washington, D.C.: Government Printing Office.
[a]Urban represents population residing in places of 2,500 or more, the population not classified as urban constitutes the rural population.

Table A–4
Regional Population Growth and Distribution, 1790–1880

Decade	Northeast Change[a]	Northeast Share[b]	North Central Change	North Central Share	South Change	South Share	West Change	West Share
1790s	33.9%	49.7%	N/A%	0.9%	33.7%	49.3%	N/A%	N/A%
1800s	32.3	48.2	472.1	4.0	32.0	47.8	N/A	N/A
1810s	25.0	45.2	194.2	8.9	27.7	45.8	N/A	N/A
1820s	27.1	43.1	87.4	12.5	29.1	44.4	N/A	N/A
1830s	22.0	39.6	108.1	19.6	21.8	40.7	N/A	N/A
1840s	27.6	37.2	61.2	23.3	29.2	38.7	N/A	0.7
1850s	22.8	33.7	40.6	28.9	23.9	35.4	245.8	1.4
1860s	16.1	31.9	42.7	33.7	10.4	31.9	60.1	2.6
1870s	17.9	28.9	33.8	34.6	34.4	32.9	81.7	3.6

Source: Adapted from Series A 172-194 in Historical Statistics of the United States, Colonial
Times to 1970. U.S. Bureau of the Census, Washington, D.C.: Government Printing Office.
[a]Change is percent change in region's population over the decade.
[b]Share is the region's share of the nation's total population at the beginning of the decade.
N/A Insufficient numbers of persons available to compute change or share.

Table A-5
Fertility Ratios by Residence and Region, 1800-1880[a]

Area	1880	1860	1840	1820	1800
United States	754	886	1,070	1,236	1,281
Urban	...	...	701	831	815
Rural	...	...	1,134	1,276	1,319
New England	498	622	752	930	1,098
Urban	...	...	592	764	827
Rural	...	...	800	952	1,126
Middle Atlantic	624	767	940	1,183	1,279
Urban	...	...	711	842	852
Rural	...	...	1,006	1,235	1,339
East North Central	757	999	1,270	1,608	1,840
Urban	...	...	841	1,059	...
Rural	...	...	1,291	1,616	1,840
West North Central	905	1,105	1,445	1,685	...
Urban	...	...	705	...	...
Rural	...	...	1,481	1,685	...
South Atlantic	851	918	1,140	1,280	1,345
Urban	...	...	770	881	861
Rural	...	...	1,185	1,310	1,365
East South Central	926	1,039	1,408	1,631	1,799
Urban	...	...	859	1,089	...
Rural	...	...	1,424	1,635	1,799
West South Central	1,043	1,084	1,297	1,418	...
Urban	...	...	846	866	...
Rural	...	...	1,495	1,522	...
Mountain	872	1,051	...	...	...
Urban	...	...	...	...	...
Rural	...	...	...	...	...
Pacific	775	1,026	...	...	...
Urban	...	...	...	...	...
Rural	...	...	...	...	...

Source: U.S. Bureau of the Census, Historical Statistics of the United States, Colonial
 Times in 1970. Bicentennial Edition, Part 2. Washington, D.C.: U.S. Government
 Printing Office, 1975. Series B 67-98.
[a]Unadjusted number of children per 1,000 white women.
...Indicates insufficient numbers of persons.

Table A-6
Net Migration of Blacks by Region, 1910–1980[a]

Period	South	Northeast	North Central	West
1910s	-454	182	244	28
1920s	-749	349	364	36
1930s	-347	171	128	49
1940s	-1,599	463	618	339
1950s	-1,473	496	541	293
1960s	-1,380	612	382	301
1970s	209	-239	-103	132

Source: Reid, John. 1982. Black America in the 1980s. Population Bulletin,
Vol. 37 (4), Table 6, pg. 19.
[a] Numbers in thousands

Table A-7
Regional Population Growth and Distribution, 1890–1980

Decade	Northeast		North Central		South		West	
	Change[a]	Share[b]	Change	Share	Change	Share	Change	Share
1890s	20.9%	27.6%	17.5%	34.6%	22.4%	32.2%	37.5%	5.7
1900s	22.9	28.0	13.5	32.4	19.8	31.9	64.3	7.7
1910s	14.7	28.0	13.8	32.1	12.7	31.2	30.1	8.7
1920s	16.1	27.9	13.4	31.3	14.3	30.7	3.8	10.0
1930s	4.5	27.2	4.0	30.4	10.1	31.5	16.7	10.9
1940s	9.7	26.1	10.8	29.4	13.3	31.2	40.4	13.3
1950s	13.2	24.9	16.1	28.8	16.5	30.7	38.9	15.6
1960s	9.8	24.1	9.6	27.8	14.3	30.9	24.2	17.2
1970s	0.2	21.7	4.0	26.0	20.0	33.3	23.9	19.1

Source: Adapted from Series A 172-194 in Historical Statistics of the United States, Colonial Times to
1970, and the 1985 Statistical Abstract of the United States, U.S. Bureau of the Census, Washington,
D.C.: Government Printing Office.
[a] Change is percent change in region's population over the decade.
[b] Share is the region's share of the nation's total popualtion at the beginning of the decade.

Table A–8
Fertility Ratios by Residence and Region, 1890–1970[a]

Area	1970	1950	1930	1910	1890
United States	503	551	485	609	667
Urban	483	479	388	469	...
Rural	558	673	658	782	...
New England	521	516	441	482	440
Urban	504	486	417	468	...
Rural	574	612	541	566	...
Middle Atlantic	486	471	424	533	547
Urban	466	432	386	495	...
Rural	568	596	590	650	...
East North Central	530	552	458	555	653
Urban	510	491	400	470	...
Rural	585	679	605	672	...
West North Central	530	600	495	630	781
Urban	497	514	365	426	...
Rural	597	702	614	760	...
South Atlantic	469	572	593	760	777
Urban	443	450	401	485	...
Rural	514	677	744	894	...
East South Central	490	631	655	817	850
Urban	453	494	414	469	...
Rural	537	720	781	922	...
West South Central	512	607	584	845	968
Urban	500	542	410	504	...
Rural	547	703	723	977	...
Mountain	542	663	582	661	757
Urban	525	584	428	466	...
Rural	596	754	712	810	...
Pacific	482	539	360	460	587
Urban	474	478	306	360	...
Rural	537	652	507	640	...

Source: U.S. Bureau of the Census, Historical Statistics of the United States,
Colonial Times in 1970. Bicentennial Edition, Part 2. Washington, D.C.: U.S.
Government Printing Office, 1975. Series B 67-98.
[a]Unadjusted number of children per 1,000 white women.
...Indicates insufficient numbers of persons.

Table A-9
Urban Population Change by Size of Urban Place, 1880–1980

	1970-80	1960-70	1950-60	1940-50	1930-40	1920-30	1910-20	1900-10	1890-1900	1880-90
1 million + more	-6.6	7.3	0.5	9.4	5.6	48.5	19.4	32.2	75.6	203.6
500,000 - 1 million	-16.4	16.7	20.9	42.3	12.0	-7.4	106.7	83.0	104.1	-57.9
250,000 - 500,000	16.4	-3.0	30.6	5.3	-1.6	75.2	15.0	38.1	16.9	88.2
100,000 - 250,000	19.1	22.6	22.9	21.6	3.3	15.7	34.7	47.9	17.6	55.7
50,000 - 100,000	18.3	20.9	54.9	21.6	13.1	23.3	26.0	54.3	33.6	113.9
25,000 - 50,000	31.3	19.4	69.7	18.8	15.4	26.6	26.1	43.6	23.4	56.9
10,000 - 25,000	29.1	21.9	48.0	19.1	9.6	29.3	26.8	27.9	25.7	57.7
5,000 - 10,000	18.8	32.1	20.2	21.8	13.3	18.7	17.8	31.6	34.4	38.8
2,500 - 5,000	16.5	6.0	16.8	29.1	6.5	7.6	17.7	28.6	27.3	40.7
Other urban territory	-12.5	51.0	33.1	---	---	---	---	---	---	---

Source: Adapted from Series A 57-72 in U.S. Bureau of the Census Historical Statistics of the United States, Colonial Times to 1970, Bicentennial Edition, Part 2, 1975; and Table 26 in U.S. Bureau of the Census, Statistical Abstract of the United States, 1984.
--- Not applicable.

Table A–10
Regional Migration Interchanges, 1955–1980[a]

	1955-60	1965-70	1970-75	1975-80
Northeast and				
North Central	-40	-53	-67	-105
South	-314	-438	-964	-1163
West	-285	-224	-311	-516
North Central and				
Northeast	+40	+53	+67	+105
South	+217	+275	+790	-849
West	-760	-415	-472	-637
South and				
Northeast	+314	+438	+964	+1163
North Central	-217	+275	+790	+849
West	-380	-57	+70	-25
West and				
Northeast	+285	+224	+311	+516
North Central	+760	+415	+472	+637
South	+380	+57	-75	+25

Source: For 1955-1960 Regional Migration Interchange, adapted from Table 2 of 1960 U.S. Census of the Population, Lifetime and Recent Migration, PC(2)-2D. For 1965-1975, Table 1-2 in Wordwell and Brown, 1980, for 1975-1980, Table 15 in Statistical Abstract of the United States, 1984.

[a] In thousands.

Table A-11
Population in Urban and Rural Territory by Metropolitan and Nonmetropolitan Status, 1950-1980

Residence	Percent Distribution			
	1950	1960	1970	1980
Urban	64.0	69.9	73.5	73.7
In Urbanized Areas	45.8	53.5	58.3	61.4
Central Cities	32.0	32.3	31.5	29.6
Urban Fringe	13.8	21.1	26.8	31.8
Other Urban	18.2	16.4	15.2	12.3
Rural	36.0	30.1	26.5	26.3
Inside SMSAs	62.5	66.7	68.6	74.8
Urban	N/A	N/A	60.5	64.2
Rural	N/A	N/A	8.1	10.6
Outside SMSAs	37.5	33.3	31.4	25.2
Urban	N/A	N/A	13.0	9.5
Rural	N/A	N/A	18.4	15.7

Source: 1985 and 1978 U.S. Statistical Abstract. U.S. Bureau of the Census, Washington D.C.: Government Printing Office.

Table A–12
Percent Change in Metropolitan and Nonmetropolitan
Population, 1950–1980[a]

Region and States	1950-60	1960-70	1970-80
Metropolitan Areas			
Northeast	13.8	10.9	-1.8
North Central	28.1	21.6	2.2
South	52.3	33.1	21.2
West	235.9	36.0	21.9
Nonmetropolitan Areas			
Northeast	10.8	5.4	12.8
North Central	1.8	-8.5	8.0
South	-4.4	-3.3	17.8
West	-44.2	-6.2	32.9

Source: Adapted from Series A 264-275 in Historical Statistics of the United States, Colonial Times to 1970 and, 1981 Statistical Abstract of the United States. U.S. Bureau of the Census, Washington, D.C.: Government Printing Office.

[a]Population change is based upon the population in metropolitan areas as defined at the time of the census. In 1950, there were 168 identified SMSAs; in 1960, 212 SMSAs; in 1970, 243 SMSAs; and, in 1980, 277 SMSAs. Thus, the population change figures take into account both demographic processes (i.e., natural increase and migration) and the effects of changing definitions of SMSAs which produced expansion in the geographic area encompassed by SMSAs.

Bibliography

Anderson, William F. "Interfarm Mobility in New York State." *Rural Sociology* 2(4): 393–401(1937).

Baker, O. E. "Rural Urban Migration and the National Welfare." *Annals of the Association of American Geography* (June 1933).

———. *The Outlook for Rural Youth*. Washington, D.C.: U.S. Department of Agriculture, Extension Service Circular #23, 1935.

Baldassare, Mark. "Local Perspectives on Community Growth." In *Nonmetropolitan America in Transition*, edited by Amos H. Hawley and Sara Mills Mazie, 116–43. Chapel Hill, N.C.: University of North Carolina Press, 1981.

Ballard, Patricia L., and Glenn V. Fuguitt. "The Changing Small Town Settlement Structure in the United States, 1900–1980." *Rural Sociology* 50(1): 99–113 (1985).

Beale, Calvin L. "Demographic Trends of the U.S. Rural Population." In *The Development of Rural America,* edited by George Brinkman, 33–50. Lawrence, Kans.: University Press of Kansas, 1974.

———. *The Revival of Population Growth in Nonmetropolitan America*. Washington, D.C.: U.S. Department of Agriculture, Economics, Statistics and Cooperative Service, ERS-605, 1975.

———. "People on the Land." In *Rural U.S.A.: Persistence and Change,* edited by T. R. Ford, 37–54. Ames, Iowa: Iowa State University Press, 1978.

———. "Rural Development in the 1980's. Selected Research and Policy Issues—The Population Dimension." Paper presented at the Rural Sociological Society meetings, Blacksburg, Va., August 1985.

Bealer, Robert C. "Theory and Rural Sociology," *Rural Sociology* 40(4): 455–77 (1975).

Beegle, J. Allan. "Social Structure and Changing Fertility of the Farm Population." *Rural Sociology* 31(4): 415–27 (1966).

Beers, Howard W. *Mobility of Rural Population.* Agricultural Experiment Station Bulletin 505. Lexington, Ky.: University of Kentucky, 1947.

Belcher, John C. "The Composition of the Population of Oklahoma Villages." *Rural Sociology* 11(3): 233–44 (1946).

Bender, Lloyd. "The Effects of Trends in Economic Structure on Population Change in Rural Areas." In *New Directions in Urban-Rural Migration: The Population Turnaround in Rural America*, edited by David L. Brown and John M. Wardwell, 137–62. New York: Academic Press, 1980.

Bender, Lloyd D., Bernal L. Green, and Roy R. Campbell. "The Process of Rural Poverty Ghettoization: Population and Poverty in Rural Regions." Paper presented to American Association for the Advancement of Science, Philadelphia, December 1971.

Bernert, Eleanor H. "Volume and Composition of Net Migration from the Rural Farm Population, 1930–40." Report for the United States Major Geographic Divisions and States. Mineograph. Washington, D.C.: Bureau of Agricultural Economics, 1944.

Bertrand, Alvin L. "Foreword." In *Rural Society in the U.S.: Issues for the 1980s*, edited by Don A. Dillman and Daryl J. Hobbs, xi–xiii. Boulder, Colo.: Westview Press, 1982.

Beshers, James M. *Population Processes in Social Systems.* New York: Free Press, 1967.

Billington, Ray Allen. *Westward Expansion: A History of the American Frontier.* New York: Macmillan, 1949.

———. *America's Frontier Heritage.* New York: Holt, Rinehard and Winston, 1966.

Binder-Johnson, Hildegard. "Distribution of the German Pioneer Population in Minnesota," *Rural Sociology* 6(1): 16–34 (1941).

Binford, Henry C. *The First Suburbs.* Chicago: University of Chicago Press, 1985.

Blackwood, Larry G., and Edwin Carpenter. "The Importance of Anti-Urbanism Determining Residential References and Migration Patterns." *Rural Sociology* 43(1): 31–47 (1978).

Blau, Peter M., and Otis Dudley Duncan. *The American Occupational Structure.* New York: John Wiley and Sons, 1967.

Bogue, Donald J. *Principles of Demography.* New York: John Wiley and Sons, 1969.

Bogue, Donald J., and Emerson Seim. "Components of Population Change in Suburban and Central City Population of Standard Metropolitan Areas: 1940 to 1950." *Rural Sociology* 21(3–4): 267–75 (1956).

Bohlen, Joe M., and Ray E. Wakely. "Intentions to Migrants and Actual Migration of Rural High School Graduates." *Rural Sociology* 14(4): 328–34 (1950).

Bouvier, Leon and Robert W. Gardner. "Immigration to the U.S.: The Unfinished Story." *Population Bulletin* 41(4): 1–50 (1986).

Bowles, Gladys K. "Migration Patterns of the Rural Farm Population, 13 Economic Regions of U.S., 1940–1950." *Rural Sociology* 22(1): 1–11 (1957).

———. "Contributions of Recent Metro/Nonmetro Migrants to the Nonmetro Population and Labor Force." *Agricultural Economics Research* 30: 15–22 (October 1978).

Bowles, Gladys K., Lloyd Bacon, and Neal P. Ritchey. *Poverty Dimensions of Rural to Urban Migration.* vol 2, chart 1974. Washington D.C.: Published jointly by the Economic Research Service; U.S.D.A.; University of Georgia, Institute for Behavioral Research; and Office of Planning Research and Evaluation, Office of Economic Opportunity, 1973.

———. *Analytic Report: Migration and Poverty in the United States, 1967.* Vol. 3. Washington, D.C.: Published jointly by the Economic Research Service; USDA; University of Georgia, Institute for Behavioral Research; and Office of Planning Research and Evaluation, Office of Economic Opportunity, 1974.

Bowles, Gladys K., and Calvin L. Beale. "Commuting and Migration Status in Nonmetro Areas." *Agricultural Economics Research* 32: 8–20 (July 1980).

Brady, Dorothy S. "Relative Prices in the Nineteenth Century." *Journal of Economic History* 26: 145–203 (June 1964).

Brown, David L., and Calvin L. Beale. "Diversity in Post–1970 Population Trends." In *Nonmetropolitan America in Transition*, edited by Amos H. Hawley and Sara Miles Mazie, 27–71. Chapel Hill, N.C.: University of North Carolina Press, 1981.

Brown, David L. and John M. Wardwell. *New Directions in Urban-Rural Migration: The Population Turnaround in Rural America.* New York: Academic Press, 1980.

Brown, James S., Harry K. Schwarzweller, and Joseph J. Mangalam. "Kentucky Mountain Migration and the Stem-Family: An American Variation on a Theme by Le Play." *Rural Sociology* 28(1): 48–69 (1963).

Brunner, Stanley D. "Changes in the Service Structure of Rural Trade Centers." *Rural Sociology* 33(2): 200–206 (1968).

Brunner, Edmund deS. "Internal Migration in the United States, 1935–40." *Rural Sociology* 13(1): 9–22 (1948).

———. "The Small Village: 1940–1950." *Rural Sociology* 17(2): 127–31 (1952).

———. *The Growth of a Science: A Half-Century of Rural Sociological Research in the United States.* New York: Harper and Row, 1957.

Bultena, Gordon, Paul Lasley, and Jack Geller. "The Farm Crisis: Patterns and Impacts of Financial Distress among Iowa Farm Families." *Rural Sociology* 5(4): 436–48 (1986).

Busch, Lawrence, and William B. Lacy. *Science, Agriculture and the Politics of Research.* Boulder, Colo.: Westview Press, 1983.

Callow, Alexander B., Jr. *American Urban History.* 2d ed. New York: Oxford University Press, 1973.

Campbell, Rex R., Daniel M. Johnson, and Gary J. Stangler. "Return Migration of Black People to the South." *Rural Sociology* 39(4): 514–28 (1974).

Campbell, Rex R., Gary J. Stangler, George H. Dailey, and Robert L. McNamara. "Population Change, Migration and Displacement along the McClellen-Kerr Arkansas River Navigation System." IWR Contract Report, 77–5. Fort Belvoir, Va.: Institute of Water Resources, 1977.

Campbell, Rex R., and Lorraine E. Garkovich. "Turnaround Migration as an Episode of Collective Behavior." *Rural Sociology* 49(1): 89–105 (1984).

Carpenter, Edwin H. "The Potential for Population Dispersal: A Closer Look at Residential Location Preferences." *Rural Sociology* 42(3): 352–70 (1977).

Cebula, R. J., and R. K. Vedder. "A Note on Migration, Economic Opportunity and the Quality of Life." *Journal of Regional Science* 13: 205–11 (1973).

Christenson, James A., and Lorraine E. Garkovich. "Fifty years of Rural Sociology: Status, Trends and Impressions." *Rural Sociology* 50(4): 503–22 (1985).

Clawson, Marion. "Land Use Trends." In *Nonmetropolitan America in Transition,* edited by Amos H. Hawley and Sara Mills Mazie, 645–67. Chapel Hill, N.C.: University of North Carolina Press, 1981.

Clifford, William B., Tim B. Heaton, Daniel T. Lichter, and Glenn V. Fuguitt. "Components of Change in the Age Composition of

Nonmetropolitan America." *Rural Sociology* 48(3): 458–70 (1983).

Cochrane, Willard W. *The Development of American Agriculture.* Minneapolis: University of Minnesota Press, 1979.

Collier, John. *Indians of the Americas.* New York: Mentor, 1947.

Commons, John R. *Races and Immigrants in America.* New York: Macmillan, 1907.

Coughenour, C. Milton, and Donald C. Wimberley. "Small and Part Time Farmers." In *Rural Society in the U.S.: Issues for the 1980's,* edited by Don A. Dillman and Daryl J. Hobbs, 347–56. Boulder, Colo.: Westview Press, 1982.

Dailey, George H., and Rex R. Campbell. "The Ozark-Ouachita Uplands: Growth and Consequences." In *New Directions in Urban-Rural Migration: The Population Turnaround in Rural America,* edited by David L. Brown and John M. Wardwell, 233–66. New York: Academic Press, 1980.

DaVanzo, Julie. *Why Families Move: A Model of the Geographic Mobility of Married Couples.* Santa Monica, Calif.: The Rand Corporation, 1976.

———. "Miroeconomic Approaches to Studying Migration Decisions." In *Migration Decision-Making,* edited by Gordon F. De Jong and Robert W. Gardner, 90–129. New York: Pergamon Press, 1981.

DaVanzo, Julie S., and Peter A. Morrison. "Return and Other Sequences of Migration in the United States." *Demography* 18(1): 85–102 (1981).

Davis, Kingsley. "The Theory of Change and Response in Modern Demographic History." *Population Index* 29: 345–65 (1963).

De Bow, J. D. *Statistical View of the United States: A Compendium of the Seventh Census.* Washington D.C.: Nicholason, 1854.

De Jong, Gordon F., and James T. Fawcett. "Motivations for Migration: An Assessment and a Valve-Expectancy Research Model." In *Migration Decision-Making,* edited by Gordon F. De Jong and Robert W. Gardner, 13–58. New York: Pergamon Press, 1981.

De Jong, Gordon F. and Robert W. Gardner (ed.) *Migration Decision-Making.* New York: Pergamon Press, 1981.

De Jong, Gordon F., and Ralph R. Sell. "Residential Preferences and Migration Behavior." Report submitted to Center for Population Research, National Institutes of Health, Department of Health, Education and Welfare. Washington, D.C.: Government Printing Office, 1975.

———. "Population Redistribution, Migration and Residential Preferences." *Annals of the American Academy of Political and Social Science* 429: 130–44 (January 1977).

Dillman, Don A. "Rural North America in the Information Society." *The Rural Sociologist* 3(5): 345–57 (1983).

Duncan, Otis Durant. "Rural Sociology Coming of Age." *Rural Sociology* 19(1): 1–12 (1954).

Easterlin, Richard. *Population, Labor Force and Long Swings in Economic Growth.* New York: National Bureau of Economic Research, 1968.

Eldridge, Hope Tisdale. "Primary, Secondary and Return Migration in the United States, 1955–1960." *Demography* 2(4): 444–55, (1965).

Falk, William W. "Making Sense of the Concept Rural and Doing Rural Sociology: An Interpretive Perspective." *Rural Sociology* 43(4): 547–58 (1978).

Farley, Reynolds. *The Growth of the Black Population.* Chicago: Markham Publishing Co., 1970.

Federal Committee on Standard Metropolitan Areas. "Documents Relating to the Metropolitan Statistical Area Classification for the 1980's." *Statistical Reporter,* 335–58 (August 1980).

Folson, J. C. and O. E. Baker. "A Graphic Summary of Farm Labor and Population." Washington, D.C.: U.S. Department of Agriculture, Miscellaneous Publication 265 (1937).

Frisbie, W. Parker, and Dudley L. Poston, Jr. "The Structure of Sustenance Organization and Population Change in Nonmetropolitan America." *Rural Sociology* 41(3): 354–70 (1976).

———. *Sustenance Organization and Migration in Non-Metropolitan America.* Ames, Iowa: University of Iowa, Iowa's Urban Community Research Center, 1978.

Fuchs, Victor R. *The Service Company.* New York: National Bureau of Economic Research, 1968.

Fuguitt, Glenn V., and Calvin L. Beale. "Population Change in Non-Metropolitan Cities and Towns." Washington, D.C.: Economic Research Service, U.S. Department of Agriculture, Agricultural Economic Report 323 (February 1976).

Fuguitt, Glenn V., Daniel T. Lichter, Max J. Pfeffer and Robert M. Jenkins. "Nonmetropolitan Population Deconcentration in the 1980s." Paper presented at the Rural Sociological Society meetings, Madison, WI, August 12–15, 1987.

Fuguitt, Glenn V., and James J. Zuiches. "Residential Preferences and Population Distribution." *Demography* 12(4): 491–505 (1975).

Garkovich, Lorraine. "Serving Small Community Information Needs through Academic Programs." *Research in Rural Sociology and Development* 2: 257–73 (1985).

Goldscheider, Galvin. *Population, Modernization and Social Structures*. Boston: Little Brown & Co., 1971.

Goldstein, Sidney. "Repeated Migration as Factor in High Mobility Roles." *American Sociological Review* 19: 536–41 (October 1954).

Graber, Edith. "Newcomers and Oldtimers: Growth and Change in a Mountain Town." *Rural Sociology* 39(4): 504–13 (1974).

Gray, Wayne T. "Population Movements in the Kentucky Mountains." *Rural Sociology* 10(4): 380–87 (1945).

Graybill, Wilson H., Claude V. Kiser, and Pascal K. Whelpton. *The Fertility of American Women*. New York: John Wiley and Sons, 1958.

Hagood, Margaret Jarman. "Changing Fertility Differentials among Farm Operator Families in Relation to Economic Size of Farm." *Rural Sociology* 13(4): 363–74 (1948).

———. "Dynamics of Rural Population." In *Rural Life in the United States*, edited by Carl C. Taylor et al., 233–44. New York: Alfred A. Knopf, Inc., 1950.

———. "Rural Population Characteristics." In *Rural Life in the United States*, edited by Carl C. Taylor et al., 233–44. New York: Alfred A. Knopf, Inc., 1950.

Hamilton, C. Horace. "Social Effects of Recent Trends in the Mechanization of Agriculture." *Rural Sociology* 4(1): 3–19 (1939).

———. "The Negroes Leave the South." *Demography* 1(1): 12–13 (1964).

Handlin, Oscar, ed. *Immigration as a Factor in American History*. Englewood Cliffs, N.J.: Prentice Hall, 1959.

Hansen, Marcus Lee. *Atlantic Migration: 1607–1860*. Cambridge, Mass.: Harvard University Press, 1940.

———. *The Immigrant in American History*. Cambridge, Mass.: Harvard University Press, 1940.

Hassinger, Edward. "The Relationship of Retail Service Patterns to Trade-Center Population Change." *Rural Sociology* 22(3): 235–40 (1957).

Hawley, Amos H. "Ecology-Human Ecology." In *International Encyclopedia of the Social Sciences*, edited by David Sills, 328–32. New York: Crowell, Collier and MacMillan, 1968.

Hawley, Amos H., and Sara Miles Mazie. *Nonmetropolitan America in Transition*. Chapel Hill, N.C.: University of North Carolina Press, 1981.

Heilbruner, Robert L. *The Economic Transformation of America*. New York: Hartcourt Brace Jovanovich, Inc., 1977.

Hill, George W., and James D. Tarver. "Indigenous Fertility in the
    Farm Population of Wisconsin, 1848–1948." *Rural Sociology*
    16(4): 359–62 (1951).
Hill, Herbert. "Anti-Oriental Agitation and the Rise of Working Class
    Racism." *Transaction: Society* 43–54 (Jan./Feb. 1973).
Hine, Robert V. *Community on the American Frontier*. Norman, Okla.:
    University of Oklahoma Press, 1980.
Hobbs, Daryl J., and Don A. Dillman. "Research for the Rural United
    States." In *Rural Society in the U.S.: Issued for the 1980's*, edited
    by Don A. Dillman and Daryl J. Hobbs, 1–9. Boulder, Colo.:
    Westview Press, 1982.
Hodge, Gerald. "Do Villages Grow? Some Perspectives and Predic-
    tions." *Rural Sociology* 31(2): 183–96 (1966).
Hoffer, Charles R. "The Development of Rural Sociology." *Rural So-
    ciology* 26(1): 1–14 (1961).
Hourwich, Isaac. A. *Immigration and Labor*. 2d ed. New York: B. W.
    Huebsch, Inc., 1922.
Humphrey, Craig R., and Ralph R. Sell. "The Impact of Controlled
    Access Highways on Population Growth in Pennsylvania Non-
    metropolitan Communities 1940–1970." *Rural Sociology*
    40(3): 332–43 (1975).
Humphrey, Craig R., Ralph R. Sell, John A. Krout, and R. Thomas
    Gillaspy. "Net Migration Turnaround in Pennsylvania Non-
    metropolitan Minor Civil Divisions, 1960–70." *Rural Sociology*
    42(3): 332–51 (1977).
Ilvento, Thomas and A. E. Luloff. "Anti-Urbanism and Nonmetro-
    politan Growth: A Re-Evaluation." *Rural Sociology* 47 (2): 220–
    33 (1982).
Jeffrey, Julie Roy. *Frontier Women: The Trans-Mississippi West,
    1840–1880*. New York: Hill and Wang, 1979.
Johansen, Harley E. "Recent Changes in Population and Business
    Activity in Rural Villages in the United States." Unpublished
    Ph.D. dissertation, University of Wisconsin, 1974.
Johansen, Harley E., and Glenn V. Fuguitt. "Changing Retail Activity
    in Wisconsin Villages: 1939–1954–1970." *Rural Sociology*
    38(2): 207–18 (1973).
Johansen, Harley E., and Glenn V. Fuguitt. *The Changing Rural
    Village in America: Demographic and Economic Trends Since
    1950*. Cambridge, Mass.: Ballinger, 1984.
Johnson, Daniel M., and Rex R. Campbell. *Black Migration in Amer-
    ica*. Durham, N.C.: Duke University Press, 1981.
Johnson, Kenneth M. *The Impact of Population Change on Business*

Activity in Rural America. Boulder, Colo.: Westview Press, 1985.

Johnson, Nan E., and J. Allan Beegle. "The Rural American People: A Look Backward and Forward." In *Rural Society in the U.S.: Issues for the 1980s*, edited by Don A. Dillman and Daryl J. Hobbs, 58–68. Boulder, Colo.: Westview Press, 1982.

Kirschenbaum, Alan. "Patterns of Migration from Metropolitan-Nonmetropolitan Areas: Changing Ecological Factors Affecting Family Mobility." *Rural Sociology* 36(3): 315–25 (1971).

Kolb, John H., and Edmund des Brunner. *A Study of Rural Society*. 3d ed. Boston: Houghton-Mifflin, 1946.

Kuhn, Thomas S., *The Structure of Scientific Revolutions*. Vol. 2, Foundations of the Unity of Science Series. 2d ed. Chicago: University of Chicago Press, 1970.

Landis, Paul H. *Rural Life in Process*. New York: McGraw-Hill, 1940.

———. "Educational Selectivity of Rural-Urban Migration and Its Bearing on Ways and Occupational Adjustments." *Rural Sociology* (3): 218–33 (1946).

Landis, Paul H., and Paul K. Hatt. *Population Problems: A Cultural Interpretation*. New York: American Book Co., 1954.

Lansing, John B., and Eva Mueller. *The Geographic Mobility of Labor*. Ann Arbor: University of Michigan Research Center, 1967.

Larson, Olaf F. "Wartime Migration and the Manpower Reserve on Farms in Eastern Kentucky." *Rural Sociology* 8(2): 148–61 (1943).

Lee, Everett. "A Theory of Migration." *Demography*. 3(1): 47–57 (1966).

Lee, Gary R., and Marie L. Lassey. "The Elderly." In *Rural Society in the U.S.: Issues for the 1980's*, edited by Don A. Dillman and Daryl J. Hobbs, 85–93. Boulder, Colo.: Westview Press, 1982.

Lichter, Daniel, Glenn V. Fuguitt, and Tim B. Heaton. "Components of Nonmetropolitan Population Change: The Contribution of Rural Areas." *Rural Sociology* 50(1): 88–98 (1985).

Linden, Fabian. "In the Rearview Mirror." *American Demographics* 9(4):4–6 (1987).

Lipset, Seymour Martin. "Social Mobility and Urbanization." *Rural Sociology* 20(3–4): 220–28 (1955).

Lively, C. E., and Conrad Taeuber. *Rural Migration in the United States*. Washington, D.C.: Works Progress Administration, Research Monograph, XIX (1939).

Long, Larry H. "Migration Differentials by Education and Occupation: Trends and Variations." *Demography* 10(2): 243–58 (1973).

Long, Larry H., and Diane DeAre. *Migration to Nonmetropolitan Areas: Appraising the Trend and Reasons for Moving.* Special Demographic Analysis, CDS–80–2, Bureau of the Census. Washington D.C.: Government Printing Office, 1980.

———. "Repopulating the Countryside: A 1980 Census Trend." *Science* 217: 1111–16 (September 1982).

Long, Larry H., and Kristen Hansen. *Reasons for Interstate Migration: Jobs, Retirement, Climate and Other Influences.* Current Population Reports, Special Studies, Series P–23, No. 81, Bureau of the Census. Washington D.C.: Government Printing Office, 1979.

Luloff, A.E. "Identifying the Locus for Action: What Local Residents Have to Say." *Small Town* 9(6): 11–14 (1978).

McCarthy, Kevin F., and Peter A. Morrison. *The Changing Demographic and Economic Structure of Nonmetropolitan Areas in the 1970s.* Report P–6062. Santa Monica, Calif.: Rand Corporation, 1979.

McKenzie, R. D. *The Metropolitan Community.* New York: McGraw Hill, 1933.

McMillan, Robert T. "Some Observations of Oklahoma Population Movements since 1930." *Rural Sociology* 1(3): 332–43 (1936).

McNall, Scott G., and Sally Allen McNall. *Plains Families.* New York: St. Martin's Press, 1983.

Mangalam, J. J. *Human Migration.* Lexington, KY: University of Kentucky Press, 1968.

Martinson, Floyd M. "Personal Adjustment and Rural-Urban Migration." *Rural Sociology* 20(2): 102–11 (1955).

Mattes, Merrill J. *The Great Platte River Road.* Vol. 25, Publications of Nebraska State Historical Society, 1969.

Mazek, Warren Ford, and William E. Laird. "City Size Preferences and Population Distribution: The Analytical Context." *Quarterly Review of Economics and Business* 14: 113–21 (1974).

Melvin, Bruce L., and E. N. Smith. *Rural Youth: Their Situation and Prospects.* Research monograph. Washington, D.C.: Works Progress Administration, 1938.

Menchik, Mark David. "The Service Sector." In *Nonmetropolitan America in Transition,* edited by Amos H. Hawley and Sarah Miles Mazie, 231–54. Chapel Hill, N.C.: University of North Carolina Press, 1981.

Merk, Frederick. *Manifest Destiny and Mission.* New York: Vintage Books, 1963.

Morrison, Peter A. "Chronic Movers and the Future Redistribution of Population." *Demography* 9(2): 171–84 (1971).

Morrison, Peter A., and J. A. Wheeler. "Rural Renaissance in America: Revival of Population Growth." *Population Bulletin* 31(3): 1976.

Mueller, Eva, and Nancy Barth. *Migration into and out of Depressed Areas.* Washington D.C.: U.S. Department of Commerce, Area Redevelopment Administration, 1964.

Murdock, Steven H. J., Baroo Parpia, Sean-Shong Hwong, and Rita R. Hamm. "The Relative Effects of Economic and Noneconomic Factors on Age-Specific Migration, 1960–1980." *Rural Sociology* 49(2): 309–18 (1984).

Namboodiri, N. Krishnan. "A Contribution to the Study of within Urban and within Rural Differentials." *Rural Sociology* 3(1): 29–39 (1966).

Nash, Roderick. *Wilderness and the American Mind.* New Haven, Conn.: Yale University Press, 1967.

Nelson, Lowry. *Rural Sociology.* New York: American Book Co., 1952.

Nelson, Lowry. "The Rise of Rural Sociology: The Pre-Purnell Period." *Rural Sociology* 30(4): 407–27 (1965).

Notestein, Frank W. "Demography in the United States: A Partial Account of the Development of the Field." *Population and Development Review* 8(4): 651–87 (1982).

Owsley, Frank L. *Plain Folk of the Old South.* Baton Rouge, LA: Louisiana State University Press, 1949.

Payne, Raymond. "Development of Occupational and Migration Expectations and Choices among Urban, Small Town and Rural Adolescent Boys." *Rural Sociology* 21(2): 117–25 (1956).

Peterson, William. *Population.* 3d ed. New York: Macmillan, 1975.

Photidias, John D. "Selected Social and Sociopsychological Characteristics of West Virginians in Their Own State in Cleveland, OH." Final report submitted to the U.S. Department of Labor, Manpower Administration, Office of Manpower Research, Morgantown, W. Va.: University of West Virginia, Appalachian Center, 1970.

Ploch, Louis A. "The Reversal in Migration Patterns—Some Rural Development Consequences." *Rural Sociology* 43(2): 293–303 (1978).

Poindexter, John R., and William B. Clifford. "Components of Sustenance Organization and Nonmetropolitan Population Change: The 1970s." *Rural Sociology* 48(3): 421–35 (1983).

Population Reference Bureau. "Population Changes in Small Communities." Executive summary, briefing to Council of State Communities Affairs Agencies, Washington, D.C. (September 21, 1981).

Poston, Dudley L., and Marion T. Coleman. "Conceptualizing and Measuring the Nonmetropolitan Turnaround in U.S. Counties: An Alternative Procedure." *Rural Sociology* 48(3): 436–46 (1983).

Potter, David M. *People of Plenty: Economic Abundance and the American People*. Chicago: Phoenix Books, 1954.

Powers, Ronald C., and Edward O. Moe. "The Policy Context for Rural-Oriented Research." In *Rural Society in the U.S.: Issues for the 1980's*, edited by Don A. Dillman and Daryl J. Hobbs, 10–20. Boulder, Colo.: Westview Press, 1982.

President's Commission for a National Agenda for the Eighties. "The U.S. in the 1980s: Demographic Trends," Population Reference Bureau, Executive Summary, Washington, D.C. (July 29, 1980).

Price, Daniel O., and Melanie M. Sikes. *Rural-Urban Migration Research in the United States: Annotated Bibliography and Synthesis*. Washington, D.C.: U.S. Government Printing Office, Center for Population Research, 1975.

Price, Michael L., and Daniel C. Clay. "Structural Disturbances in Rural Communities: Some Repercussions of the Migration Turnaround in Michigan." *Rural Sociology* 45(4): 591–607 (1980).

Pursell, Carroll W., Jr. "Machines and Machine Tools, 1830–1880." In *Technology in Western Civilization*, vol. 1, edited by Melvin Kranzberg and Carroll W. Pursell, Jr., 392–405. New York: Oxford University Press, 1967.

Rank, Mark R., and Paul R. Voss. "Patterns of Community Involvement: A Comparison of Residents and Recent Immigrants." *Rural Sociology* 47(2): 197–219 (1982).

Ravenstein, E. G. "The Laws of Migration." *Journal of the Royal Statistical Society*, 48(2): 167–235 (1885).

———. "The Laws of Migration." *Journal of the Royal Statistical Society*, 52(2): 241–301 (1889).

Redfield, Robert. "Rural Sociology and the Folk Society." *Rural Sociology* 8(1): 68–71 (1943).

Reuss, Carl Frederick. "A Qualitative Study of Depopulation in a Remote Rural District: 1900–1930." *Rural Sociology* 2(1): 66–75 (1937).

Rindfuss, Ronald, and James A. Sweet. *Postwar Fertility Trends and Differentials*. New York: Academic Press, 1977.

Ritchey, P. Neal. "Effect of Marital Status on the Fertility of Rural-Urban and Urban-Rural Migrants." *Rural Sociology* 38(1): 26–35 (1973).

———. "Explanations of Migration." In *Annual Review of Sociology*, vol. 2, edited by Alex Inkeles, 363–404. Palo Alto, Calif.: Annual Reviews, Inc., 1976.

Roberts, Roy L. "Significance of Varying Population Densities and Regional Development in the Ecology of Kansas." *Rural Sociology* 3(22): 145–52 (1938).

Robinson, Warren C. "Changes in the Rural Population of the U.S. by Metropolitan and Nonmetropolitan Status, 1900–1960." *Rural Sociology* 30(2): 166–83 (1965).

Rocha, Rodolfo. "Early Ranching along the Rio Grande." In *At Home on the Range: Essays on the History of Western Social and Domestic Life*, edited by John R. Wunder, 3–18. Westport, Conn.: Greenwood Press, 1985.

Rogers, Susan Carol, and Sonya Salamon. "Inheritance and Social Organization among Family Farmers." *American Ethnologist* 10(3): 529–50 (August 1983).

Rutman, Gilbert. "Migration and Economic Opportunities in West Virginia: A Statistical Analysis." *Rural Sociology* 35(2): 206–17 (1970).

Salamon, Sonya. "Ethnic Differences in Farm Family Land Transfers." *Rural Sociology* 45(2): 290–308 (1980).

Salamon, Sonya, and Shirley M. O'Reilly. "Family Land and Development Cycles among Illinois Farmers." *Rural Sociology* 44(3): 525–42 (1979).

Sanders, John. "The Depressed Area and Labor Mobility: The Gaskin Kentucky Case." *Journal of Human Resources* 4(4): 437–50 (1969).

Schaefer, Donald E. "A Statistical Profile of Frontier and New South Migration: 1850–1860." *Agricultural History* 59(4): 563–478 (1985).

Schlesinger, Arthur M. *Paths to the Present.* New York: Macmillan, 1949.

Schlissel, Lillian. *Women's Diaries of the Westward Journey.* New York: Schocken Books, 1982.

Schultze, Rolf, Jay Artis, and J. Allan Beegle. "The Measurement of Community Satisfaction and the Decision to Migrate." *Rural Sociology* 28(3): 279–83 (1963).

Schwarzweller, Harry K., and James S. Brown. "Social Class Origin, Rural-Urban Migration, and Economic Life Chances: A Case Study." *Rural Sociology* 32(1): 5–19 (1967).

Schwarzweller, Harry K., James S. Brown, and Joseph J. Mangalam. *Mountain Families in Transition.* University Park, Pa.: The Pennsylvania State University Press, 1971.

Sell, Ralph and Gordon F. De Jong. "Toward a Motivational Theory of Migration Decision-Making." *Journal of Population*, 1(4): 313–35 (1978).

Seward, Rudy Ray. *The American Family: A Demographic History*. Beverly Hills, Calif.: Sage Publications, 1978.

Sewell, William H. "Rural Sociological Research 1936–1965." *Rural Sociology* 30(4): 428–51 (1965).

Shannon, Fred A. *The Farmer's Last Frontier: Agriculture 1860–1897*. New York: Farrar and Rinehart, 1945.

Shryock, Mary S., and Jacobs Siegel and Associates. *The Methods and Material of Demography*. vol. 2. Washington, D.C.: U.S. Bureau of the Census, 1973.

Skinner, Constance Lindsay. *Pioneers of the Old Southwest*. New Haven, Conn.: Yale University Press, 1921.

Smith, Henry Nash. *Virgin Land: The American West as Symbol and Myth*. Cambridge, Mass.: Harvard University Press, 1970. Reissued.

Smith, Richmond Mayo. *Emigration and Immigration*. New York: Charles Scribner's & Sons, 1890.

Smith, T. Lynn. "The Role of the Village in American Rural Society." *Rural Sociology* 7(1): 10–21 (1942).

———. *The Sociology of Rural Life*. New York: Harper and Brothers, 1953.

Smith, T. Lynn, and Martha Ray Fry. *The Population of Selected "Cut-Over" Area in Louisiana*. Baton Route: Louisiana Agriculture Experiment Station Bulletin 268, 1936.

Sofranko, Andrew J., and Frederick C. Fliegel. "Rural-to-Rural Migrants: The Neglected Component of Rural Population Change." Growth and Change, 2 (April 14, 1983): 42–49.

Sofranko, Andrew J., and James O. Williams, eds. *Rebirth of Rural America: Rural Migration in the Midwest*. Ames, Iowa: North Central Regional Center for Rural Development, Iowa State University, 1980.

Sorokin, Pritirim A., and Carie C. Zimmerman. *Principles of Rural-Urban Sociology*. New York: Henry Holt & Co., 1929.

Speare, Alden. "Residential Satisfaction as an Intervening Variable in Residential Mobility." *Demography* 11(2): 173–83 (1974).

Steahr, Thomas E., and A. E. Luloff. *The Structure and Impact of Population Redistribution in New England*. University Park, Pa.: Northeast Regional Center for Rural Development, Publication 39, 1985.

———. "Analytical Framework for Migration in New England." In

The Structure and Impact of Population Redistribution in New England, edited by Thomas E. Steahr and A. E. Luloff, 37–51. University Park, Pa.: Northeast Regional Center for Rural Development, Publication 39, 1985.

Stinner, William F., and Michael B. Toney. "Migrant-Native Differences in Social Background and Community Satisfaction in Nonmetropolitan Utah Communities." In *New Directions in Urban-Rural Migration: The Population Turnaround in Rural America*, edited by David L. Brown and John M. Wardwell, 313–32. New York: Academic Press, 1980.

Stoeckel, Richard H. "The Economic Foundations of East-West Migration during the 19th Century." *Explorations in Economic History* 20: 14–36 (January 1983).

Stokes, C. Shannon, and Michael K. Miller. "A Methodological Review of Fifty Years of Research in Rural Sociology." *Rural Sociology* 5(4): 539–60 (1985).

Stratton, Joanna L. *Pioneer Women: Voices from the Kansas Frontier*. New York: Simon and Schuster, Touchstone Books, 1981.

Stuart, Nina G. "The Older Metropolitan Migrant as a Factor in Rural Population Growth." In *Rebirth of Rural America: Rural Migration in the Midwest*, edited by Andrew J. Sofranko and James D. Williams, 153–70. Ames, Iowa: Iowa State University, North Central Regional Center for Rural Development, 1980.

Taeuber, Conrad. "The Movement to Southern Farms, 1930–35." *Rural Sociology* 3(1): 69–78, 1938.

Taeuber, Conrad, and Irene B. Taeuber. *The Population of the United States*. New York: John Wiley and Sons, 1957.

Taeuber, Karl E. "The Residential Redistribution of Farm Born Cohorts." *Rural Sociology* 32(1): 20–36 (1967).

Taeuber, Karl E., Leonard Chiazze, Jr., and William Haenszel. *Migration in the United States: An Analysis of Residence Histories*. Public Health Monograph 77, U.S. Department of Health, Education and Welfare. Washington, D.C.: Government Printing Office, 1968.

Tarver, James D. "Gradients of Urban Influence on the Educational, Employment and Fertility Patterns of Women." *Rural Sociology* 34(3): 356–67 (1969).

Tarver, James D., and Calvin L. Beale. "Population Trends of Southern Nonmetro Towns, 1950–1960." *Rural Sociology* 33(1): 19–29 (1968).

Tarver, James D., and William R. Gurley. "The Relationship of Selected Variables with County Net Migration Rates in the U.S., 1950–1960." *Rural Sociology* 30(1): 3–12 (1965).

Tetreau, E. D. "The People of Arizona Irrigated Areas." *Rural Sociology* 3(2): 177–87 (1938).

———. "The Location of Heirs and the Value of Their Farm Inheritances: Farm and City Values." *Journal of Land and Public Utility Economics* 16(4): 416–29 (1940).

Thomas, Dorothy Swain. "Selective Migration." *The Milbank Memorial Fund Quarterly* 16: 403–07 (1938a).

———. *Research Memorandum on Migration Differentials*. New York: Social Science Research Counsel Bulletin 43, (1938b).

Thompson, Warren S. and P. K. Whelpton. *Population Trends in the United States*. New York: McGraw Hill Book Co., 1933.

Thompson, Wilbur R., and James J. Mikesell. "Housing Supply and Demand." In *Nonmetropolitan America in Transition*, edited by Amos H. Hawley and Sarah Mills Mazie, 551–88. Chapel Hill, N.C.: University of North Carolina Press, 1981.

Till, Thomas E. "Manufacturing Industry: Trends and Impacts." In *Nonmetropolitan America in Transition*, edited by Amos H. Hawley and Sara Mills Mazie, 194–230. Chapel Hill, N.C.: University of North Carolina Press, 1981.

Tilly, Charles B. and Harold C. Brown. "On Uprooting Kinship and the Auspices of Migration." *International Journal of Comparative Sociology*. 8(1): 139–64, (1967).

Trewartha, Glenn T. "The Unincorporated Hamelt: An Analysis of Data Sources." *Rural Sociology* 6(1): 35–42 (1941).

Tucker, C. Jack. "Changing Patterns of Migration between Metropolitan and Nonmetropolitan Areas in the United States." *Demography* 13(4): 435–43 (1976).

Turner, Frederick Jackson. *The Frontier in American History*. New York: Henry Holt & Co., 1921.

Tweeten, Luther. "Employment." In *Rural Society in the U.S.: Issues for the 1980's*, edited by Don A. Dillman and Daryl J. Hobbs, 175–84. Boulder, Colo.: Westview Press, 1981.

Uhlenberg, Peter. "Noneconomic Determinants of Nonmigration: Sociological Considerations for Migration Theory." *Rural Sociology* 38(3): 296–311 (1973).

U.S. Bureau of the Census. *Reasons for Moving: March 1962 to March 1963*. Current Population Report, Series P–20, No. 154. Washington, D.C.: Government Printing Office, 1966.

———. *Statistical Abstract of the United States: 1984*. Washington, D.C.: Government Printing Office, 1983.

———. *Geographical Mobility, March 1982 to March 1983*. Current Population Reports, Population Characteristics. Series P–20,

No. 393. Bureau of the Census. Washington, D.C.: Government Printing Office, 1984.

Vining, Daniel R., Jr., and Thomas Kontuly. "Population Dispersal from Major Metropolitan Regions: An International Comparison." *International Regional Science Review* 3(1): 49–73 (1978).

Wade, Richard. "Urban Life in Western America, 1790–1830." In *American Urban History*, 2d ed., edited by Alexander B. Callow, Jr., 109–21. New York: Oxford University Press, 1973.

Wakeley, Ray E., and Mohiey Eldin Nasrat. "Sociological Analysis of Population Migration." *Rural Sociology* 26(1): 15–23 (1961).

Wardwell, John M. "Equilibrium and Change in Nonmetropolitan Growth." *Rural Sociology* 42(2): 156–79 (1977).

———. "Toward a Theory of Urban-Rural Migration in the Developed World." In *New Directions in Urban-Rural Migration: The Population Turnaround in Rural America*, edited by David L. Brown and John M. Wardwell, 71–114. New York: Academic Press, 1980.

———. "The Reversal of Nonmetropolitan Migration Loss." In *Rural Society in the U.S.: Issues for the 1980s*, edited by Don A. Dillman and Daryl J. Hobbs, 23–33. Boulder, Colo.: Westview Press, 1982.

Wardwell, John M. and C. Jack Gilchrist. "Employment Deconcentration in the Nonmetropolitan Migration Turnaround." *Demography* 17(1): 145–58 (1980).

———. "Nonmetropolitan Migration: Facts of the 1980's, Theories of the 1970's." Paper presented to the annual meetings of the Rural Sociological Society, Madison, Wisc. (August 1987).

Warner, Sam Bass, Jr. *The Urban Wilderness*. New York: Harper and Row, 1972.

Webb, Walter Prescott. *The Great Plains*. New York: Grosset and Dunlap, 1931.

Whelpton, Peter K. "Industrial Development and Population Growth." *Social Forces* 6: 462 (1928). As cited in *Rural Life in Process*, by Paul H. Landis 44. New York: McGraw-Hill, 1940.

White, Morton, and Lucia White. *The Intellectual Versus the City*. Cambridge, Mass.: Harvard University Press and M.I.T. Press, 1962.

Wilcox, Walter F. *Studies in American Demography*. Ithaca, N.Y.: Cornell University, 1940.

Williams, James D., "The Nonchanging Determinants of Nonmetropolitan Migration." *Rural Sociology* 46(2): 183–202 (1981).

Williams, James O., and David B. McMillen. "Migration Decision-

Making among Nonmetropolitan Bound Migrants." In *New Directions in Urban-Rural Migration: The Population Turnaround in Rural America*, edited by David L. Brown and John M. Wardwell, 189–212. New York: Academic Press, 1980.

———. "Location Specific Capital and Destination Selection among Migrants to Nonmetropolitan areas." *Rural Sociology* 48(3): 447–57 (1983).

Willits, Fern, and Robert C. Bealer. "The Utility of Residence for Differentiating Social Conservation in Rural Youth." *Rural Sociology* 28(1): 70–80 (1963).

———. "An Evaluation of a Composite Definition of Rurality." *Rural Sociology* 32(27): 165–77 (1967).

Woofter, T. J., Jr. "Trends in Rural and Urban Fertility Rates." *Rural Sociology* 13(1): 3–9 (1948).

Yoder, F. R., and A. A. Smick. *Migration of Farm Populations and Flow of Farm Wealth*. Washington, Agricultural Experiment Station, Bulletin 315. Pullman, Wash., 1935.

Yoesting, Dean R., and P. G. Marshall. "Trade Pattern Changes of Open-County Residents: A Longitudinal Study." *Rural Sociology* 34(1): 85–90 (1969).

Zelinsky, Wilbur. "Is Nonmetropolitan America Being Repopulated?" *Demography* 15(1): 12–39 (1978).

———. "Coping with the Migration Turnaround: The Theoretical Challenge." *International Regional Science Review* 2(winter): 175–78 (1977).

Zuiches, James J. "In-Migration and Growth of Nonmetropolitan Urban Places." *Rural Sociology* 35(3): 410–20 (1970).

———. "Residential Preferences in the United States." In *Nonmetropolitan America in Transition*, edited by Amos H. Hawley and Sara Miles Mazie, 75–115. Chapel Hill, N.C.: University of North Carolina Press, 1981.

Zuiches, James J., and David L. Brown. "The Changing Character of the Nonmetropolitan Population, 1950–1970." In *Rural U.S.A.: Persistence and Change*, edited by Thomas R. Ford, 55–74. Ames, Iowa: Iowa State University Press, 1978.

Zuiches, James J., and Glenn V. Fuguitt. "Residential Preferences: Implications for Population Redistribution in Nonmetropolitan Areas." In *Commission Research Reports*, vol. 5, edited by Sara Mills Mazie, 617–30. Washington, D.C.: Government Printing Office, 1972.

———. "Residential Preferences and Mobility Expectations." Paper presented to American Sociological Association, New York (August 1976).

Zuiches, James J., and Jon R. Reiger. "Size of Place Preferences and Life Cycle Migration: A Cohort Comparison." *Rural Sociology* 43(4): 618–33 (1978).

Name Index

Anderson, William F., 91
Artis, Jay, 112

Bacon, Lloyd, 116
Baker, O. E., 114, 115, 124, 165
Baldassare, Mark, 158, 159
Ballard, Patricia L., 139, 140
Barth, Nancy, 127
Beale, Calvin L., 93, 94, 97, 99,
    118, 119, 127, 128, 144, 146,
    147, 155, 156, 169, 180
Bealer, Robert C., 23, 163
Beegle, J. Allan, 25, 112, 120,
    121
Beers, Howard W., 112
Belcher, John C., 119
Bender, Lloyd D., 127, 142, 144
Bernert, Eleanor H., 114
Bertrand, Alvin L., 177, 178
Beshers, James M., 7, 16
Billington, Ray Allen, 31, 61
Binder-Johnson, Hildegard, 79
Binford, Henry C., 36, 67
Blackwood, Larry G., 150, 158
Blau, Peter M., 6
Bogue, Donald J., 10, 100

Bohlen, Joe M., 112
Bouvier, Leon, 132
Bowles, Gladys K., 114, 116,
    146, 147
Brady, Dorothy S., 32
Brown, David L., 146, 147, 150,
    154, 155, 156
Brown, Harold C., 19
Brown, James S., 13, 105, 115,
    165, 183
Brunner, Edmund des., 99, 109,
    112, 114, 124, 125, 168
Brunner, Stanley D., 125
Bultena, Gordon, 174
Busch, Lawrence, 175

Callow, Alexander B., 32, 35, 87
Campbell, Rex R., 44, 52, 59, 60,
    79, 95, 99, 113, 114, 117, 127,
    133, 150, 157, 158
Carpenter, Edwin, 150, 158
Cebula, R. J., 19
Christenson, James A., 150,
    171, 172
Clawson, Marion, 158
Clay, Daniel C., 158, 159

Clifford, William B., 147, 148, 154, 155, 156
Cochrane, Willard W., 38
Coleman, Marion T., 5, 140
Collier, John, 27
Commons, John R., 52
Coughenour, C. Milton, 141

Dailey, George H., 117, 150, 157, 158
DaVanzo, Julie S., 7, 11, 14, 17, 149
DeAre, Diane, 141, 147
DeBow, J. D., 57, 58
De Jong, Gordon F., 4, 6, 7, 8, 9, 11, 19, 140, 145, 148, 149, 154, 165, 181
Dillman, Don A., 43, 177, 178
Duncan, Otis Dudley, 6
Duncan, Otis Durant, 164, 167

Eldridge, Hope Tisdale, 116

Falk, William W., 23
Farley, Reynolds, 105
Fawcett, James T., 4, 6, 7, 8, 9, 19, 148, 181
Federal Committee on Standard Metropolitan Statistical Areas, 21
Fliegel, Frederick C., 140, 154, 155
Folson, J. C., 124
Frisbie, W. Parker, 5, 9, 147
Fry, Martha Ray, 70
Fuchs, Victor R., 45
Fuguitt, Glenn V., 93, 94, 128, 137, 139, 140, 144, 149, 150, 153, 154, 155, 156, 180

Gardner, Robert W., 132, 165
Garkovich, Lorraine E., 44, 150, 171, 172

Geller, Jack, 174
Gilchrist, C. Jack, 137, 145, 149
Gillaspy, R. Thomas, 22
Goldscheider, Galvin, 13
Goldstein, Sidney, 14
Graber, Edith, 158, 183
Gray, Wayne T., 99
Graybill, Wilson H., 75, 120
Green, Bernal L., 127
Gurley, William R., 19, 104, 113, 146

Hagood, Margaret Jarman, 92, 97, 120
Hamilton, C. Horace, 102
Hamm, Rita R., 113, 147
Handlin, Oscar, 52, 68, 81, 91
Hansen, Kristen, 147
Hansen, Marcus Lee, 53, 54, 69, 71
Hassinger, Edward, 125, 144
Hatt, Paul K., 83, 91, 92, 94, 108, 109
Hawley, Amos H., 5, 45, 137, 140, 143, 145, 158, 179
Heaton, Tim B., 139, 151, 153, 154, 155, 156, 180
Heilbroner, Robert L., 102, 104
Hill, George W., 120
Hill, Herbert, 58
Hine, Robert V., 57, 59, 60, 67, 71, 72, 79
Hobbs, Daryl J., 177, 178
Hodge, Gerald, 144
Hoffer, Charles R., 164
Hourwich, Isaac A., 81
Humphrey, Craig R., 22
Hwong, Sean-Shong, 113, 147

Ilvento, Thomas, 150

Jeffrey, Julie Roy, 32, 55, 56, 64, 70, 80, 82

Jenkins, Robert M., 137
Johansen, Harley E., 125, 128, 144, 180
Johnson, Daniel M., 52, 59, 60, 95, 99, 113, 114, 133
Johnson, Kenneth M., 126
Johnson, Nan E., 25

Kirschenbaum, Alan, 22, 126
Kiser, Claude V., 120
Kolb, John H., 109, 124
Kontuly, Thomas, 129
Krout, John A., 22
Kuhn, Thomas S., 2

Lacy, William B., 175
Laird, William E., 151
Landis, Paul H., 61, 70, 83, 91, 92, 94, 108, 109, 112, 168
Lansing, John B., 104
Larson, Olaf F., 114
Lasley, Paul, 174
Lassey, Marie L., 156
Lee, Everett, 10, 106
Lee, Gary R., 156
Lichter, Daniel T., 137, 139, 153, 154, 155, 156, 180
Linden, Fabian, 41
Lipset, Seymour Martin, 113
Lively, C. E., 114, 168
Long, Larry H., 113, 141, 147
Luloff, A. E., 150, 152, 157, 158, 179, 182

McCarthy, Kevin F., 150
McKenzie, R. D., 122
McMillan, Robert T., 92
McMillen, David B., 7, 148, 149, 150, 152
McNall, Sally Allen, 57, 66, 81, 86
McNall, Scott G., 57, 66, 81, 86
McNamara, Robert L., 150

Mangalam, Joseph J., 8, 13, 105, 165, 183
Marshall, P. G., 144
Martinson, Floyd M., 112
Mattes, Merrill, J., 55
Mazek, Warren Ford, 151
Mazie, Sara Miles, 45, 137, 140, 143, 145, 158, 179
Melvin, Bruce L., 115
Menchik, Mark David, 45, 146
Merk, Frederick, 26
Mikesell, James J., 40
Miller, Michael K., 166, 171, 181
Moe, Edward O., 172
Morrison, Peter A., 7, 14, 17, 137, 149, 150
Mueller, Eva, 104, 127
Murdock, Steven H. J., 113, 147

Namboodiri, N. Krishnan, 23
Nash, Roderick, 33
Nelson, Lowry, 28, 164
Notestein, Frank W., 167, 168, 174

O'Reilly, Shirley M., 80
Owsley, Frank L., 73

Parpia, Baroo, 113, 147
Payne, Raymond, 112, 115
Peterson, William, 10, 51, 53, 123
Pfeffer, Max J., 137
Photidias, John D., 117
Ploch, Louis A., 150, 151, 158
Poindexter, John R., 147, 148
Population Reference Bureau, 146
Poston, Dudley L., 5, 9, 140, 147
Potter, David M., 26, 30, 71
Powers, Ronald C., 172

Price, Daniel O., 101, 115, 127,
    166
Price, Michael L., 158, 159
Pursell, Carroll W., 32

Rank, Mark R., 183
Ravenstein, E. G., 10, 17
Redfield, Robert, 23
Reiger, Jon R., 149
Reuss, Carl Frederick, 117
Rindfuss, Ronald, 120
Ritchey, P. Neal, 3, 4, 10, 12,
    116, 121, 181
Roberts, Roy L., 94
Robinson, Warren C., 22
Rocha, Rodolfo, 59
Rogers, Susan Carol, 80
Rutman, Gilbert, 104

Salamon, Sonya, 80
Schaefer, Donald E., 72, 73
Schlesinger, Arthur M., 61, 64,
    74
Schlissel, Lillian, 56, 69, 70, 71,
    76, 80
Schultze, Rolf, 112
Schwarzweller, Harry K., 13,
    105, 115, 165, 183
Seim, Emerson, 100
Sell, Ralph R., 11, 22, 140, 145,
    149, 154
Seward, Rudy Ray, 75, 77
Sewell, William H., 163, 166
Shannon, Fred A., 66, 105
Shryock, Mary S., 20, 178
Siegel, Jacobs, 20, 178
Sikes, Melanie M., 101, 115,
    127, 166
Smick, A. A., 125
Smith, E. N., 115
Smith, Henry Nash, 26, 29, 30
Smith, Richmond Mayo, 79

Smith, T. Lynn, 22, 52, 70, 78,
    115, 118, 119, 120
Sofranko, Andrew J., 140, 141,
    150, 151, 154, 155
Sorokin, Pritirim A., 22, 179
Speare, Alden, 7
Stangler, Gary J., 133, 150
Steahr, Thomas E., 152, 179,
    182
Stinner, William F., 158
Stoeckel, Richard H., 73
Stokes, C. Shannon, 166, 171,
    181
Stratton, Joanna L., 70, 80
Stuart, Nina G., 150
Sweet, James A., 120

Taeuber, Conrad, 76, 92, 114,
    168
Taeuber, Irene B., 76
Taeuber, Karl E., 114
Tarver, James D., 19, 104, 113,
    120, 144, 146
Tetreau, E. D., 94, 125
Thomas, Dorothy Swain, 116
Thompson, Warren S., 119
Thompson, Wilbur R., 40
Till, Thomas E., 146
Tilly, Charles B., 19
Toney, Michael B., 158
Trewartha, Glenn T., 169
Tucker, C. Jack, 136
Turner, Frederick Jackson, 72,
    73
Tweeten, Luther, 146

Uhlenberg, Peter, 107
U.S. Bureau of the Census, 20,
    97, 132, 141, 143

Vedder, R. K., 19
Vining, Daniel R., 129
Voss, Paul R., 183

Wade, Richard, 64
Wakely, Ray E., 112
Wardwell, John M., 106, 129,
   136, 137, 143, 145, 147, 149,
   150, 151, 152, 157
Warner, Sam Bass, 37, 39
Webb, Walter Prescott, 72
Wheeler, J. A., 137
Whelpton, P. K., 119, 120
White, Lucia, 44
White, Morton, 44
Wilcox, Walter F., 75
Williams, James D., 7, 19, 113,
   147, 148

Williams, James O., 7, 141, 150,
   151, 152, 154
Willits, Fern, 23
Wimberley, Donald C., 141
Woofter, T. J., 120

Yoder, F. R., 125
Yoesting, Dean R., 144

Zelinsky, Wilbur, 147
Zimmerman, Carie C., 22, 179
Zuiches, James J., 10, 22, 146,
   149, 150, 154, 155

Subject Index

Administrative concepts, 178
Affinity models, 7
Age: attributes, 154, 155, 156; selectivity, 113–14, 116, 117; structure, 118–23
Age-sex structure, 77–78
Agglomeration, 106, 152; effect, 35; efficiencies, 34
Aggregate: approach, 165–66; data, 4, 165, 181; measures, 8, 181; models, 16, 19–20
Aging in place, 156
Agrarian: democracy, 29; frontier, 32
Agricultural: communities, 126–27; economics, 165, 166; economy, 67; labor, 102; mechanization, 102; migrants, 73; practices, 70; productivity, 70, 172
Agricultural Experiment Stations, 167, 168, 169, 170, 171, 172
Agricultural Extension Service, 170
Agriculture: changes in, 102, 103, 175; development of, 59;

industrialization of, 38–39; mechanization of, 38–39, 173; reorganization of, 44–45
Alternative destination, 108
Amenities, 4, 93, 105, 126, 144, 148, 150, 154, 159
American Indians. See Native Americans
Annexation, 35
Antiurban sentiments, 44
Antiurbanism, 150
Appalachians, 105, 108, 109, 115, 117, 121
Approaches, methodological, 165
Area, 17
Area attributes, 2
Attitudes, 169
Attributes, 2
Auspices of migration, 19

Beech Creek, 183
Behavior, 165–66, 169
Beliefs, 165
Blacks, 79, 95–97, 108, 130–31; migration of, 52, 59–61, 95–97, 105, 112, 113, 114, 115,

116, 118, 122, 132–33; regional distribution of, 95; urbanization of, 95–97
Boosterism, 64
Braceros program, 91
Branch families, 105
British: crown, 27, 30, 31, 59; loyalists, 54
Bureau of Agricultural Economics, 164, 167

California Gold Rush, 51
Capital, 81, 173; economic, 124–25; human, 124–25; land as, 29, 30
Case study, 170, 171, 182–83
Celtic heritage, 53–54
Census, 13, 19; 1790, 52; 1920, 35; 1930, 94; 1980, 129; of Agriculture, 1920, 38; data, 16, 18, 76, 166, 170, 171, 181, 182; decennial, 16, 18, 166, 170
Central Plains, 60
Centrifugal force, 134
Chain migration, 53
Cherokees, 56
Children ever born, 76
Choice. See Volition
Cities: attractions of, 64, 66, 67; building of, 31–32; expansion of, 35; migration to, 35
City buiding, 31, 66
Civil rights movement, 130
Civil War, effects of, 77, 132
Cognitive-behavior: approach, 148, 151; model, 10, 18, 107–8, 181
College communities, 117, 126
Commercial structure, 125–26
Communication networks, 143, 152
Communities: ethnic, 87; socio-

economic patterns of, 80–81; sociopolitical consequences of, 81–82
Community: development, 170; of destination, 19; of origin, 13; processes, 175
Commuting, 146, 152
Concept clarification, 178–80
Conceptual: frameworks, 175; orientation, 164–65
Continental destiny, 26
Cornbelt: fertility in, 120; outmigration from, 127
Cottonbelt, fertility in, 120
Counterstream: of blacks, 132–33; of migrants, 116–18
Country Life Commission, 164
County level data, 22, 181–82
Current Population Survey, 129

Danneborg, Nebraska, 57
Data: county level, 22, 181–82; population, 170; sources of, 16–18, 20, 22, 165–66
Decennial census, 16, 18, 166, 170
Decision-making process, 7, 8, 10, 11, 15, 18, 105, 107, 108, 113, 170
Deconcentration movement, 145
Defense: migration, 108; mobilization, 108
Demographic: composition, 155–57; research, 167, 168, 170, 171, 174, 180
Demography, 167–68, 169, 174
Dependency ratio, 123–24
Dependents, burdens of, 123–24
Differential economic opportunities, 165
Diseconomies, urban, 107
Distance, 64, 107, 113, 121, 143, 144, 151

Division of Farm Life Studies, 164, 167
Dust Bowl, 94

East, 72
Ecological: model, 5, 147–48; structure, 144, 151; diversity in, 126–27; theory, 179, 120–21
Economic:
—base, type of, 126
—capital, 124–25
—crises, 41
—development, 32–34, 40, 46, 58, 59, 80; government involvement in, 41–42
—development programs, 169
—enterprises, rural, 41
—framework, 19
—growth, 34, 39
—models, 3–4, 6, 113, 145, 147, 175; operationalizing, 18–20
—motivations, 66, 104, 108, 173
—opportunity, 9, 60, 70, 74, 68, 84, 86, 113, 126, 165, 173; differentials in, 44, 45, 46
—specialization, 125
—structure, 165; transformation of, 183
—trends, 166
Economic Research Service, 169
Economies of scale, 34, 38, 40, 106, 152
Economy: farm, 91; structural transformations of, 44–46
Education: aspirations for, 111–13, 115–16; attributes for, 153, 154, 155; attainment of, 111–13
Educational selectivity, 111–13, 117–18
Emigration, 53–54
Employment: differentials, 104, 146, 148; manufacturing, 38,

45, 86, 93, 128, 145; opportunities, 45, 86, 104, 107, 113, 145–46, 148, 183; structure, 147
Ethnic: communities, 57, 87; groups, 122; migration, 52–54; structure, 86
European immigrants, 53, 57, 58
Ever-married women, 76
Exclusion Act, 58
Expansion: geographic, 26–28, 33, 35, 36; territorial, 120
Expectancy, 11
Expected benefits, value of, 4
Extension: programs, 170; specialists, 170

Family: composition selectivity, 114–15; income, nonmetro vs. metro, 146; influence in migration, 15, 148–49; members, 15, 16, 19; size, 76–77; median, 75–76; structure, 76–77, 80
Farm:
—business cycles, 84
—commodity prices, 84
—economy, 91
—foreclosures, 84–86
—inheritance, 125
—labor, 168; displacement of, 38
—population, changes in, 92, 93, 97–99, 109, 114–15, 124, 126–27, 140–41, 168–69
—villages, 79
Farm-born migration, 168–69, 172
Farmers, 71, 72–73, 112; hobby, 141; part-time, 141
Farms: settlement patterns of, 79–80; size of, 38; subsistence, 92

Farmsteads, 29, 31, 70, 79–80, 127
Federal Emergency Relief Administration, 168
Federal government: involvement in economic development, 42; role in land dispersal, 27–30; role of, 46–47
Federal Housing Administration (FHA), 36, 39–40
Federal land disposal programs, 29
Federal programs, 36, 39–40
Federal Transfer payments. *See* Transfer payments
Federal, investment, 106–7
Fertility, 74–76, 77, 119–21, 156–57, 173, 174; norms, 75; rate, 77; ratio, 75, 77; rural, 75–76; urban, 75
Five Civilized Tribes, 27
Forced migrations, 51, 52, 59
Forecasts, 170
Foreign-born residents, 54, 57, 86
Freeholders, 31, 78
Free immigration, 89
Free migrations, 51, 52, 53
Friends, influence in migration, 148–49
Frontier, 54, 55, 56, 57, 58, 70, 71, 72–73, 74, 79, 80, 81, 83; agrarian, 32, 33, 35; of agriculture, 74; of commerce and industry, 74; thesis of, 30; of science and entrepreneurship, 47; urban, 86, 435
Frontier family, 76–77
Frontier migrant, 73, 78
Full employment, level of, 46

Galpin, Charles J., 164, 167, 172

Gentrification, 44
Geographic: center, of population, 55; expansion, 26–28, 33, 35, 36, 152; location, 80; mobility, 6, 18, 70, 73, 77; space, 13; territory, 121
German-American Alliance, 87
Goods-producing industries, 145
Goods production, 130
Government, investment in infrastructure, 106–7
Governmental programs, 130
Great American Desert, 55
Great Depression, 41, 86, 92, 105, 168
Great Lakes, 93, 129, 148
Great Migration, 95, 122
Great Plains, 55, 71, 72, 75, 81, 99, 127, 156
Great Society programs, 169
Gross interchange, 17
Gross migration flows, 19, 182
Gross National Product, 40, 130
Group behavior, 72
Growth: absolute, 139, 141; of cities, 84; economic, 34, 39; nonmetropolitan, 129–30, 131, 152–53; population, 49, 52, 53, 54, 55, 60–61, 86, 131–32, 144; relative, 139, 141; rural, 139; of suburbs, 100; of towns, 139–40
Growth rate, 35, 153; rural, 170; urban, 31, 33, 74, 122–23

Hamlets, 169
Highway system, 37, 100, 106, 107, 123, 143
Highway trust fund, 100
Hinterland, 33, 35, 42, 64, 67, 74, 84, 144
Hispanics, 121
Hobby farmer, 141

Homestead Act, 29, 75
Homesteads, 79, 83
Household maximization, 6
Human capital, 124–25, 168,
    173; investments in, 165;
    maximization, 6

Immigrant streams, 51–54
Immigrants, 80–81
—ethnic groups, 52–54, 57;
    Asians, 122, 132; Austrians,
    54, 86, 87; Belgians, 54; Brit-
    ish, 89; Chinese, 53, 58;
    Dutch, 54; English, 53, 58, 68,
    78; Finnish, 86; French, 53;
    Germans, 52–53, 54, 57–58,
    78, 79, 80, 89; Greeks, 86;
    Hungarians, 86, 87; Irish, 58,
    68, 78, 79; Italians, 86, 89;
    Latin Americans, 132; Latvi-
    ans, 86; Lithuanians, 86;
    Mexicans, 122; Polish, 86;
    Prussians, 54; Rumanians, 87;
    Russians, 86, 87; Scandinavi-
    ans, 53, 54, 57; Turkish, 86;
    Scottish, 78; Spaniards, 58–
    59; Swedish, 53, 80; Welsh,
    58; Western Hemisphere, 89,
    91
—first generation, 87
—religious groups, 52, 57
—settlement patterns of, 78–80
Immigration, 86–91, 131–32; ef-
    fects of, 89–91; laws, 87–91;
    reasons for, 68–69
Impelled migrations, 51, 52
Incentive, 11
Income: attributes, 154; differ-
    entials, 146–47, 151; gap, 104,
    130; migration effect on, 151;
    models, 151; selectivity, 115
Indentured servants, 51, 52
Independent freeholders, 31

Indian nations, 27
Indian Removal Act, 27
Individual, 8; attributes, 2; mo-
    tivations, 5, 181; perceptions,
    10; as unit of study, 15, 20
Industrial change, rural, 144
Industrialization, 37, 39, 86; ag-
    ricultural, 38–39; economic,
    36–39; rural, 127
Industrial structure, 130
Industries, location of, 183
Inflationary pressures, 45
Information society, 183
Infrastructure, 29, 30, 143, 157;
    government investment in,
    39, 41, 43, 45, 46, 47, 106–7;
    improvement of, 106–7; public
    investment in, 41; rural, 40
Inheritance, of farm, 125
In-migration, to farm, 141
Innovations: scientific, 42; tech-
    nological, 32–34, 41, 42; tele-
    communication, 46–47;
    transportation, 33, 36
Institutional context, 166–72,
    174–76
Institutions, mission orientation
    of, 167, 170, 171, 173
Interarea differentials, 183
International nonmetropolitan
    growth, 129
Intervening obstacles, 106
Intra-area migrants, 154

Japanese-Americans, 108

Kansas Exodus, 60
Kinship networks, 105–6, 183

Labor, 37, 45, 58, 59–60, 102,
    148, 168, 173; demand,
    changes in, 99, 102; mobility,

studies of, 4; productivity,
102; surplus, 102
Laborers, farm, displacement of,
38
Labor force, 37, 41, 42, 130, 147,
152, 172; models, 113, 147,
151
Labor market: differentials, 4;
needs, 183; opportunities, 145
Land: abundance of, 71; acquisition of, 70, 73; attraction of,
72; as capital, 29, 30; desire
for, 70; dispersal, 27–30; do-
nations, 29; government investment in, 28; grants, 30–
31; price of, 73, 83; public, 29,
30; sales, 28; speculation, 28;
value, 28
Land-grant system, 166, 167,
171, 173, 177
Landholders, independent, 78
Land-use planning, 157, 158
Land-use policies, 28–30
Land values, 157, 158
Laws of migration, 9
Life-cycle: changes, 15, 70;
model, 6–7
Lindsborg, Kansas, 57
Locational: perceptions, 70, 108;
theory, 148; values, 10
Locations, alternative, 148
Location-specific capital, 7, 149–
52

Marco approach, 2–5, 8–12, 17
Macro level data sources, 166
Manifest destiny, 26, 33, 49
Manufacturing, 74, 145–46;
firms, 37–38; growth of, 130;
employment, 38, 45, 86, 93,
128, 145; sector, 45, 130, 183
Market conditions, 165
Mass migrations, 51, 52, 53

Mennonites, 57, 80, 81
Methodology: approaches to,
165–66; improvements in,
181–83
Metropolitan areas, 20–23, 178;
emergence of, 122–23; growth,
133, 134–37, 152; population
in, 134–36; rural areas inside,
134; urban areas inside, 134
Metropolitan Statistical Area,
21
Micro approach, 2, 5–12, 18
Midwest, 56, 83, 99, 139, 148,
151, 154, 156
Migrants, characteristics of,
111–18; composition of, 132;
counterstream of, 116–18;
family composition of, 114–15;
intra-area, 154; return, 116–
17; rural-to-urban, 121; sex
composition of, 114–15; urban-
to-rural, 121
Migration: analysis unit in, 15–
16, 20; adjustment to, 106; approaches to, 2; of blacks, 91–
93, 95–97, 113; consequences
of, 153–59; decision making,
107; defense, 108; definition
of, 12–13; demographic consequences of, 118–23; differentials, 8, 145; economic models
of, 73, 74, 113; economic motivations for, 104–5, 108; epi-
sodic, 108; factors in, 1; to
farms, 140–41; farm-to-farm,
61; farm population, 168–69;
geographic mobility in, 9;
guidebooks, 56; institutional
significance of, 172–74; interchanges, 133–43, 155, 173; internal, 67; interpreting, 68–
74; metropolitan-to-metropolitan, 133; metropolitan-to-

small towns, 133; nonmetro-to-nonmetro, 154–55; motivations for, 9, 19, 108; noneconomic factors in, 147–48, 165; noneconomic motivations for, 108; operationalizing, 12, 18–20; political consequences of, 157–59; push factors in, 61; reasons for, 12, 19, 20, 69–74, 83, 104; research, 172–74; rural, 73; to rural areas, 93–94, 117–18; rural farm-to-urban, 97–99; rural nonfarm-to-urban, 99; rural-to-urban, 124, 133, 140; selectivity, 111–18, 168; social system in, 8; societies, 56; socioeconomic conditions in, 8; socioeconomic consequences of, 123–28; structural transformations of, 106–7; theoretical explanations of, 165; trends of, 169; types of, 13–15, 51; urban, 61–67, 73; to urban fringe, 100; urban-to-rural, 93, 140; volition in, 8; wartime, 109–10; westward, 54–61, 94–95
Migration behavior: aggregate level, 181; individual level, 181
Migration decision making, 181
Migration flows, 19; gross, 182
Migration streams, 86–101, 131–33, 152; analysis of, 17–18, 182; composition of, 61, 86–91, 132, 153–55; consequences of, 74–82; definition of, 17; demographic consequences of, 155–57; measures of, 17; metro-to-nonmetro, 153–54; nonmetro-to-metro, 155; regional variations in, 154; retirement, 152, 154,

155, 156; size of, 153; types of, 51; urban, 97–101
Migration theory, development of, 180–81
Military communities, 117
Mining communities, 127
Mobility, 6, 18, 67, 71, 77, 81, 182
Modernization, 143
Mormons, 54, 79
Morrill Act, 29–30
Motivational theory, 11, 19
Motivations, 9, 104, 105, 106, 108, 165, 173, 181; economic, 19, 66; individual, 11, 19
Motives, 8, 14, 15, 16, 20, 165
Moving, reasons for, 19

National affairs, government influence in, 39–40
National: prosperity, 40–42; trends, 181
Native Americans, 26–28, 51, 56
Native-born persons, 56
Natural decrease, 118–19, 155
Natural increase, 49, 66, 102, 130, 153, 155, 156, 157
Natural Resources Committee, 119–20
Natural resources, 68
Net in-migration, in nonmetropolitan areas, 130
Net interchange, 17
Net migration, 182; calculation of, 16–17; residual method of, 17
Net migration flows, 19
New England, 76, 92
Nicodemus, Kansas, 60
Noneconomic factors, in migration, 148, 165
Noneconomic models: in marco

approach, 4–5; in micro approach, 6–7
Nonlabor market factors, in macro approach, 3
Nonmetropolitan:
—adjacency, 117, 121, 126, 137, 140, 152, 153, 158
—areas, 20–23, 178, 179
—growth: components of, 139–40; regional variations in, 137
—population, rural, 180
—population change, 129–30, 131, 139, 153, 157–59, 180
Norms, 163
North Central region, 57, 76, 95, 102, 103, 104, 132, 136, 137, 141
Northeast, 61, 70, 78, 80, 92, 93, 95, 104, 119, 136, 137, 139
North, 60, 95, 130–31, 132

Occupational: aspirations, 104, 112–13, 115–16; attributes, 154, 155; diversity, 107; opportunity, 112; selectivity, 115, 117
Open country residents, 180
Opportunities, economic, 9
Oregon Societies, 56
Out-migration: from farms, 92, 97, 124, 114–15, 126–27; from metropolitan areas, 133; from nonmetropolitan areas, 145; from rural areas, 118–19, 123–24, 164–65, 173
Overland trails, migration on, 56
Ozarks, 5, 109, 121, 127, 129, 148, 154, 157

Pacific Coast, 93, 95
Part-time farmer, 141

Perceptions, 10, 11, 107; of destinations, 108
Physical space, 143
Place of origin, 108
Plains, 99, 109
Plantations, 31, 78–79
Plunkett, Sir Horace, 164
Political-administrative boundary, 13
Political freedom, 69
Population:
—age composition of, 77
—change: absolute vs. relative, 139, 141; farm, 97–99, 109, 114–15, 126–27; net rural, 49, 173; net urban, 49; nonmetropolitan, 129–30, 131, 139, 153, 157–59; rural, 118–19, 123–24, 131, 139, 157–59
—data, 170
—distribution, 132, 134, 136
—estimates, 170
—ethnic, 122
—farm, 168–69
—geographic center of, 55, 132
—growth, 49, 52, 54, 55, 60–61, 86, 87, 92, 93–94, 100, 108–9, 131–32
—loss of farm, 97, 109
—racial, 122
—regional distribution of, 61
—research: rural, 163–76; support for, 66
—rural, 119
—sex composition of, 78
—structures, 5
—trends, 166, 170, 173, 175, 183–84
—urban, 122–23
Postindustrial society, 183
Pre-emption Act, 29, 31
Prejudices, ethnic and racial, 87
President's Commission on Im-

migration and Naturalization, 89
President's Commission on Population Growth, 148
Primary migration, 14
Production: mechanized, 97–99; organizational structure of, 38–39
Productivity, 40, 45, 173
Professional: standards, 170; values, 163
Prorural sentiments, 44, 150
Prosperity, national, 40–42
Prourban attitudes, 44
Proximity to place, 179
Public: assistance programs, 4; policy, 169; relief programs, 105; services, 156, 157–58
Publication outlet, 171
Puritans, 52
Purnell Act, 167, 177
Push-pull model, 9, 70, 71, 72, 103, 104, 105, 115, 149, 165, 173

Quakers, 52
Quality of life, 41, 104, 149, 150, 158, 167

Race relations, 131–32
Racial: attributes, 153, 154; composition, 122
Railroads, 30, 33, 36, 37, 57, 64, 72
Rectangular survey, 28, 31, 79
Religious: freedom, 69; migration, 52
Repeat migration, 15
Research: agenda, 177, 178–84; challenges for, 177–84; funds for, 174
Residential: desirability, 181; diversity, era of, 42–47, 143–53, 159–62; histories, 18, 114; mobility, 13, 15; preferences, 149; turnaround, 10
Residual method, 17
Resources, 183
Retail businesses, loss of, 125
Retirement: communities, 126; migration, 147, 152, 154, 155, 156
Return migration, 15, 116–17, 127, 150
Right of passage, 69
Roads, 37, 39, 64, 106, 107, 143
Rural, 180
—America, study of, 163–76
—areas, 21, 66; birth rates in, 119; fertility in, 119–20; loss of capital, 124–25; out-migration from, 173; sex ratio in, 119
—communities: changing age structure in, 119; ecological structure of, 126–27; migration consequences on, 153–59
—development, 170
—development programs, 170
—dominance: era of, 49–82; events of, 25–26; stage of, 25–34
—dominance migration: farm-to-farm, 61; rural-to-urban, 61–67; urban-to-rural, 67–68; westward, 54–61
—economies, structural change in, 144
—employment, growth of, 45
—fertility, 119–21
—industrial change, 144
—infrastructure, 40, 47
—nonmetropolitan population, components of, 180
—operationalizing, 20–23
—people, attitudes of, 43

—population change, 129–30,
131, 139, 170, 173; reasons
for, 101–9
—population studies, 22, 177;
federal support for, 172; influences of, 163–76; institutional
context of, 166–72; institutional significance of, 172–74
—relief, 168
—sociology, 177, 178; departments of, 166; research, 166
—turnaround, 153, 165, 169,
170
Rural Electrification Act, 41
Rural Free Delivery, 36
Rural Sociological Society, 177
Rural Sociology, 171, 172
Russian Mennonites, 57

Safety valve thesis, 72
Selectivity: educational aspirations, 111–13; occupational
opportunities, 112–13
Sentiments: antiurban, 44; prorural, 44
Service: functions, 169; industries, 45, 145, 183; sector, 45;
employment in, 45; public, 156,
157–58; production, 130
Settlement, patterns of, 30–32,
57–59, 78–80
Sex: ratio, 119; selectivity, 114–
15; structure, 119
Size of place, 179
Slave trade, 59–61, 79
Slaves, black, 51, 52, 53, 59–60
SMA. *See* Standard Metropolitan Area
Social: class origin, 115; mobility, 47, 73, 83, 91, 104; models
of, 6; problems, 164–65, 167,
168; relations, 158–59; structure, 165; welfare, 175

Social scientists, 163–66
Societies, migration of, 56
Sociopolitical conflicts, 158–59
South, 52, 53, 56, 59, 60, 70, 79,
92, 95, 99, 102, 105, 113, 114,
118, 121, 122, 131, 132, 136,
137, 139
Southeast, 59, 132
Southwest, 122, 132, 154
Space, geographic, 13
Standard Metropolitan Area
(SMA), 123, 179, 134–36; cri-
teria for, 20–21; definition of,
20; history of, 21–22
Standard Metropolitan Statisti-
cal Area, 21
Standard of living, 41, 42, 45,
47, 105, 107, 183
State, investment in infrastruc-
ture, 106–7
Stem family, 105–6
Structural: change, 144, 169,
175; factors, 9; transforma-
tions, 106–7
Suburban rings, 100, 137
Suburbs, 35, 36, 39, 67, 100
Sunbelt, 5
Surplus population, 101–2
Survey of Economic Opportu-
nity, 116
Sustenance organization, varia-
tions in, 147

Technological: change, 38, 47,
168; innovations, 84, 99, 123,
143
Technology, agricultural, 127
Telecommunications, 46–47; diffusion of, 107
Territorial expansion, 26–28,
120
Teutonic heritage, 54

Theoretical: paradigm, 165; perspectives, 18, 175, 179
Theory construction, 180–81
Towns, 66
Trade centers, 144
Trail of tears, 27
Transfer payments, 45
Transportation system, 30, 37, 53, 64, 143, 146, 152
Tribal lands, 27
Turnaround, rural, 165
Turnaround county, 157

Upper Great Lakes, 154
Upper Midwest, 60
Urban:
—areas, 21, 113, 115; attitudes toward, 44;
—centers, 35–36, 39, 66, 74, 84;
—era, 83–110, 111–28;
—fertility, 120–21;
—fringe, 21, 100, 123, 134;
—frontier, 86;
—gentrification, 44;
—growth, 31, 33, 123, 133, 134–37; era of, 34–42; reasons for, 74;
—hinterland, 42;
—influences, 43;
—labor force, 37;
—lifestyle, 144;
—migration, 60, 61–67;
—operationalizing, 20–23;
—places, population in, 87, 108–9, 123;
—vs. rural, 22–23
Urbanization, 36, 39, 84, 120, 152, 169; effects on fertility, 121
Urbanized areas, 134

USDA. *See* U.S. Department of Agriculture
Utility maximization, 74, 165
U.S. Bureau of the Budget, 20
U.S. Department of Agriculture, 164, 167, 168, 169, 170, 171, 172, 173, 177

Vacation homes, 149
Value-expectancy model, 181
Values, 10, 11, 151, 163, 165, 168, 169, 176
Veteran's Administration (VA), 36
Villages, 31, 66, 169
Vital statistics, 171
Volition, individual, 8

Wage differentials, 146
War of 1812, 28
Wartime migration, 109
Waterways, 64
West, 56, 58, 119, 132, 136, 137, 139
West Coast, 58
Westward migration, 69–74, 94–95
Westward movements, of immigrants, 56–61, 132
Works Progress Administration, 168
World War I, effects of, 84, 87, 95, 104
World War II, effects of, 36, 86, 92, 95, 99, 104, 108, 120

Young persons, migration of, 114–15, 116, 124

Zoning, 157

About the Author

LORRAINE GARKOVICH is Associate Professor of Sociology at the University of Kentucky, College of Agriculture. Her research focuses on consequences of population change for rural communities and patterns of family and work roles in farm households. Her articles have appeared in *Rural Sociology,* *Teaching Sociology,* and the *Journal of the Community Development Society,* and her chapters have appeared in books on community development, American farm women, and rural policy. She is a member of the Rural Sociological Society, the Population Association of America, and the Community Development Society.

www.ingramcontent.com/pod-product-compliance
Lightning Source LLC
Chambersburg PA
CBHW070240290326
41929CB00046B/2207